This guide is dedicated to the amazing CM and VM of Team Adventure. I couldn't be more proud of you both.

Always brave. Ever, ever, ever.

Forever in my heart - Dad

Disclaimer:

The Legend of Zelda: Tears of the Kingdom is a registered trademark of Nintendo. The screenshots and artwork shown in this publication were taken from "The Legend of Zelda: Tears of the Kingdom", a game developed and published by Nintendo.

This educational guide is a 100% independent and unofficial publication which is in no way, licensed, authorized, or endorsed by Nintendo. This guide book is for general information and entertainment purposes only.

Names, brands, and logos mentioned within this publication may be protected by trademark or other intellectual property rights of one or more jurisdictions. It is not implied that there is any commercial, or other relationship, between the publisher and the trademark holder.

Table of Contents

The sequel to Nintendo's largest Zelda game (well, it was until Tears of the Kingdom came along and said "Hold my Rupees") is finally out and what a game!

The Zelda series has always held a special place in our hearts. The author of the guide you're holding has very vivid memories of playing A Link to The Past on his SNES back when he was only 14. He started at 7pm, went for a snack a "little later", and checked the clock to see it was 4am!

We told him that wasn't healthy. Although, we don't think he heard us, as he was too busy fusing-together his next diabolical Korok-torture device courtesy of the new Ultrahand ability. It really is something special. And nuts. If you don't believe us, check out the YouTube QR code we added on page 33.

We've pulled together our biggest guide to-date and have genuinely worked tirelessly around the clock to bring you a guide that we trust you'll find helpful in your journey through the skies, surface, and underground hell that is The Depths (shudders).

As always, if you've found our guide helpful, or have any feedback for us, please leave a review on the digital shop you bought our guide from. We genuinely read them all.

Our sincerest gratitude,

The Alpha Strategy Guides team

TOP TIPS!

 *The Benefit Of Our Hindsight*

This game is - quite simply - massive and jam-packed with **many** different things to pay attention to (some of which, such as cooking, aren't even fully explained in-game).

While it carries across a *lot* of similarities with the Breath of the Wild (BotW), it still has quite a few new surprises tucked-up its Zonai-device powered sleeves.

And that's where this section comes in. We'll help bring you up-to-speed on what's new and also provide a refresher if you never played the BotW.

So, let's get off to a great start in this sprawling, complex, and challenging game...

Cooking up a Storm

This is one critical area that the game provides **zero** guidance on.

Cooking certain combinations of Materials (such as fruits and vegetables) bestow you with recipes that replenish your health, stamina, etc.

Or, create **temporary** buffs (such as extra hearts, increased defenses, or attacks, cold/heat resistance, and more).

This is a *critical* aspect to learn from the start, so head to page 23 for the full low-down on how to become a master chef.

Weapon/Item Durability

Annoyingly, this has carried over from BotW. Basically, every time you use a weapon or an item takes damage, it's one step closer to breaking.

Weaker items (such as wooden sticks) will break *much* quicker than weapons made of solid metal (such as swords).

However, unlike in BotW (where you had to keep a ton of replacement weapons/items to hand), you can now use the new **Fuse** ability to combine materials to weapons/items *increasing their durability* (**and strength**)!

The developers have allowed you to go pretty nuts here as well. While you can fuse a rock to a wooden stick to turn it into a heavy-hitting, block-breaking pole, you can also fuse a bookcase to a sword (and many more)!

Until you find stronger weapons later on, fusing items together will be your best "bang for your buck" when it comes to both durability *and* attack power.

Armor Upgrades

If you're looking for stronger armor, you'll need to visit the (classic) Great Fairy Fountains scattered throughout the map.

There are four of them in total, and to unlock access, you'll need to complete side adventures related to the music troupe.

Once you have a Great Fairy available, you can upgrade your armor by providing the required monster materials and enough Rupees.

The Great Fairy informs you about the specific materials and Rupee cost for each upgrade.

It's important to note that you can't add special features like cold-resistance to the outfits, but you can make them more durable.

Keep in mind that not all pieces of armor can be upgraded in Tears of The Kingdom. Initially, the Great Fairies have a limit on how much you can upgrade your armor, so it's *crucial* to unlock all of them.

Creativity FTW!

It's fair to say that the developers are *encouraging* you to go all-out with how you approach enemies and puzzles.

The game takes a **heavy** approach to physics-based solutions, so let your imagination run wild as you build up your skills and arsenal.

This is leaning towards creative solutions (that work, even though they let you skip huge chunks of puzzles) is magnified by the combination of the new Abilities and the numerous weapons/items/materials and Zonai Devices that you come across.

Can't get up a mountain (or don't want to go through the cave route)?

Attach some Zonai fans to some fused wood/platforms and take the - new - lift up to the top!

Many Shrines can be defeated *far* more quickly (than their "intended route") with a bit of imagination, some materials, and a sense of ambition.

The most important thing here is to just have fun trying out loads of different ideas.

However, it's probably a good idea to create a manual save *before* you commit materials and time to a big project (just in case it doesn't work out as expected).

Heat/Cold Resistance

The elements play a key role in this game. There's quite a few either very hot, or very cold areas.

You can tell whether an area is hot or cold by looking at the thermometer located to the left of the mini-map in the bottom right-hand corner of the screen.

If you go into such an area without suitable clothing/armor on (which have special heat/cold resistant properties), then you'll find Link will quickly start to lose health.

However, one way around this is to cook special recipes that grant Link a limited amount of immunity from the extreme heat or cold.

For example, cooking five Spicy Peppers together grants you a - very handy - 12 mins and 30 seconds of invulnerability to the freezing cold.

Caution: Eating a new recipe (while one is still active), causes the older temporary buff/resistance to stop working!

Blood Moon Nightmares

It's worth noting that the game gets noticeably harder when it turns night-time.

Every seven *in-game* days (around three hours in real-time), the sky turns crimson red and all (non-story) enemies respawn again.

They also drop all of their resources once again (and re-spawned bosses now drop some **very** useful new loot for defeating them more than once)!

You can use a campfire, fire pit, or Inn to manually change the time of day.

> **Top Tip:** *Look for skeletal Bokoblins to appear at night-time. They go down in one hit (and require a further hit to their skull to finish them off for good) and their - fragile -* **Bokoblin Arms** *have a base attack of 20!*
>
> *They may break quickly, but they also prove to hit hard against some of the tougher enemies (such as Blue Bokoblins or Lizalfos).*

The Test of Heart

BotW fans who finished the game will likely remember a key moment that required them to have **a lot** of stamina to obtain a certain item.

The same requirement applies once again in the sequel *hint, hint*. However, it's worth your while adding a few more Hear Pieces as enemies hit much harder in this game!

Lightning Fast Reflexes

If you find yourself in a thunderstorm, you will find electricity building up around Link if he's wearing *anything* metallic.

Immediately swap out any metal armor or shields to prevent the strike hitting you.

However, you *can* throw metallic objects at enemies and let the lightning strike it, causing massive damage *and* a fire to finish off any enemies too! Ha!

A Positive Ascension

While we cover this ability in greater detail a bit later on in the guide, it's worth noting that as long as the aiming pointer turns **green**, then Link can ascend up through *whatever* object is above him (be that mountain or otherwise).

However, instead of *immediately* popping up and out, it's worth staying half-way out for a few seconds.

If you don't like where you end up, you can press **B** again to descend back to where you came from. Very handy in case your cheeky shortcut landed you in a tight spot.

Assassin's Freed

If you never played BotW before, then to uncover more of your map, you must unlock and ascend the **Towers** found in each key area.

Doing so unlocks a new portion of the map, making it *much* easier to navigate.

Top Tip: *Take advantage of the fact you get launched right up into the sky when you unlock a new Skyview Tower. You can paraglide to the sky islands up here and look for high-level loot!*

Gatcha Zonai!

You'll find yourself collecting **Zonai Charges** as you battle and defeat the Construct enemies.

These Charges can be dropped into a Device Dispenser and - depending on the size and the amount of the Zonai Charges dropped into it - you'll be rewarded with a loads of different one-time-use Zonai Devices.

Also, once you've used a dispenser at least once, check it out in the map view to see just how many of each Zonai Devices remain.

Heart and Stamina

Upgrades

Unlike in classic Zelda games (where you collect four Heart Pieces to increase your health by one), in this you need to complete Shrines to earn a **Light of Blessing**.

You can now trade in four of these at a stone statue for *either* an upgrade to your health, or an upgrade to your stamina.

You also earn a full heart container after key bosses.

Speedy Travels

One other great aspect of finding Shrine (even if you chose not to enter it), is that doing so unlocks a new **fast travel** point on the map.

You can now create a large network of fast travel points which will prove to be *invaluable* as you navigate the Sky Islands, Surface, and the Depths.

Deeper Underground

Finally, you can access the enemy-packed Depths of Hyrule by recklessly diving into the red pit in the middle of the map. It's gigantic, tough, and **full** of very strong boss-like enemies to fight.

Of course, this also means that you'll find a **lot** of *very* powerful weapons as a reward for dispatching of said bosses...

> **Top Tip:** *Use a skeletal horse to safely ride over the red Gloom that causes you to lose access to your hearts (until you reach the surface again at least).*

Shining Lightroots

If you're struggling to locate one of the 120 Shrines on the surface, then keep an eye our for Lightroots in The Depths.

Each Lightroot is actually the base of the corresponding Shrine directly above it on the surface!

Stand under the Lightroot and check your surface map to see if you've found this Shrine yet or not. If not, place a marker on the map so you can go back to it later.

> **Did You Know?** *The name of the Lightroot is the name of Shrine above it - but* **backwards**.

A Warmer Welcome

There are a pair of leggings that you can find in the Great Sky Island that provides a very useful resistance to the cold.

One you complete the Ascend ability Shrine here (*Gutanbac Shrine*), look right for a rock ledge sticking out nearby.

Ascend up here and open up the chest on the right for a pair of **[Archaic Warm Greaves]**.

These provide immediate protection against the less-harsh icy conditions, meaning that you don't need to create (and eat) quite as many Cold Resistant meals.

A Mounting Problem

Upon landing in Hyrule, it's definitely worth finding a **solid colored** horse for riding along the great open-world on. Just as in BotW, solid color horses are harder to tame, but they also come with better stats by default.

Head to the *New Serenne Stable* (west of *Hyrule Castle*) and then look on the map for the *Passeri Greenbelt* (southwest of *Lookout Landing*).

You'll have a higher chance of finding better quality horses to tame and mount here.

If you find that you're startling the horses too easily, then you can create an Elixir made of **Sunset Fireflies** to up your sneaking skills for a little while.

Once you find one to your liking, you can head back to **Sprinn** at the *New Serenne Stable* and he'll register your first horse for free!

Collect the Rod that it drops and you can now shoot long-range electric bolts at your enemies.

However, it becomes even *more* powerful during a rainstorm. The bolts are amplified and it creates a huge Area-of-Effect attack that can impact groups of enemies.

Finally, shocked enemies drop their weapons and shields, making them *much* easier to pick up!

> **Did You Know?** *If you have a BotW save file on your Switch where you had a horse already saved, then take the first new horse back with you to register it and Sprinn informs you that you've already registered a horse!*
>
> *Your old BotW horse (complete with previous stats and Bond) will now be available for use in this game! Sweet!*

A Shocking Discovery

Located on a sole Wizard enemy, you can pick up a **[Topaz Rod]** that has a unique property.

To find this Electric Wizard, head to the grid reference: *-1557, 0578, 0025* (west of the *Breach of Demise*) and take it out as soon as you see it (headshots with your arrows are quite effective).

ABILITIES

Your Creativity Unleashed!

There are a whole new range of amazing abilities waiting for you to solve tons of puzzles, or beating baddies into submission.

You start to unlock them as you progress through the story and the first four abilities are unlocked as you complete the **Great Sky Island** area at the beginning of the game.

On their own, each ability is pretty cool. However, when you start mixing and matching them together… well… it boggles the mind just how many ideas you come up with (that are also likely to work too)!

We'll cover the key benefits of each ability in turn and we will then pick a few of our favorite combinations (which allowed us to skip difficult sections or complete tougher Shrines with the minimum of frustration, and the most fun).

First up, **Ultrahand**.

Ultrahand

The first ability you access allows (from Shrine one) Link to pick up almost any object in the world and manipulate it in 360 degrees.

However, what makes this ability *extra special* is the fact that when you put two objects close together (while using Ultrahand), the items will **automatically** stick together!

It's the gluing of objects together that allows you to build all sorts of crazy contraptions.

Admittedly, trying to accurately line up objects together (to get them to stick together properly), *can* be very fiddly.

Fuse

The second ability you access (via the second Shrine on Great Sky Island), allows you to stick weapons and other items together, allowing you to come up with some surprisingly effective combinations.

A basic example is fusing a rock to a wooden stick. On its own, the wooden stick is weak. However, by fusing it to something like a rock, increases both its durability (how long it lasts before it breaks) and its attack strength.

You can even fuse items to your shield, allowing you to turn what was a defensive item, into a formidable attacking weapon!

Some gems can also add some elemental damage to your weapons! A few examples include:

- **Ruby:** *Adds fire damage to weapons, or fire resistance to shields.*

- **Sapphire:** *Adds cold damage to weapons, or cold resistance to shields.*

- **Topaz:** *Adds electricity damage to weapons, or electricity resistance to shields.*

Ascend

The third ability (unlocked in the third Shrine), allows Link to travel up *through* certain solid objects.

The key indicator to whether or not an object can be passed through, is if the portal is green.

It's definitely worth paying *very* close attention to parts of the world where you wouldn't *normally* expect to be able to ascend through.

Quite often you'll find that you can pass right up through *very* tall mountains, or up onto ledges that allow you to save a **ton** of time (see: Tears of the Kingdom speedruns on YouTube for some awesome examples of this in action).

And, just in case you missed it in our **Top Tips!** Chapter earlier, it's worth noting that you can *descend* from an ascension - as long as you remain halfway in the ground.

As soon as you pop up to that new level, you can't return.

Recall

The fourth ability to learn (the final one on the Great Sky Island) is the ability to rewind the time of any physical objects.

What this effectively means is that you can reverse the movement of an object (whether it's flying, rolling, or floating over water).

You'll soon find that many shrines and bosses require you to freeze their projectiles, and use the Recall ability to send them right back where they came from!

However, it's important to keep in mind that the Recall ability only has a finite amount of time on it (although you can stop it at any point before it runs out).

As you'll see in a moment, this ability works *exceptionally* well with Ultrahand (and Ascent as too).

Autobuild

This ability allows you to immediately access your Zonai Device constructions by recording your creations and then saving them to memory.

They're accessible from a pop-up menu with the following options:

- *Favorites*
- *Schematics (Blueprints)*
- *History*

As long as you have enough materials and Zonai resources to build the saved contraption, then it'll be built right in front of you!

If you've spent *ages* creating kick-ass device, then you can now save it as a favorite for accessing later.

You can also collect **[Schema Stones]** to unlock blueprints for existing designs/builds.

Now, this ability *usually* requires you to complete the Quest: "Camera Work in the Depths" first (from Josha at *Lookout Landing*) before it's unlocked for you via the quest after this.

However, it's possible to pre-preemptively skip the triggering of both quests and instead, you can plunge right into the Depths in the *Eastern Abbey* of *Hyrule Field*.

One you land, explore the nearby building, look for the track, and stick some fans on the nearby mine-cart.

Here you'll encounter the checkpoint required to unlock the Autobuild ability! Sweet!

Camera

If you go for the Autobuild ability via the main quest-line, then you are awarded the Camera ability first. However, we've added it last here as it's not as useful as the other abilities.

To access it, you need to unlock the Paraglider (by speaking with Purah) and then travel to the following coordinates in the Depths: -0789, -0443, -0470

Activate the Lightroot here and speak with Robbie, where he activates this ability on your tablet.

Everything you take a photo of is added to the **Hyrule Compendium** and you can even use it to take a selfie of Link! While holding the camera, press **X** and then use the left stick to strike a pose and hold **ZL** to modify the pose.

What's the best photos *you* can take?

COOKING

Piping hot enhancements

Cooking is back and, like before, you can use different ingredients to cook all sorts of meals that give Link unique (and temporary) buffs to specific stats. Basically, it's *super* handy to know as the meals can be **very** powerful.

However, if you've never played Breath of the Wild, then it's *critical* that you pay attention as the sequel *also* doesn't bother telling you how to put the food into the pots that are littered throughout the game (which is rather important as you can't simply drop the food into the pots).

How to Cook

Once you find a lit pot (either one that's pre-lit, one you had to light yourself with flint and an iron weapon, or a single-use Portable Pot), go into the **Materials** menu option and select the first piece of food that you want to cook.

Select the **'Hold'** option that appears and Link will hold one of that item in his hands. You can now select (and hold) up to four more items.

Each food-type gives you an idea of what type of buff to expect (whether that's cold-resistance, heart replenishments, increased stamina, or more).

There's hundreds of recipe combinations and it's helpful to know what recipes give you your best "bang for your buck."

That's why you'll find the complete list of recipes on the following pages (along with what buffs they offer).

Once you've chosen the food you want to cook, press **B** to go back to the game and then press **A** to cook the food.

A few seconds (and a song and dance) later, Link holds a dish, and on-screen appears the recipe name with a list of how many hearts it replenishes, along with any specific buffs it applies (and, crucially, how long that buff is active for).

However, **do not** mix buff ingredients! They just cancel each other out, wasting them. Also, **do not** mix Monster Parts with Food! It creates **Gross Food**!

Toasty!

Another option available to you (if there isn't a pot nearby), is to start a fire with some wood and some flint. However, the best you can do here is to toast individual items.

You *do* get an additional boost to their buffs (versus the uncooked version), but try not to use them on the rarer foods.

Speaking of rarer foods…

Quality Counts

Different qualities of some foods exist as well. "Hearty" versions of food provide greater boosts to your buffs, in comparison to their basic varieties.

However, if you attempt to mix food with Monster Parts (such as a **Keese Wing**), then you'll find that you'll end up cooking something *so* revolting, that the dish is pixelated out!

Elixirs

However, keep those Monster Parts safe as they should be combined with a bug, frog, or lizard at a cooking pot to make powerful Elixirs!

Elixirs act in a similar way to cooked meals, in that the more of a certain item you use, the stronger the buff effects are (and the longer they last for).

Status Effects

Here's what each recipe's status effect means:

- **Dark** - *Gloom resistance*
- **Electro** - *Shock resistance*
- **Enduring** - *Adds stamina*
- **Energizing** - *Restores stamina*
- **Fireproof** - *Fire resistance*
- **Hasty** - *Speed up*
- **Hearty** - *1-5 Extra Hearts*
- **Icy/Chilly** - *Heat resistance*
- **Mighty** - *Attack up*
- **Sneaky** - *Stealth up*
- **Spicy** - *Cold resistance*
- **Sticky** - *Grip up*
- **Sunny** - *Heals Gloom damage*
- **Tough** - *Defense up*

Quick Cooking

Finally, if you have already cooked a recipe with an item before, then you can select **Select for Recipe** to get a list of *every* recipe you've unlocked with *that* material. If you have all the ingredients required, it'll cook it all for you!

Our Favorite Recipes

With well over 200 different recipes to cook up, we're going to focus our attention on the recipes and elixirs that we feel offer some of the best "bang for your buck".

Clearly this isn't an exhaustive list, but this does allow you to focus on the most useful materials to keep an eye out for on your adventure.

Recipe	Ingredients	Status Effect
Bright Fish Skewer	Glowing Cave Fish	Restores health and causes Link to glow (useful in the Depths)
Energizing Elixir	1 x Restless Cricket 1 x Monster Part	Fully restores your stamina (Crickets found in Hyrule Field)
Hearty Elixir	4 x Hearty Lizards 1 x Monster Part	Full recovery + 16 extra hearts!
Hearty Fried Wild Greens	5 x Hearty Radishes	Full recovery + 25 extra hearts!
Warding Dark Stew	1 x Dark Clump 1 x Raw Meat 1 x Any Fish	Increases Gloom Resistance + restores 4 hearts
Enduring Fried Wild Greens	1 x Endura Carrot	Restores 4 hearts, full stamina recovery, and 1/3 extra stamina
Sunny Steamed Meat	1 x Sundelion 1 x Raw Meat	Repairs 3 broken hearts, + 2 hearts restored
Mighty Simmered Shroom	4 x Ironshrooms	+ 3 Defense + 5 hearts restored
Mighty Simmered Fruit	1 x Mighty Bananas	+3 Attack Power + 5 hearts restored
Spicy Sauteed Peppers	5 x Spicy Peppers	12:30 Cold Resistance + 5 hearts restored
Sneaky Mushroom Skewers	5 x Silent Shrooms	10 minutes of stealth + 5 hearts restored

POWER START!

How to Find Great Gear Early

Due to the game's open-world nature, it's possible to find a few key items very early on to make your life *much* easier from the start (when you know where to look for them that is).

So, we've focused on a key balance of how easy/quick the item is to acquire, and also how much benefit it offers in return for the risks involved in obtaining it.

Link's Hylian Shield

This legendary shield is back and this time it's hidden in a hard-to-find tunnel.

Head to Hyrule Castle, and go to the eastern side and stand by the cliff edge at -0127, 1040, 0080.

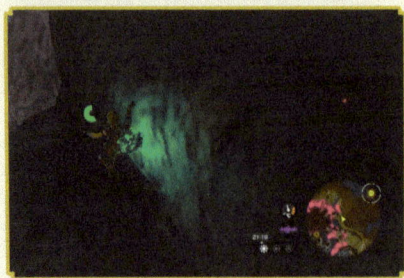

Drop down two small ledges and there's a tunnel here.

Run to the end and use a fire arrow on the pit in the middle to reveal the shield in a chest!

Just be careful with it! It *may* have a defense rating of 90, but it can definitely be broken! However, it's *miles* better than any other regular early-game shield.

Easy Early Rupees

Look out for Addison who's hugging every post in Hyrule. This is a mini-puzzle where you need to construct something so the post doesn't fall over when you ask him to let go.

Use fuse + nearby items to build something and he'll give you rupees, meals, and some materials every time you help him out! Use these easy Rupees to buy better armor/items early on.

Barbarian Armor

Head to the tunnel located on the west side of *Crenel Hills* (north of *Orsedd Bridge*) and take some explosives with you.

Ignore the **Stone Talus** boss in the middle of the room (it's the pile of rocks) and look for the large cluster of green and black rocks on the wall.

Blow it up with a bomb arrow and use the armor from the chest, boosting your attack power!

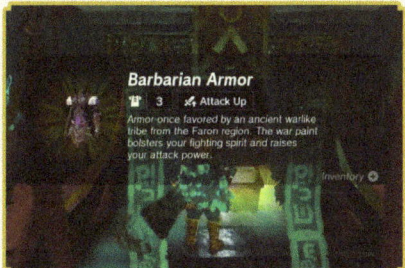

Champion's Leathers + Weapons

Get some height from the first Tower you unlock and use any stamina-boosting items you have to glide all the way over to the platform located northeast of Princess Zelda's Room. Enter the room here.

BotW players will immediately recognize this room. Light both fires either side of the stairs and open the chest that unlocks in the stone area behind you.

Once collected, you can also pick up a few really powerful Royal weapons here (such as a sword and spear), and they'll all give you a solid boost at the start of the game.

Magic Staff

Finally, make your way to *Susub Shrine* (which is hidden underground inside a well near *Deya Village Ruins*). Enter the Shrine, open the chest, and fuse a gem to the staff to turn it into an elemental cannon that can rapidly fire off three balls of energy!

AMIIBO!

Unlocking Those Freebies

If you happen to have an amiibo character from the collection, then you can place it on your Switch to unlock some cool rewards at any point in the game.

Although, note that you can only scan an amiibo once per 24hrs *and* you can only start to use them once you reach the *Temple of Time's* closed door (and try to open it) in the main story-line.

How to use

1. *Enter the Save and Load screen,*
2. *Select options, then amiibo,*
3. *Activate amiibo functionality,*
4. *Check the abilities menu,*
5. *Select amiibo,*
6. *Tap your amiibo on the Switch.*

You can now choose where you want the freebies to drop on the map.

Here's a list of what amiibo unlocks what items (although, do note that not all items drop every time, and some are rare too).

amiibo	Unlocks
8-bit Link	Arrows, Knight's Broadsword, Knight's Shield, Rare: Sword of the Hero, Tunic of the Hero
Bokoblin	Meat, Boko Bow, Spiked Boko Shield, Rare: Bokoblin Fabric
Breath of The Wild Link	Arrows, Fish, Meat, Soldier's Bow, Rare: Tunic of Memories
Breath of The Wild Zelda	Herbs, Gems, Rare: Hyrule-Princess Fabric

amiibo	Unlocks
Daruk	Amber, Flint, Rock, Salt, Cobble Crusher, Rare: Goron-Champion Fabric
Ganondorf	Meat, Gems, Rare: Dusk Claymore, Gerudo Claymore
Guardian	Grilled Fish, Rusty Claymore, Rusty Halberd, Rusty Shield, Rare: Ancient Blade, Ancient-Sheikah Fabric
Archer Link	Arrow, Fish, Meat, Soldier's Bow, Rare: Ancient Blade, Tunic of Memories
Link Rider	Mushrooms, Soldier's Broadsword, Rare: Hylian Hood Fabric
Link's Awakening	Arrows, Soldier's Broadsword, Rare: Tunic of Awakening
Majora's Mask	Mushrooms, Knight's Broadsword, Rare: Fierce Deity Mask, Majora's Mask Fabric
Mipha	Fish, Zora Sphere, Rare: Zora-Champion Fabric
OoT Link	Meat, Soldier's Claymore, Rare: Trousers of Time
Revali	Apples, Arrows, Swallow Bow, Rare: Falcon Bow, Vah Medoh Divine Helm
Sheik	Mushrooms, Eightfold Blade, Phrenic Bow, Rare: Sheik Fabric, Sheik Mask, Shield of the Mind's Eye
Skyward Sword Link	Arrows, Knight's Broadsword, Knight's Shield Rare: Sword-Spirit Fabric, Trousers of the Sky, Tunic of the Sky
TotK Link	Mushrooms, Knight's Broadsword Rare: Champion's Tunic Fabric
Twilight Princess Link	Herb, Soldier's Bow, Rare: Dusk Bow, Princess of Zelda Fabric
Young Link	Meat, Soldier's Claymore Rare: Biggoron's Sword

This is where you get to be *really* creative as these devices can often be stuck together with Ultrahand to create some *exceptionally* useful devices (especially in some of those more difficult Shrines!).

Whether it's a Mech Warrior, a Strike Bomber, a Laser Beam trap, or almost anything else your brain can imagine. Zonai Devices can be often either found out "on the field," or they can be found in a single-use Zonai capsule.

Just be sure to keep them charged with batteries to prevent them failing at the worst possible time!!!

Name	Icon	Description
Balloon		Rises when filled with hot air. Add to a metal base if you plan on using fires to keep it flying high!
Battery		Provides temporary power to other Zonai devices.
Beam Emitter		Shoots a light beam from its horn. Works well fused on top of a Construct Head.
Big Battery		Holds multiple times as much energy as a normal battery.
Big Wheel		It's a big, mean wheel that tears through environments that might challenge smaller wheels (such as shallow water).
Cannon		Fires shots in intervals. The shot explodes when hitting the target.
Cart		Built to move efficiently over flat surfaces. Apply force to get it moving, so long as it has a power source.

Name	Icon	Description
Construct Head		Always faces whatever it deems an enemy. Attach a combat Zonai device to the head for homing attacks.
Fan		Produces wind with its internal propeller. Use vertically to lift things up, horizontally to push things forwards.
Flame Emitter		Shoots flames from its mouth. Works well fused on top of a Construct Head.
Frost Emitter		Shoots icy air from its mouth (freezing smaller enemies). Fusing it with some materials when in icy mountains to change its property.
Homing Cart		Heads straight for the nearest monster. Attach an explosive device to it to cause serious damage and havoc!
Hover Stone		Floats in mid-air. Fuse with a fan to create a "hoverboard."
Hydrant		Shoots water. Works well fused on top of a Construct Head.
Light		Basically a torch. Fuse with a Mirror to greatly extend its range and effectiveness.
Mirror		Focuses and reflects light. Works well when fused with a Light or Beam Emitter.
Portable Pot		Allows you to cook a single recipe on it pretty much anywhere.

Name	Icon	Description
Rocket		Thrusts whatever it's fused to forwards. Fuse one of these to the back of a shield for portable high-speed transport!
Shock Emitter		Shoots a lightning bolt from its horn. Works fused on top of a Construct Head.
Sled		Allows you to travel quicker over grass and sand. Fuse a Rocket or a Fan and small wheels to this for maximum speed benefits.
Small Wheel		Use this on flat or smooth surfaces only.
Spring		Bounces anything off of anything that it touches/touches it. Fuse them to a shield to create high-jump opportunities, or to push attacks away!
Stabilizer		Remains upright. Use to prevent constructions from flipping over.
Stake		Can be fixed to walls or into the ground.
Steering Stick		Activates all powered devices fused to the same construction. Perfect for creating directional cars, planes, etc. Found at the Hudson Construction Site Dispenser, N/E side of the map.
Time Bomb		Creates an explosion *and* this explosion can also activate any other nearby unpowered Zonai devices in its radius!
Wing		Used to glide long distances. Add a Steering Stick and some Fans to it to turn it into a fast plane. Fuse an Emitter to it to turn it into a Fighter Plane!

YouTube

Scan the QR code or use this URL:

That should keep you entertained for a while!

MAIN QUESTS

How to Beat the Story

This part of our guide covers each of the main story missions that ultimately lead you to the final battle and the ending.

Now, it's important to note that once you leave the tutorial Sky Island, you can effectively do the whole game in any order that you like (and, yes, that *does* include going straight to the final boss - well, as soon as you've acquired your Paraglider that is).

Therefore, rather than trying to force you to play this - massively open-world game - in any linear way, we're going to simply allow you to find the quest you want to do as-and-when you want to try and beat it.

Technically speaking, nearly all of the main story missions are optional. However, if you want to see the extended "True" ending, then you'll need to complete **all** of the missions listed on the right.

There's 23 main story missions and some can only be unlocked when previous missions have been completed.

- *Find Princess Zelda*
- *The Closed Door*
- *To the Kingdom of Hyrule*
- *Crisis at Hyrule Castle*
- *Camera Work in the Depths*
- *A Mystery in the Depths*
- *Impa and the Geoglyphs*
- *Regional Phenomena*
- *Find the Fifth Sage*
- *Trail of the Master Sword*
- *Recovering the Hero's Sword*
- *Tulin of Rito Village*
- *Yunobo of Goron City*
- *The Sludge-Covered Statue*
- *The Broken Slate*
- *Restoring the Zora Armor*
- *Clues to the Sky*
- *Sidon of the Zora*
- *Riju of Gerudo Town*
- *Secret of the Ring Ruins*
- *Guidance from Ages Past*
- *The Dragon's Tears*
- *Destroy Ganondorf*

Hyrule Castle Depths

Let's dive straight in, beginning right under the grand Hyrule Castle. Your initial task is simple: follow Zelda, have a chat along the way, and inspect the intriguing findings deep under Hyrule Castle.

As you stroll down a narrow hallway adorned with statues, you'll have a surprise encounter with some pesky *Keese*.

Vanquish them and watch the ensuing cutscene unfold. Once it wraps up, make your way through the corridor emanating red smoke. (What could possibly go wrong, right?) Continue down the corridor.

Link's Awakening

Once you regain consciousness, grab the **[Decayed Master Sword]**. Even in its shoddy state, it'll serve its purpose, allowing you to slice through the vine-ridden doorway.

The subsequent room houses a radiant green circle with a hand emblem. Feel free to interact with it.

After this interaction, a fresh set of doors will open for you. Make your way down this new tunnel, diving into bodies of water and scaling walls until you stumble upon a chest, which contains the Ancient Legwear.

It's advisable to don these as they offer Link some much-needed armor.

Continue through the doorway leading outdoors and make the plunge down to the *Great Sky Island*!

Great Sky Island

Welcome to the Great Sky Island – your starting point. Your first port of call is the *Temple of Time*. As you embark on this journey, we suggest you gather any **[Tree Branches]** and food items you encounter.

On landing in the pond peppered with lilypads, swim ashore and descend the staircase. Stick to the path, and you'll soon confront a *Zonai Soldier Construct.*

After you've dealt with it, you'll find a quaint stone structure that houses a **[Wooden Stick]** - a significant upgrade to your tree branches.

Continue along the path until you bump into a friendly *Steward Construct* who gifts you the

[Purah Pad], the game's equivalent of the Shiekah Slate from Breath of the Wild.

Quest: Closed Door

With the Purah Pad in your possession, it's time to pay a visit to the *Temple of Time.*

Before you do, interact with another green circle to the right of the Steward Construct. This activates a bridge for you to cross.

Once you've crossed, follow the path to a platform overlooking a pond ripe for diving. Take the plunge.

Welcome to a grander portion of the Great Sky Island. While our guide offers a more direct route to each if the key locations in the game, you are welcome to explore this vast area at your own pace.

Temple of Time

Our route to the Temple of Time involved exiting the pond flanked by two stone stands and following the path that begins at their base. We tackled any *Soldier Constructs* along the way until we reached the steps to the temple.

Upon reaching the temple, swim through the water to find the steps and ascend. Here, you'll face a shield-wielding *Soldier Construct.* After defeating it, try to make your way into the *Temple of Time.*

After the cutscene, you'll automatically embark on the main quest – **The Closed Door.** Your mission is to explore the shrines dotted across the Great Sky Island. Your first stop?

The *Ukouh Shrine*, where you'll unlock the first key ability in this game - **Ultrahand**.

Shrine

 Story

 Weapon

 Zonaite

 K. Seed

Charge

The *Ukouh Shrine*, situated directly to the west of the *Temple of Time* on the expansive *Great Sky Island*, is a significant landmark in Zelda: Tears of the Kingdom.

Its silhouette is easy to see in the distance when you stand outside the temple.

This page describes the route we used to reach the *Ukouh Shrine*. However, if casual exploration is more your thing (and there's lots to discover here), then feel free to come back to this page for direct guidance when you're ready to head to the first shrine.

To the Shrine

Your first goal is to descend the somewhat decrepit steps to the west, a stone's throw away from the Temple of Time's entrance.

Then, keep your course set westward, toward the hill where the shrine proudly stands.

As you head there, a couple of *Zonai Soldier Constructs* may cross your path. If you're up for the challenge, feel free to engage them for some Zonai materials.

Once you find yourself at the base of the hill, swim across the petite pond and commence your uphill journey.

At certain junctures, you'll have to flex your climbing skills to bridge the gap left by missing stairs.

Your stamina is limited, but you can speed things up by pressing X to jump up/across a wall (but at a cost of a chunk of Stamina). You'll find the first shrine (of many) at the top.

Shrine: Ukouh

This shrine bestows you with the **Ultrahand** ability. You'll immediately begin using it to solve each of the three key puzzles in this Shrine.

Bridging the Gap

Jumping right into our Ultrahand puzzle, we kick-off with a straightforward task: just grab that wooden plank and lay it across the gap, serving as your makeshift bridge.

You can twist and turn the plank for the perfect fit by turning the left joytsick and using the D-pad for horizontal or vertical adjustments.

longer bridge. Lift it up, place it across the wider gap, and cross it.

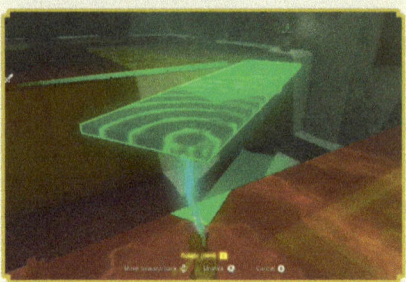

Hooked on it

First, grab the plank from the wall and lay it down. Now take off a hook, rotate it so it's base is level with the plank below it, and attach it right in the center of the plank.

Now lift your newly crafted hook-and-plank combo and latch it onto the metal zip-line.

Don't be Con-fused

Grab the plank on the wall and then rotate it so it's flat. Lower it down and as you bring the wood closer together, a few attachment options will present themselves.

Carefully attach the ends of the planks together to make a

As soon as it hooks, be ready to hop on - it'll likely start moving immediately.!Enjoy the ride to the end of the shrine, where your first **[Light of Blessing]** awaits.

KEY:

- Shrine
- Weapon
- K. Seed
- Story
- Gemstone
- Charge

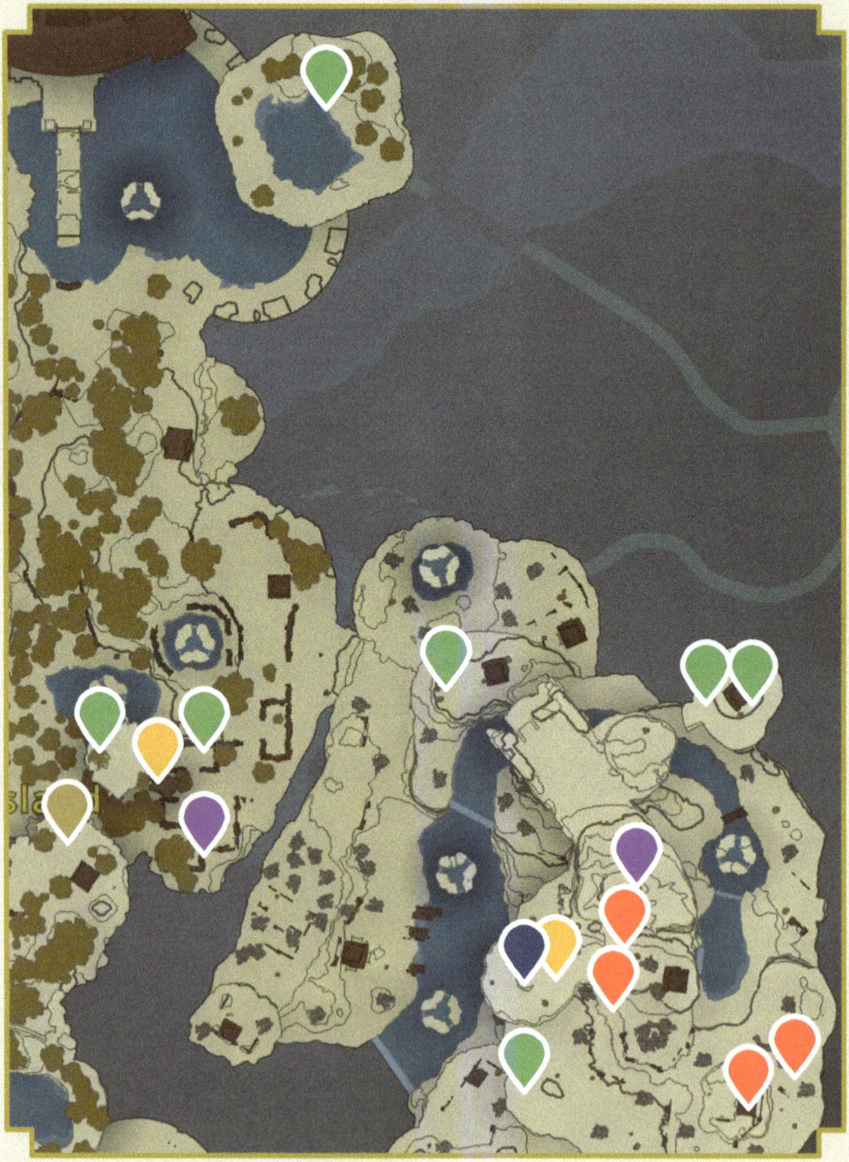

The Gutanbac Shrine resides in the frigid, snow-blanketed part of Sky Island.

Our journey started at the *Ukouh Shrine*. We backtracked our path to the sizable pool situated at the base of the main stairs leading to the Temple of Time.

From this point, we set course southeast, passing a stone platform that emerged from the ground, followed by a descent down a flight of stairs.

This led us to an open space, inhabited by a *Zonai Soldier Construct* and a stove. After dispatching the Construct, our attention turned to the building housing the stove.

Ooh! Toasty!

Nearby, **[Spicy Peppers]** can be found flourishing in the bushes. We recommend collecting these peppers and utilizing them to whip up a range of dishes that offer **Cold Resistance**.

Combining two Spicy Peppers with one Raw Meat yields a **Spicy Pepper Steak,** providing 5:30 minutes of Cold Resistance. Alternatively, cooking three Spicy Peppers results in **Spicy Sautéed Peppers,** offering 7:30 minutes of Cold Resistance.

To gain a hefty 12:30 minutes of Cold Resistance, cook five peppers together.

Once you're prepared, ascend the slope behind the building. Be sure to munch on one of your prepared meals as the temperature plummets to prevent Link from sustaining damage.

Turn right at the crest of the slope, picking up more **[Spicy Peppers]** along the way. This path eventually guides you to a lake, where a Maker Construct is stationed, overseeing some rafts.

River Crossing

The **Energy Cell** is a critical tool, enabling the use of **Zonai Devices**. These devices range from Portable Stoves to Flamethrowers to Fans, useful for propelling various vehicles.

As the name suggests, the Energy Cell stores the energy needed to operate these devices and recharges automatically when not in use. As you progress, you'll unlock the capability to augment the power capacity of the Energy Cell.

To acquire the Energy Cell, engage in a conversation with the Maker Construct near the lake in the frosty region of the Great Sky Island, who's maintaining the rafts.

Once you possess your Energy Cell, board one of the rafts afloat in the water and strike the Fan with your weapon or an arrow. This action activates the Fan, propelling the raft across the water.

Upon reaching the other side of the lake, veer left and ascend the stairs. Reach the summit by clambering up the rocks and cliffside.

You'll find yourself at a small river with a waterfall. Turn right to find a rock you can leap onto. From its top, follow the path leading behind the waterfall.

At the summit, a bridge and Soldier Construct await.

Nearby, you'll spot a stove and **[Spicy Pepper]** bushes in the vicinity of the Construct, handy for preparing additional Cold Resistance meals, if required.

Next, scale the stairs near the stove and follow the path around the pool until you find yourself on the opposite side of the waterfall.

Here, start your ascent of the cliff face. There should be a resting spot approximately halfway up to recover stamina before resuming your climb.

Upon reaching the peak, you'll spot a stone building housing a stove. To your right, the *Gutanbac Shrine* awaits.

Shrine: Gutanbac

This shrine bestows you with the **Ascend** ability. You'll immediately begin using it to solve each of the three key puzzles in this Shrine.

Puzzle 1

Upon reaching this elevated area, you'll notice two pillars on the rightmost wall, both of which you can ascend. The left one leads to a chest, the right one leads to the next level of the Shrine.

Once the bridge has dropped, circle around and ascend onto the bridge.

Puzzle 3

The concluding puzzle is straightforward. Stand under the moving platform ahead and patiently wait until it's directly above you to ascend onto it.

Puzzle 2

Entering the next area, you'll spot a **Construct** enemy looming ahead. Eliminate it as necessary, then veer to the right.

If you destroy the nearby crates and ascend, you can claim the **[Construct Bow]** up here.

Proceed towards the ropes suspending a bridge. Sever the rope using a sharp weapon by striking the loops on the ground, or simply ignite it with a fiery arrow.

Once aboard, time your next ascend to the platform above to reach the shrine's end, where you can receive your third **[Light of Blessing]**. One more to go before your first upgrade!

Key:

- Shrine
- Story
- Weapon
- Gemstone
- K. Seed
- Charge

Great Sky Isla

The *In-Isa Shrine* is located southwest of the Temple of Time.

If you've completed the Gutanbac Shrine previously, descending the snowy mountain is your next task.

A simple way to achieve this is by using Ascend on the hollow tree near the Gutanbac Shrine and employing the Zonai Wings on the other side of the tree to glide down to the vicinity outside of the *Temple of Time*.

Don't forget to collect the **[Archaic Warm Greaves]** from within this tree (as they automatically add some Cold Resistance by default).

Our trek to the In-Isa Shrine commenced atop the hill south of the Ukouh Shrine. After descending a flight of stairs, we discovered a railing leading to the next segment of the *Great Sky Island*.

Echoing the Ukouh Shrine challenge, nearby planks and hooks are to be utilized to construct a platform to ensure safe passage to the next section of the island.

Upon reaching there, you'll notice a broken bridge, making it necessary to build your own bridge using Ultrahand to cross.

We accomplished this by fastening four logs together in a two-by-two horizontal shape, then positioning it over the gap.

Plenty of logs are scattered around this area for experimentation. If you need more, you can fell some trees. Next to the Zonai Construct - one of many you'll encounter on this path who will impart knowledge about the game's mechanics - you'll find a Stone Axe to assist you in this task.

After creating your bridge and crossing to the other side, you need to veer east and traverse another, intact, bridge.

Along this route, you'll encounter a Zonai Construct with a set of [10 arrows] and an [Old Wooden Bow] nearby for your taking.

From this Zonai Construct, follow the river southward. On your journey, you may come across a Construct ready to offer a quick cooking lesson and three Soldier Constructs. Defeating these Soldier Constructs will unlock a chest containing an [Opal].

If you plan on bringing the Korok along, attaching two hooks is a smart move.

Once prepared, hook your platform onto the railing, hop on, and savor the stunning view as you glide through the sky.

Eventually, you'll find yourself at a cliff's edge, with a panoramic view of a lake and the shrine on the opposite side. From here, head west until you encounter another railing.

At this point, you need to use logs, hooks, and Ultrahand to create another platform for crossing the railing.

We suggest cutting down a tree for a log, ensuring enough room to transport the nearby Korok to their companion on the next island.

Once you land on the subsequent small island, deliver the Korok to their friend if you've brought them along. Doing so rewards you with *two* [Korok Seeds].

Don't worry, there's only another 998 Korok Seeds to find in Tears of the Kingdom!.

Regardless of whether you've transported the Korok or not, you will need to seize the sail on the ground with Ultrahand and affix it to the side of your platform.

Once secure, shift the platform onto the next railing before hopping on yourself.

You'll now find yourself at the lake's edge. But before you can set sail, you'll need to detach the hooks from your platform and position the sail upright on it.

Once it's ready, place the raft on the water and hop aboard. If the wind shifts direction while you're sailing, simply use Ultrahand to adjust the sail.

Upon reaching the lake's other side, follow the path to a set of stairs leading to the *In-Isa Shrine*.

Along the way, be prepared to face a couple of ChuChus and a Soldier Construct.

IN-ISA SHRINE

This shrine bestows you with the **Fuse** ability. You'll immediately begin using it to solve each of the three key puzzles in this Shrine.

Sword + Boulder

Choose a boulder to fuse with your weapon, creating a super handy "Boulder" fused weapon. To proceed, you'll need to employ this boulder weapon to bash through the stone obstruction in your way.

Firestarter

Head down the left corridor where you'll be greeted by two rows of fiery fruit trees. Harvest some **[Fire Fruit]** and arm your bow.

With your bow drawn, hit the **UP** button on the D-pad to access your inventory and select the fire fruit to fuse it with your bow.!

Take aim at the leafy upper part of the wall ahead with your fiery bow.

The resulting blaze will consume the leaves and wooden shelf, causing the chest to plummet. Inside, you'll find a **[Small Key]**. This newly acquired key unlocks the nearby door.

Fused Combat

With the door open, you're now in the shrine's final puzzle room. Your task here: battle a **Captain Construct** Construct I, who also wields the **Fuse** ability!

You can either choose to battle it (use fiery arrows to set the leaves on the ground on fire, then smash it) and grab the Bow it drops.

Or, simply smash the rocks behind it, and finish the Shrine! The choice is yours!

After wrapping up both the Gutanbac Shrine and In-Isa Shrine, your next destination is back to the Temple of Time.

Once there, open the temple door to conclude The Closed Door main quest. Then, step inside and touch the tear-shaped crystal.

After a brief cutscene, you'll be granted the **Recall** ability, which lets you reverse an object's movement and halt it whenever you please.

Your next task is to employ Recall on one of the wheels at the temple's rear, reversing their rotation to access the platform above.

Here, you'll find a **Goddess Statue**, but you're one **Light of Blessing** short of receiving an upgrade from it. Doh!

For now, try to unlock the door behind the Goddess Statue. You'll come up short, but fret not - this door won't remain locked for much longer.

The Nachoyah Shrine

To get to the Nachoyah Shrine you'll need to first use your map to travel back to the *Room of Awakening*.

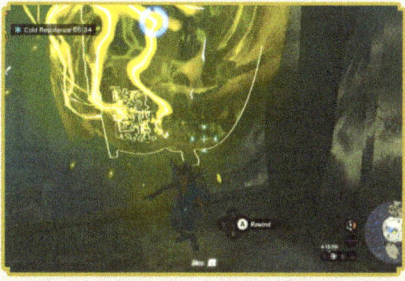

Once you've arrived, activate Ascend beneath the platform on the left side of the room. Then, use Recall to reverse the rotation of the wheel in front of you and climb onto it.

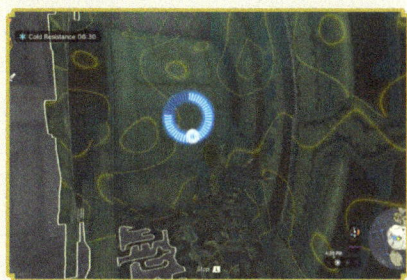

When the moment is right, leap over to the next wheel, and from there, you can make your way to a passage in the rock. You might need to utilize Recall a second time while doing this.

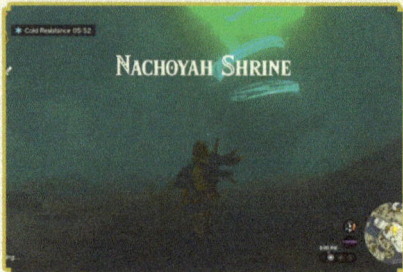

Follow the passage, and you'll soon arrive at the Nachoyah Shrine.

It's worth mentioning that a Crystal Refinery is situated near the shrine.

This refinery can be used to generate Energy Wells, enhancing the capacity of your Energy Cell and thereby allowing you to power Zonai Devices for longer stretches of time.

For the time being, you won't be able to use the refinery, but remember its location for future use.

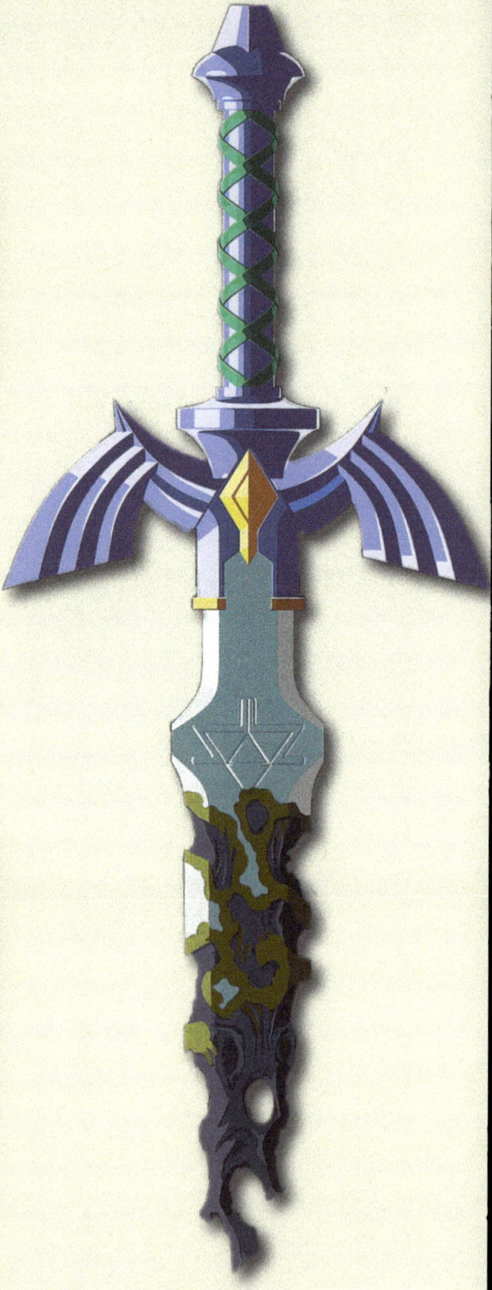

Shrine: Nachoyah

Map: 0388, -1660, 2299
Region: Great Sky Island

This shrine bestows you with the **Recall** ability. You'll immediately begin using it to solve each of the three key puzzles in this Shrine.

Water Crossing

As you venture into the shrine, you'll observe a raft drifting towards you downstream. Proceed to the ledge, activate **Recall** on the raft, and promptly hop on.

This carries you upstream, helping you traverse the strong currents to reach the other side. Here, a second raft awaits the same treatment, with the added twist of ascending a waterfall as it reverses!

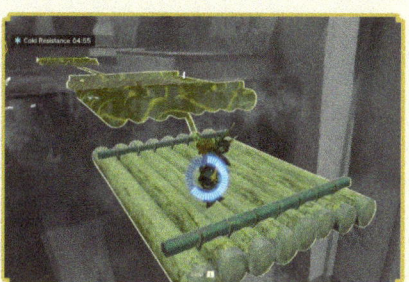

Clock Hands

The solution to this (initially awkward looking) puzzle is unexpectedly straightforward: as the hands cross each other, activate recall on one of the clock hands.

This causes them to move in unison!

With this adjustment, you'll have ample time to pass through the door. Following this, you can cancel recall to restore the clock to its original state!

Beyond this door lies the end of the shrine, where you can claim the fourth **[Light of Blessing]**.

Now head back to the *Temple of Time* and exchange your four Lights of Blessing for a **Heart Container**.

Use Ascend to cross the broken bridge and the cutscene signals the end of the tutorial area and the game starting properly!

Hyrule Field

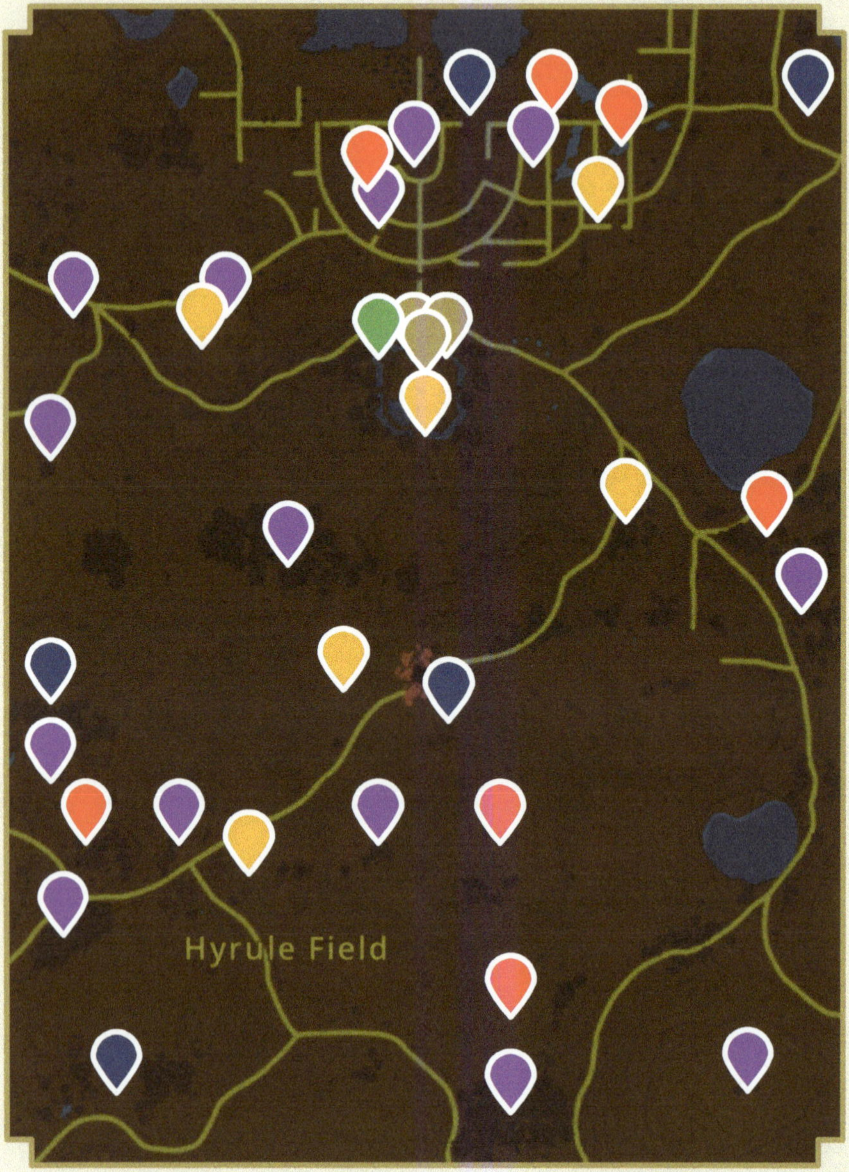

> **Top Tip:** *While it's not mandatory to do so, we recommend that you get the first few key story-line missions completed out of the way. Doing so now unlocks a bunch of key upgrades (such as the Paraglider) and the final two abilities.*

After surviving that unbelievably high base jump down to the surface level, it's time to begin the game in earnest.

Head to Lookout Landing

Your first destination should be *Lookout Landing*, positioned on the periphery of the *Hyrule Castle Town Ruins*.

To get there, you'll need to navigate towards *Hyrule Castle*, which is quite hard to miss (given its floating nature and the red smoke enveloping it).

During your journey, you'll come across **Bokoblins** that you can defeat to gather materials and weapons.

You'll also encounter heaps of building supplies, handy for constructing a vehicle if you're in the mood for a quicker way to get around the vast open world.

Once you arrive at *Lookout Landing*, you'll bump into **Robbie**, who'll direct you to have a chat with **Purah**. She's located on the second floor of the building equipped with a telescope aimed at *Hyrule Castle*.

Once you're there, have a word with Josha, and Purah will come out to greet you.

After your conversation with Purah, the To The Kingdom of Hyrule quest will wrap up, and the Crisis at Hyrule Castle main quest will kick off automatically.

As noted earlier, we'd also advise you to complete the initial part of the *Crisis at Hyrule Castle* quest before delving deeper into Hyrule, as it will unlock some crucial features, like the **Paraglider**.

KEY:

Shrine
Weapon
K. Seed
Story
Gemstone
Tower

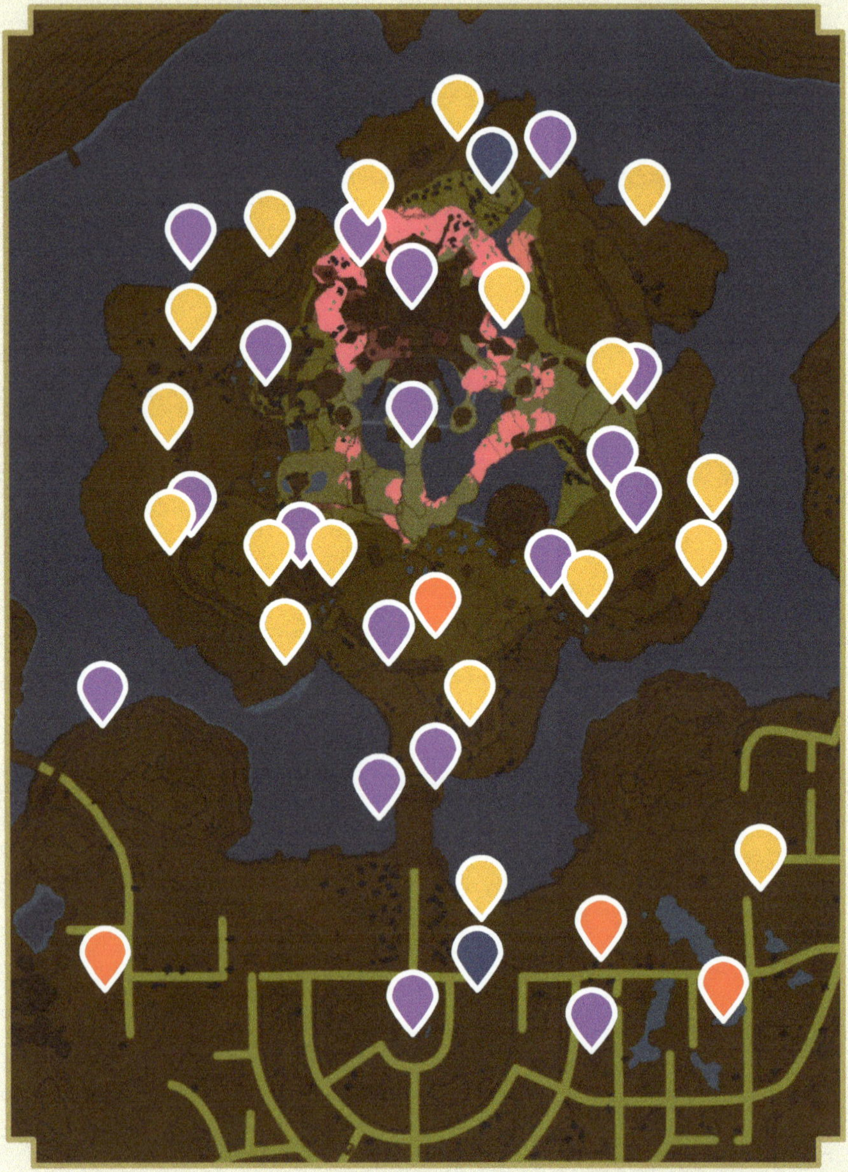

Find Hoz

Your initial task in the *Crisis at Hyrule Castle* main quest involves syncing up with Hoz, the skipper of Princess Zelda's search party.

At present, he's at *Hyrule Castle*, so exit *Lookout Landing* and navigate through the remnants of Hyrule Castle Town until you find yourself at the castle gates.

On your way, you'll have the opportunity to gather additional weapons and, if you feel inclined, tackle the challenge presented by the *Kyononis Shrine* (see page 169 for the solution to this shrine).

Upon reaching the castle gates, you'll soon realize that they're simply too massive for you to pry open.

The workaround is to leap over the side of the walkway adjacent to the gates and go around them.

Having made it to the other side, you can have a word with Raseno, who'll inform you that Hoz is stationed at the castle's first gatehouse.

To locate this gatehouse, just follow the path until you come across the building.

Upon arriving at the gatehouse, make your way inside and scale one of the walls until you reach the first balcony.

From here, continue your upward climb along the exterior walls until you reach the gatehouse's next level, where you'll find Hoz.

Engage in conversation with Hoz, then kick back and relish the ensuing cutscene.

Now it's time to loop back to *Lookout Landing* where you'll acquire the **[Paraglider]**.

Acquiring the Paraglider

After your dialogue with **Hoz**, your next stop is *Lookout Landing* to reconnect with **Purah**. So, whenever you're ready, backtrack along your previous route.

If you've managed to conquer the *Kyononis Shrine*, you can speed up your return by teleporting to it.

Purah will be exactly where you last saw her, in the company of Josha.

Post-chat, you can indulge your curiosity and explore the emergency shelter or simply make a beeline to the *Skyview Tower* and engage **Purah** in conversation once more.

Following a brief cinematic, examine the console situated nearby and, after a subsequent chat with **Purah**, she will present you with the **[Paraglider]**.

Now it's time to step onto the luminescent blue circle within the *Skyview Tower* to augment your map with *Central Hyrule*.

Having touched ground again, make your way back to the building housing the telescope and initiate another discussion with **Purah**.

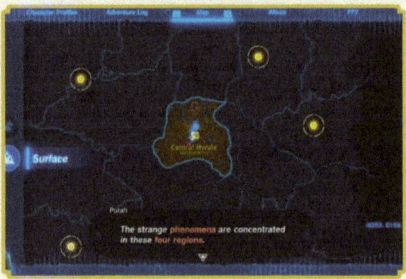

This dialogue will trigger the Regional Phenomena main quest, charging you with traversing Hyrule to assist the **Rito**, **Zora**, **Gorons**, and the **Gerudo**. The whole of Hyrule is now yours to discover!

Your next move is entirely up to you! Will you hunt for shrines, progress the main story-line, or scout the terrain for hidden gems?

However, it's important to note that this particular quest is *far* from over. You won't be able to finish it until *a f t e r* completing the *R e g i o n a l Phenomena* quest (which is very big and long).

Before that quest, we do **strongly** suggest spending some time on the *Camera Work In The Depths* quest, initiated by **Josha**.

This quest not only serves as an orientation to the chasms, but also provides access to the **Camera** ability.

To continue the *Regional Phenomena* quest, you need to either make your way to *Hebra* for the **Rito** quest, *Eldin* for the **Goron** quest, *Gerudo Desert* for the **Gerudo** quest, or *Lanayru* for the **Zora** quest.

Lastly, you can take on the *Impa and* the *Geoglyphs* quest, which will enable you to start amassing memories across Hyrule and trigger *The Dragon's Tears* quest.

KEY:

 Lightroot   Weapon   K. Seed

Story   Shield Armor

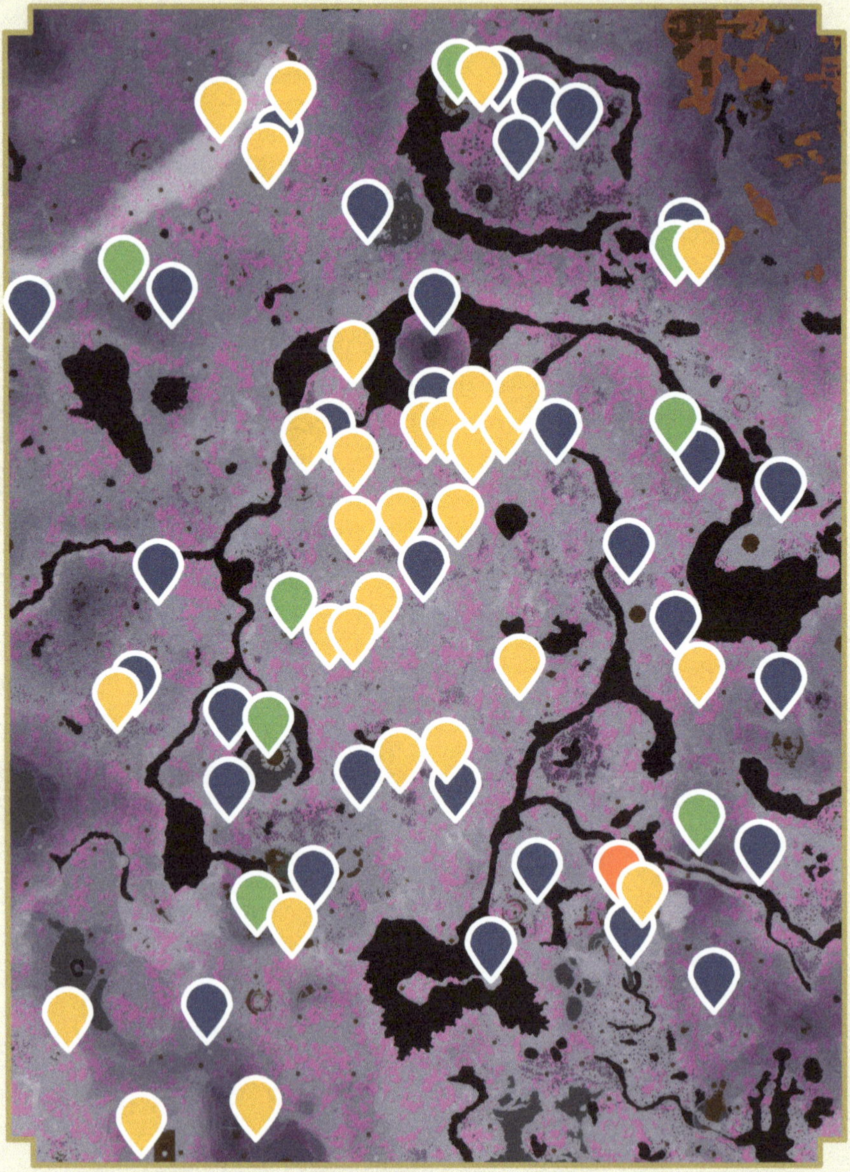

Caution! *The questline for 'A Mystery in the Depths' initially calls for the completion of any one section of the primary story-line quest, 'Regional Phenomena'. Just make sure to clear one area so it's removed from your quest log.*

After checking off your chosen area, seek out *Josha* at *Lookout Landing*. She'll share her belief about a temple hidden in the Depths, accessible via a series of statues that guide your way.

She'll hand over **[10 Giant Brightbloom Seeds]** and **[10 Arrows]** for assistance. However, considering the vast expanse of the Depths, we recommend a much larger stash of lights for your expedition…

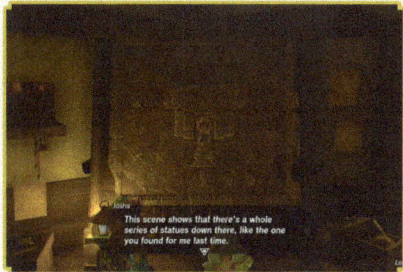

How to unlock Autobuild

To get your hands on the **Autobuild** ability, your journey starts with a fast-travel to *Layusus Lightroot*.

Here, you'll notice the statues' gaze directing you - heed their silent guidance. Their general pointing is south, but keep a sharp eye to avoid straying into the dark unknown.

A few statues later, you'll stumble upon *Nihcayam Lightroot*. Ignite it to unlock a fast-travel point and brighten the surrounding area. Then, stick to the statues, moving southward.

Three statues in, an open space filled with red Gloom greets you. Checking your mini-map, you'll see you're on the lit edge of *Nihcayam Lightroot*. Caution is advised here as a mini-boss, **Frox: Scourge of the Depths**, lurks to the right!

Mini-Boss: Frox

You can circumvent the Gloom patch and continue south if you wish to avoid conflict. However, if you decide to engage Frox, beware its devouring breath attack and crushing bounce.

Keep a safe distance and aim for its eye to stun it. Once stunned, scale its back and strike the rock outcrops for damage.

Defeating it earns you a bounty of [**Zonaite**], a [**Large Crystallized Charge**], [**Frox fangs**], and [**Frox Fingernails**].

Keep moving south, tackling or dodging enemies along the way. A large statue-less gap awaits, but persist.

Pass an ancient ruin housing a Wing and some Zonai devices - a sign you're on the right path. Small fires in the distance can guide your way.

As you draw near, drop Brightbloom Seeds to illuminate a potentially tricky rock ledge.

Traverse the ledge and deal with a camp of Gloom-infected **Moblins** and **Bokoblins**.

You can also snatch the two Grand Poe on the left. Then, press on until you reach the *Great Abandoned Central Mine*.

Here, activate the construct to receive **Autobuild**.

This ability lets you instantly replicate your Ultrahand-made creations, recalling past projects for quick repetition, and also awards you Schema Stones for common and useful projects.

For now, follow the NPC's instructions to repair the car by reattaching its wheel. Then, use Autobuild to duplicate the car on the opposite side.

Boss: Master Kohga

You now face a boss battle with a Yiga clan member, Master Kohga in Zelda: Tears of the Kingdom. They'll use their own car to attempt to run you over.

Phase 1

Stun them with a bow shot and knock them off their structure, then charge in for a sword attack. (Autobuild can be used to create your own car, but we didn't find this particularly useful.)

Phase 2

In the second phase, the Yiga clan member's car will sport a front barrier, but it won't stop your arrows.

Phase 3

The third phase upgrades the car with a windshield and sides, forcing you to attack from the rear. Persist with your arrow attacks and the fight should be manageable.

Once you've beaten the Yiga clan, open the chest to procure a **[Huge Crystallized Charge]**.

Then, interact with the constructs as directed. You'll receive your first **[Schema Stone]** that crafts a Fanplane! Sweet!

You'll also secure the parts necessary to test it out, so give it a whirl and slot it into the groove, heading towards the nearby *Lightroot*.

Feel free to snag some **Poes** along the way, but remember that doing so may land you down a small cliff from the Lightroot, obscuring it from view. You might need to drop a Brightbloom Seed or two to re-orient yourself.

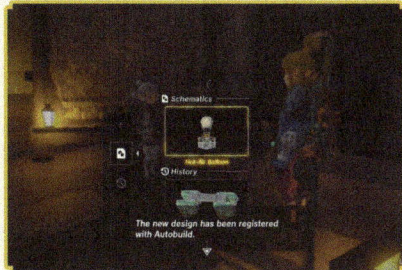

Once you've activated *Koradat Lightroot*, you're free to explore more, but return to **Josha** when you feel ready.

She'll present another Schema Stone, which crafts a hot air balloon. After her conversation, head outside and repair the balloon. She'll reward you with a **[Large Zonaite]** for your efforts.

While this technically wraps up the quest, you'll automatically inform **Josha** about the Yiga clan, leading her to share more about the statues and setting up your subsequent Depths mission.

You're now eligible to converse with **Robbie** to kick off the *Hateno Village Research Lab* quest, which unlocks several upgrades for the Purah Pad, including the **[Travel Medallion]**, **[Shrine Sensor]**, and **Hero's Path** mode.

This quest has you going to four different regions (each with their own elemental challenges) that you need to visit.

We're going to offer our recommendation of the order in which we believe you should try. Of course, the choice is ultimately up to you.

Our recommended order is:

- **Rito Village** - *Hebra*
- **Goron City** - *Eldin (northeast of Lookout Landing)*
- **Zora Domain** - *Lanayru (east of Lookout Landing)*
- **Gerudo Town** - *Gerudo (southwest of Lookout Landing)*

Rito Village Tips

Let's get you set for the Rito Village. It's chilly up there, so packing some **Cold Resistant** gear is crucial.

Don't forget those spicy pepper dishes and any Cold Resistant attire you might've snagged from the Great Sky Island.

When you reach the village, keep an eye out for the **[Snowquill Armor Set]**. It'll give Link an extra shield from the biting cold.

Goron City Tips

Onward to *Eldin* and the Goron story-line. Things get hot here, so fire resistance is key. Brewing up some fireproof elixirs with fireproof lizards and monster parts should do the trick.

Oh, and in *Goron City*, you'll find the **[Flamebreaker Armor Set]**, just like in BotW. Just a quick note - fireproof and heat-proof are *not* the same thing.

Your cooling elixirs won't save you from the lava-filled caverns of *Eldin*.

Zora Domain Tips

No weather issues here, just plenty of water. But no worries - the Zora Armour is part of the story-line. So, you're all set!

Do pack some blue Chuchu jelly for cleanup duty though. Trust me, you'll understand what we mean when you get there...

Gerudo Town Tips

The Gerudo Desert tests both your cold resistance and your heat resistance. You can get the **[Desert Voe]** set from the Gerudo region to keep you cool during the heat.

Getting to Rito Village

Once you hit the cliffside near *Rito Village,* you'll see the bridge is out of commission. Fear not. Look for **[Hylian Pinecones]**, they're usually scattered in front of the *Lucky Clover Gazette.*

Take these to the fire near the busted bridge and chuck 'em in. Watch as the fire roars up and creates a draft that can take your glider sky-high. From this vantage point, glide over to *Rito Village.*

Once you've touched down in Rito Village, don't forget to trigger the *Gatakis Shrine.* It'll be your warp point back to town.

Quest: Tulin of Rito Village

Locating Hebra South Summit Cave

> **Top Tip:** *Grab the Snowquill Armor from the local shop in the village! Hebra Mountains can kill you without sufficient Cold Resistant armor/ recipes.*

To begin your journey from Rito Village, set your course to *Hebra Trailhead Lodge.* Paraglide from *Revali's Landing* to the small rock pillar mid-way across *Lake Totori.*

Catch your breath, then glide the rest of the way over the lake, heading north towards the lodge.

Upon entering the lodge, have a chat with **Harth**. He'll guide you towards your next target - **Tulin**, who's hanging out in Hebra South Summit Cave.

Apparently, the cave is northeast of the lodge, marked by a hard-to-miss bonfire.

Climb the ladder and begin your uphill journey on the Mountain Climbing Path. There's a handy detour available: activating the *Rospro Pass Skyview Tower,* just left of the climbing path.

After sorting out the tower, continue along the snow-lined path. Expect some Ice Keese and a Bokoblin to cross your path. Keep your eyes peeled to your left for a large bonfire - that's your ticket into *Hebra South Summit Cave!*

Tulin's Location

Once you're in *Hebra South Summit Cave,* find **Laissa**, a Rito chilling in the cave. She'll hint that Tulin's somewhere deeper in the cave.

Right beside Laissa, you'll see some pesky bramble thorns partially blocking the way.

No fire fruit or fire-fueled weapon? A torch will do to burn those brambles. If you'd rather, you can squeeze past them to a large cavernous room.

A draft from below gives you the chance to take your paraglider for a spin. Aim for a small opening in the opposite wall.

You'll encounter a Horroblin here. Arrow him to drop him down, then finish him off with more arrows or a melee weapon.

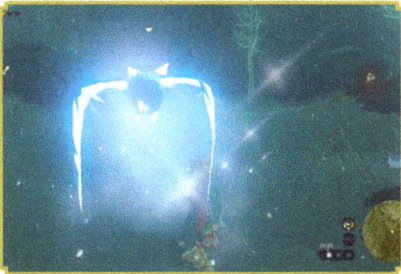

Deeper into the cave, there's a small room with a campfire, flint, and barrels. Look up to see more brambles.

You'll need to either fly and glide over or burn the brambles and climb up. Either way, you'll need a campfire, built using the flint.

Hopefully, you've collected some Hylian Pine Cones from Rito Village and Hebra region. Throwing them on fires creates gusts of wind, which can give your paraglider a lift to the ledge.

No pine cones? Use the fire to light your arrows and burn the brambles or opt for Fire Fruit.

On the ledge, there are more brambles. Drop a flint near them, strike it with a metal or stone weapon and watch the thorns go up in flames.

In the next room, defeat a Bubbulfrog to score its Bubbul Gem! Head up the ledge on the back wall to proceed out of the cave.

Surprisingly, Tulin's not in the cave! Out of the cave, it's time to scale the mountain.

After a bit of climbing, you'll find a winding path leading you to the summit. There, at last, you'll find Tulin!

However, this was just the first part of this particular mission. It's now time to go find one of the classic Zelda components that was missing from BotW - Dungeons!

So, let's go find it!

Reaching The Wind Temple

Caution! *Don't forget to pack a handful of cold-resistant meals and don your warmest outfit. You're about to scale a frosty mountain, after all!*

After securing Tulin's bow from the monster and clearing out the enemies, Tulin gains the green light to venture to the blizzard's origin.

Linking up with him unlocks a new skill, a gust-enhancer, perfect for giving your glider a speed boost mid-flight!

Next stop: the sky region, gateway to the dungeon. From this point, simply follow the platforms and pillars northeast to Hebra Peak's summit, then rise into the sky!

With Tulin back under your control, leap and glide to the next pillar, employing his gust to aid your journey.

Repeat this maneuver to scale the ruins and reach the mountain's peak. Easy, just watch your stamina!

Once you reach the Summit, employ Gust to cross the first batch of floating platforms. Start ascending the towering structure.

At the top, hop across to the platform and use your Ascend ability to float higher into the sky.

Rising Island Chain

A cutscene shows Link and Tulin discovering a floating boat. Now the challenge truly begins. Hop onto the ship's sail and glide towards the Mayaumekis Shrine. Activating it offers a convenient fast travel point.

Next, head to the ruins on your left. Break the ice here for a chest containing five arrows.

MAYAUMEKIS SHRINE
Hebra Mountains Sky

Use Gust to reach the next floating ruin, defeat the Construct waiting for you, and proceed to the next boat sail.

Two more Constructs and a towering climb later, stack two sets of cubes under the pillar's ledge. Now, use Ascend to climb up easily.

Keep heading forward, gliding into an alcove with icicles and employing Ascend. Congrats, you've moved up a sky ruin level!

A large gate looms ahead. Use Gust to reach it and the next set of ruins (watch out for another Construct!).

Onwards, break the ice blocking your path with an arrow (Bomb flower attachments work wonders!) and glide towards the next sail.

Navigate towards another island, use the sail to move forward, break the obstruction on the next island, and glide across to the floating ship.

Here, glide onto the sail, traverse to the next, and be cautious of the flying enemies. Once at the temple-like ruin, glide to the next set of ruins, blocked by monsters.

Careful, the bridge beyond the Constructs collapses underfoot! To cross, climb up on the arch before the bridge and use your glider and Gust to make it across safely.

Navigate through some more Constructs before arriving at an area with broken parts. Here, you'll assemble a hot air balloon to continue.

With the balloon assembled, strike the dragon head with a weapon, and watch as it ascends. Glide over to the next pillar and use Ascend to reach the next sky ruin level.

From there, climb up the ruin walls, and get ready for another sail and a pair of floating ships.

Take a leap onto the first sail, then glide to one of the ships to drop onto its sail. Break the ice ahead and use the sail to ascend.

At this point, Tulin will warn you about the bone-chilling cold. Make sure Link is kitted out with at least one piece of cold-resistant armor and has enjoyed a spicy dish. Then, activate the Kahatanaum Shrine for another teleport point.

Need more cold-resistant food or better gear? Seize this moment to gear up. Next, hop onto the sail and start utilizing the ships circling the storm's eye to ascend further.

At the pinnacle, the blizzard dissipates. Work your way up onto the final ship's sail and leap onto it.

With a combination of Gust and your glider, glide into the storm's heart and make your descent. Now, it's time to proceed into the *W i n d Temple.*

 # THE WIND TEMPLE

KEY: Turbine Weapon Gem

1F

B1

B2

Skyward bound above Hebra, you'll find yourself at the Wind Temple, also known as The Legendary Stormwind Ark.

Your mission? Disengage five Wind Turbine-style locks to confront the boss and end the blizzard. Get ready to traverse the highs and lows of this ship with Tulin and Link.

Lock Hunt

After touchdown on the massive boat, interact with the Ouroboros statue for a teleport point. A cutscene will then reveal the blizzard's cause.

One lock is already activated, leaving five others for you to locate across the ship's three levels.

Unlocking these five locks can be done in any sequence, but kicking off with the ones directly in front of you post-temple-unlock is recommended.

You must find five different ship entry points to reach all locks.

Lock 1 - Upper Stern

Your first lock is tackled by advancing towards the ship's stern and three locked doors. Ignore the large middle door upstairs—it's unopenable.

Instead, go left and use Ultrahand to yank the lever, unveiling a gate and a construct with a Flame-emitter Spear.

After defeating him, claim the spear—it'll come in handy later. Also, nab the treasure chest down the hall.

Exiting the room, turn left and spot an icicle. Using Ultrahand, move it to the lever across you without a handle. Place it correctly at the end of the lever handle, then pull with Ultrahand.

Incorrect positioning might render the lever inoperable. Once the gate's open, head in and find a gigantic wind turbine. Give it a whirl with Tulin's Gust to unlock the first lock.

Lock 2 - Ship's Propeller

Next, return to the ship's core and catch the gust upwards. Aim to land on the ship's highest part, where two gigantic doors will be visible. Equip Ultrahand, yank one door open, and head towards the Temple's propeller.

Dive down with your glider, alternating between opening and closing it due to the current. Above the propeller, a room on the south end houses the next wind turbine.

Ignite it with Tulin's Gust. After that, grab the Soldier Blade from the chest across the propeller room, then teleport back to the Temple's start.

Lock 3 - Ship's Base

For the third lock, jump and glide towards the ship's center. Near the bottom, glide into a damaged opening housing a Construct.

Dispatch him for an uninterrupted interaction with the wind turbine. Activate it with Gust, claim the treasure chest in the left corner, then warp back to the Temple's start.

Lock 4 - Left Basement

Facing the ship's stern, veer left and jump off the closest platform to the ship's front. Glide down to an icicle-covered opening and land there.

Beware of the ship's energy-shooting cannons. Smash through the icicles, turn right, and find a massive windmill. Use Recall to reach the other side safely.

The next room houses a gate-trapped windmill. Pull the lever in front to open the ship door. Equip your bow and shoot down ceiling-hanging icicles.

Drag an icicle near the door with Ultrahand, connect the gears, and the nearest set will spin, opening the gate.

Once inside, use Gust on the wind turbine to unlock the fourth lock. Teleport back to the Wind Temple's start.

Lock 5 - Right Basement

For the final lock, head right, opposite the fourth lock. Jump down near the ship's stern and enter an opening on the ship's side.

Turn right, dispose of the Keese, use Gust to cross a hole, and take down the Construct. You'll find yourself in a room with wall fragments.

Look up to see the room extend upwards, then use Ascend from the back of the room to reach the second level.

On the second level, follow the right hallway to find a movable pole. Use Ultrahand to attach a nearby broken wall piece to the pole's bottom.

Rotate the pole a little past when the gate opens. Then, using Recall near the ladder that leads to the locked gate, quickly climb up and dash through the gate as it opens.

Proceed upwards via the long ladder on your right and take down the Construct guarding the wind turbine. Employ Gust to undo the final lock, and the gate in front of you will open.

Return to the Ouroboros Statue and interact with it to summon the boss, *Colgera*.

A teleport option will become available once it materializes, allowing you to gather necessary supplies for your showdown.

This boss is armored with rocks on three parts of its body. After some flying, it begins to hurl rocks upwards.

To avoid them, descend while swerving side to side. Once positioned directly above the boss, collapse your glider to let Link plummet through the ice, injuring Colgera and causing it to summon a portal.

Aim to hover in the middle and relocate as Colgera ascends from another portal below; use arrows to shatter the ice on its belly.

Reiterate the process of shattering the ice, now located mid-body.

It will mimic his prior tactics upon breaking the first ice segment, so evade him as he emerges from the portal, then shatter the ice near his tail, ushering in Colgera's second phase.

The method of harming Colgera stays the same, but you'll need to perform it three more times since the ice on its belly has reformed.

Colgera conjures a barrier of tornadoes, so navigate to his side and around him.

One you notice it shedding its initial rock layer. Utilize Tulin's Gust to rapidly cross the ice, dodge the airborne rocks, and have Link plunge through Colgera's body for damage.

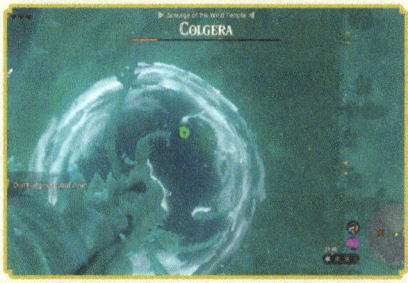

Next, it summons a portal and reappear beneath you, dodge this, and he'll call upon his second tornado wave. As Colgera flies in the tornadoes' eye, shedding rocks, use Gust to speed over and shatter the ice in his midsection.

Expect another portal and a follow-up attack from below, then more tornadoes. Dodge these and apply Gust to reach the last patch of ice. After Link successfully pierces it, you've bested Colgera!

Shrine Weapon K. Seed

Story Gemstone Tower

Eldin Canyon

To successfully complete this mission, Link needs Flame Guard-equipped armor for protection against extreme heat.

Goron City Rescue

Preparation

The urgent task at hand is dealing with the intense heat. *Goron City* might be OK for Link, but the scorching caves around *Death Mountain* and the Fire Temple *require* the **Flamebreaker Armor**.

Equipped with **Flame Guard**, this gear prevents Link from overheating and sustaining damage.

Thankfully, a complete set *isn't* required; a single piece suffices. **The Flamebreaker Tunic**, retailing at 700 Rupees, is available at *Goron City's Armor Shop*.

The Flamebreaker Armor set pieces are priced as follows:

- **Flamebreaker Helm:** *1,400*
- **Flamebreaker Armor:** *700*
- **Flamebreaker Boots:** *1,200*

Should you overlook the tunic in the store, it can be acquired before facing **Yunobo** at *YunoboCo HQ*, located in the worker's store opposite his cave. Prices remain consistent here.

In addition to the Flamebreaker Armor, ensure you have non-wooden shields and weapons to prevent them bursting into flames due to the extreme heat.

Likewise, when navigating extremely hot regions , all arrows morph into flame arrows, their tips set alight by the intense heat.

On the bright side, it shouldn't be too difficult lighting a pot for cooking recipes and elixirs in.

Locating and Conquering
Yunobo

To locate Yunobo, seek out the three Goron in the city center, adjacent to the mammoth Rock Roast pile.

Run inside the cave and approach Yunobo, causing a cut-scene to trigger and a battle to commence!

Observe his peculiar conduct, after which he will dispatch Offrak and Slergo back to YunoboCo HQ. To get there, proceed out of town past the Marakuguc Shrine.

Here, a cart system is present. Utilize the right cart and an adjacent fan to traverse the track, leading straight to YunoboCo HQ.

Once at the HQ, look for a cave with Offrak and Slergo outside.

Remember to don your Flamebreaker Armor, or enter YunoboCo HQ to purchase it for 700 Rupees.

Interact with the two petite Gorons to gain access to Yunobo, who is conversing with Princess Zelda.

Post-cutscene, Yunobo will attack using a charge maneuver. Evasion is critical as he charges rapidly; aim to coax Yunobo into crashing into rocks. Successful attempts result in stars circling his head, providing an attack opportunity.

A trio of strikes will shatter Yunobo's mask and halt his frenzy. Simply position Link before a flat cave rock, dodge when he begins to charge, and strike upon seeing the stars.

Following the combat, a rock slide ensues. Utilize Yunobo's ability to slam him into the rocks, freeing the group.

The adventure continues to the top of Death Mountain.

Ascending Death Mountain

After you've calmed Yunobo, the quest for Princess Zelda leads you to *Death Mountain.*

The journey and ascent are simplified by rail tracks for minecarts; you just need to know your route.

Exiting the cave, reuse the cart that brought you to YunoboCo HQ and follow the rails up. At the top, descend to the rail track below, placing a rail cart on it.

This track leads straight to Death Mountain. Notably, while cart-riding, Yunobo's attack becomes useful for clearing large rocks obstructing the rail track

Don't fret if the cart seems slow on parts of the track; a single fan provides sufficient power for the entire trip.

Arriving at Death Mountain's base lands you in a Goron work zone. The next track is directly ahead. Set a rail cart on it.

From here, Yunobo's ability becomes more crucial due to rocks at the track's start and enemies that attack during the ascent.

Aim Yunobo at them to knock them off or kill them if they are **Keese**. His attack recharges quickly, so overuse isn't a concern. Midway up the mountain, the cart stops at a platform with **Black Bokoblin**. Dispatch them and proceed with the next cart.

Set it on the other side of the blockage and climb in to continue the journey. Yunobo helps to fend off enemies and clear the track from sizable rocks, as before.

Overcoming Moragia

Upon reaching the summit, jump out of the cart. A cut-scene triggers, followed by the emergence of a creature named **Moragia** from the mountain crater.

Ground-based combat is futile, but **Zonai Wings** nearby, already pre-built with fans, a Steering Stick, and infinite Energy Cells, provide the solution. How handy!

Liberate the Wings from the rock and set them upright, facing the cliff. Grab the steering wheel and pilot it off the cliff to activate the Wings.

No battery level concerns exist, ensuring unlimited flying. Yunobo readies an attack on the wingtip. Ascend to a vantage point for launching him at Moragia's three heads.

Each head succumbs to a single hit, but dodging the rocks that Moragia spews from its mouths is vital.

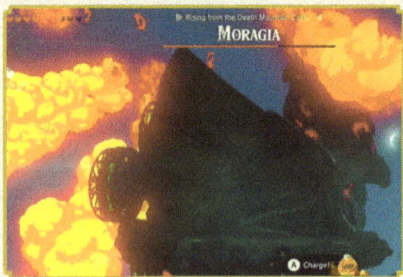

Aiming is simplified by the dotted line. Yunobo's rapid recharge time allows for a few missed shots without worry.

After striking the last head, Moragia disintegrates, and Death Mountain becomes accessible.

To advance the story-line, plunge into the Death Mountain Depths. This is the location of the forthcoming temple, the Fire Temple.

Navigating to the Fire Temple

Distinct from the rest, the Fire Temple is located in The Depths, not suspended in the sky.

After triumphing over Moragia atop the mountain, you must plunge into the mountain itself.

First-time explorers of The Depths should proceed with extreme caution, as it vastly differs from the sky and surface.

Landing with your glider, you'll find yourself enveloped in darkness. Head to the *Mutis Lightroot* and activate it.

With the area lit, converse with Yunobo, stationed near the Lightroot. He informs you of a voice emanating from deeper within The Depths.

Follow the voice, using Brightbloom Seeds for lighting. Depending on your chosen path, encounters with enemies such as Black Bokoblins and Fire Chuchus are likely. Stay vigilant.

Lava streams throughout The Depths, and contact with it results in Link's demise, or re-positioning at the lava's edge. Navigate towards the statues.

You'll eventually encounter an area populated by *Poe* and a *Zonai Dispenser*. Collect the Poe, useful for trading with statues for Gloom Resistant gear.

Notable features here include a lava cascade from a dark cliff and a path before the Zonai Dispenser. Light up the wall for climbing.

From here, Brightbloom Seeds become integral to navigation, especially when reaching more cliffs and a Zonai car.

Place a Brightbloom Seed in the wall ahead and climb up, disregarding the car as it lacks the capacity to climb such steep walls, risking a fall into the lethal lava.

Atop the longer wall, a minecart track and distant Black Bokoblins come into view, along with the *Fire Temple* itself.

Eliminate the **Black Bokoblins**, place an available minecart on the track, and attach the fan. Climb in and start it for a swift journey to the *Fire Temple*.

The route is filled with enemies like **Horriblin**, who can be neutralized using Yunobo's attack, sparing Link from damage.

Soon, you'll reach the stairs leading to the *Fire Temple* itself, triggering the next cut-scene.

THE FIRE TEMPLE

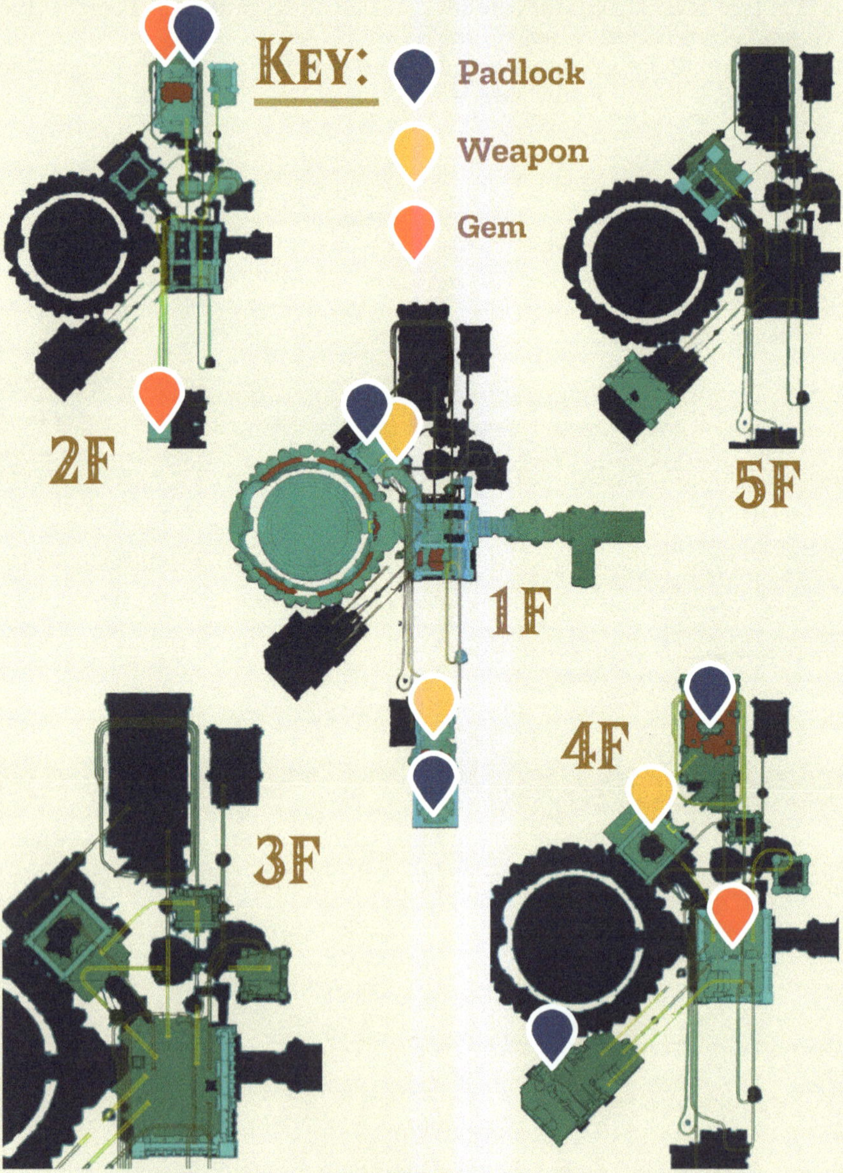

KEY:

Padlock

Weapon

Gem

2F

1F

5F

3F

4F

Don't be fooled by the labyrinth of minecart tracks in the Fire Temple.

It's actually a simple journey through five levels to reach the boss room. Be ready for some minecart rides, a sprinkle of gliding, and some climbing as well.

Getting Through the Five Locks

Upon reaching the Temple, you'll find a massive boulder barricading it. With Yunobo's help, smash through it and engage with the statue on the right.

Your mission? Unlock five padlocks by striking Gongs with Yunobo to access the boss room. Beware, the Fire Temple, unlike the Wind or Water Temples, can be harder to get lost in (if you're not careful).

1st Padlock 1 (1F)

Heading towards the Temple entrance, take the right route for the first padlock. You'll know you're in the right place when you encounter a Construct waiting for

a fight. In the room, leap onto the floating rocks to cross the initial lava river.

There, you'll see several Hydrants. Trigger one, pick it up with Link, and carry it to the extensive lava pond, allowing the water to momentarily flow onto the lava.

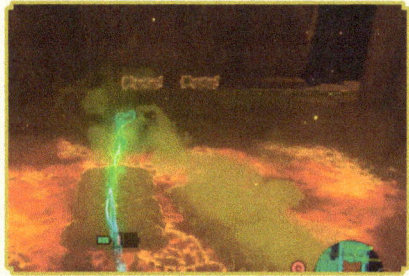

This action forms a stepping stone on which you can transport the hydrant. Repeat until you reach the minecart on the other side.

Hop in the Minecart, and soon you'll spot a large device showcasing a glowing arrow. Swap to Yunobo to change the track's direction and proceed to the next section.

Miss it, and you're back to square one. Once you land in the next area, you'll see some Zonai Capsules. Pick them and a Hydrant, and tread down the Fire Like path.

Use the Hydrant to douse it, and then hit the exposed ball to defeat it. A treasure chest containing a robust Zonaite Shield is your reward.

Use the Hydrant on the lava river to create rock fragments. Use Ultrahand to combine these fragments, creating a bridge for Yunobo to roll over and shatter the huge rock obstructing your path.

Once the rock's out of the way, proceed into the room housing the first Gong. Yunobo will activate it, releasing the first padlock.

2nd Padlock: (2F)

Make your way back to the original minecart. There's a switch beside the track's gate; strike it and hop back into your minecart to ascend to the second level.

An obstructing rock and a Construct in a minecart await you. Use Yunobo to obliterate both.

Upon reaching the second level, stop at the small room, hit the switch to reroute yourself, then promptly strike the sizable device with Yunobo to delve deeper into the second level.

Remember to leap out or halt the cart at the mid-islands inhabited by the *Flaming Rock Likes*.

You'll need a weapon tipped with a rock to vanquish these foes.

Proceed to the next minecart track and strike the nearby switch. This action lowers the tracks ahead, allowing you to cross.

Once you've entered the next room, pick up the Hydrant and create a bridge for Yunobo to shatter the massive rock.

This move allows water to flow onto the lava, forming a bridge for Link and Yunobo to cross. This path leads you to the second Gong, which Yunobo will unlock.

3rd Padlock: (5F)

To reach the third floor, fire an arrow across the Temple to strike the switch you previously used to lower the track. This brings it back up, allowing access to the third floor.

Mount your minecart and head to an area teeming with divergent tracks and a Construct. Follow the track at the top right corner of the room, noting a break in the rail.

Put a minecart on the track and affix Rockets (found left of the track). When ready, ignite the devices and the minecarts will launch.

They'll likely derail, but the altitude will be sufficient to glide onto the fourth floor. Defeat the Construct ahead and momentarily ignore the hook-attached minecarts.

Head straight and ascend the small fallen bridge. Using Ultrahand, manipulate the two metal grates to form a ramp and align them with the half-bridge near the minecart tracks.

Remember to collect the Arrows from the chest underneath.

Attach the grates to the bridge's end, forming a ramp for Yunobo to shatter the large rock. Upon completion, ascend to where the rock once was.

Looking upward, you'll see the fifth floor, devoid of tracks. From this point, climb up to the fifth floor. There are ample resting spots if your stamina needs refreshing.

Once at the top, proceed to the third Gong, strike it with Yunobo to release another padlock. Destroy the large rock and descend back to the fourth floor.

4th Padlock: (4F)

Return to the intertwined minecarts. Disentangle them, place the hook in one minecart's center, attach a Fan at its rear, and set it on the right rail.

Ride it to the subsequent room, using the temple's external walls to navigate the left side to another room with minecarts. Follow the track leading upward, watching out for a minecart-housed Construct at the top.

In the next room, peer downward for the room hosting the fourth Gong. Glide down and upon landing, the next Gong, perched on a cliff in a lava pool, is in sight.

There's also a small ramp and another cliff with a destructible rock. Descend the ramp and use Yunobo's attack to crush the rock.

Fire Hydrants rest on another cliff; trigger them with an arrow and they'll start transforming cooled lava into rocks. Swiftly shift the rocks so more can form and use Ultrahand to construct a ramp.

Once set, you can launch Yunobo off the ramp to hit the Gong. You could also build a full bridge, but this consumes more time.

The task may seem complicated initially, but with proper height and placement, hitting the Gong becomes effortless. This undoes the fourth padlock, with the fifth accessible from a room directly behind you.

5th Padlock: (1F)

In the room housing the fourth Gong, you'll find another room containing a large breakable rock. Build a ramp using rocks formed by the Hydrants pouring into the water pool.

The challenge here lies in achieving the right height and positioning the ramp correctly for Yunobo to soar over the hall and smash the boulder.

After breaking the rock, raise the ramp to allow Link a safe glide to the room.

Once inside, head towards the floor's hole. Jumping in takes you back to the first level, behind the locked door hosting a Gong. Strike it to undo the final padlock.

Your final task involves hitting the switch to open the gate and walking back to the statue. Interact with it, and the bridge to the boss room unfolds.

Inside, you'll face the Marbled Gohma Boss.

The Marbled Gohma, a creature that has been a part of previous Zelda games, resembles an imposing spider with four potent legs.

You must avoid its stomping feet and its hurled rock explosives to make it through the battle.

In order to inflict damage on Marbled Gohma, strike its eye with an arrow. Speed things up by directing Yunobo towards its legs.

When Yunobo lands a hit, it shatters the leg. Repeat this twice, and Gohma collapses.

Climb its body and keep attacking until it starts to rise. Leap off just as it draws back.

Repeat this cycle until its health bar decreases by half, marking the beginning of its second, arguably easier, phase.

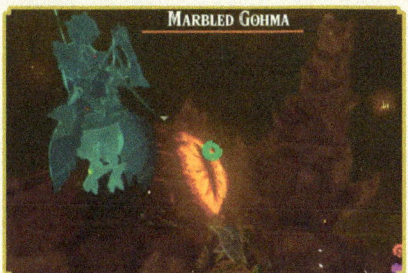

During Marbled Gohma's second phase, it clings to the ceiling. The strategy here is simple: launch Yunobo down the room's center to strike one of its legs, swiftly forcing it back to the floor.

When it crashes, it'll be disoriented, providing an opportunity to climb atop it and target its eye. As it readies itself to rise, disembark, and it'll ascend to the ceiling again.

Its subsequent attack involves hurling three size-able exploding rocks at Link. Maintain constant movement to dodge these.

If Yunobo's aim is precise, you can efficiently topple it each time it returns to the ceiling before it manages to attack you.

After the successful battle, retrieve the Heart Container. Post the cut-scene, the Rock Roast vanishes, and you're teleported back to Goron City.

KEY: Shrine · Weapon · K. Seed · Story · Gemstone · Tower

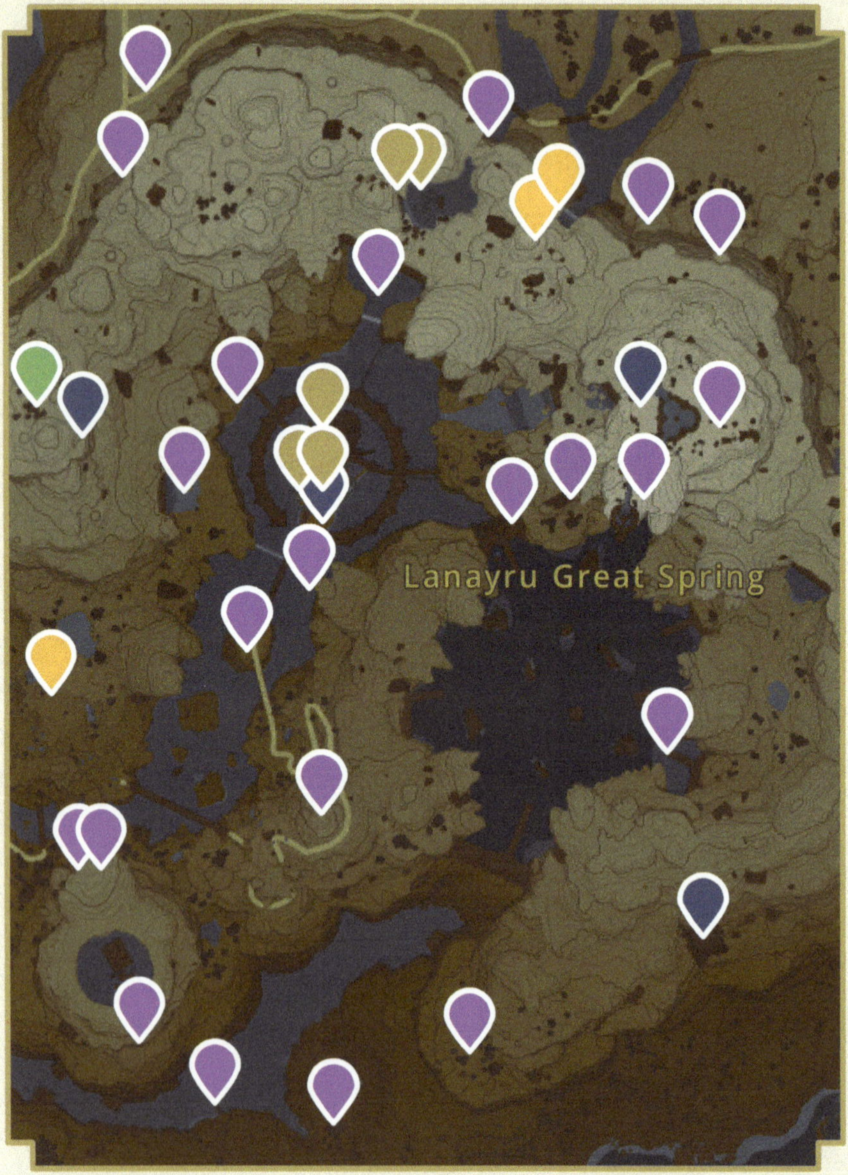
Lanayru Great Spring

Make your way to the middle of *Lanayru* and look for the *Mogawak Shrine*, activating it as a handy Fast Travel point.

To beat the upcoming dungeon, you're going to need to get hold of the Zora Armor. This armor allows you to swim up waterfalls!

The Sludge Covered Statue

Start by finding **Yona** near the statue in Zora Domain plaza. Cleanse the statue using a Water Fruit, prompting Yona to head further into Zora's Domain to assist injured Zora.

Meet **Yona** at the infirmary, and she'll inform you about the near-completion of Link's Zora Armor. However, an Ancient Arowana is needed to fully restore the tunic.

Chat to **Dento** at the general store, then go to *Mipha Court*.

Fast travel to the *Great Sky Island* and you'll find **Ancient Arowana** in loads of ponds.

Fast travel back to Yona to receive the **[Zora Armor].** Once equipped, it enables you to ascend waterfalls and it's **essential** for entering and beating the upcoming dungeon.

Unearthing the Sky Fish

The puzzles leading up to this dungeon is rather challenging. You must discover the Zora King, a fish-shaped floating island, and then a floating teardrop to begin before you can head to the dungeon.

Fixing the Tablet

Upon speaking with Sidon, he mentions that a researcher, Jiahato, is investigating the muck's source. Head over to Toto Lake.

Once there, you'll learn he's examining a damaged tablet missing a significant part. The missing section can be found nearby, coated in muck.

Utilize a Water Fruit to clear it, and then Ultrahand to re-position it. Once the tablet is restored, Jiahto informs you about the need for Zora King's Scale and the whereabouts of the elusive Sky Fish.

Discovering King Zora

The next task involves finding King Zora. King Zora is at the Pristine Sanctum. The best entry strategy is to glide in; the entrance can be easily spotted from Lulu Lake. Inside, you'll encounter the King, injured by the muck.

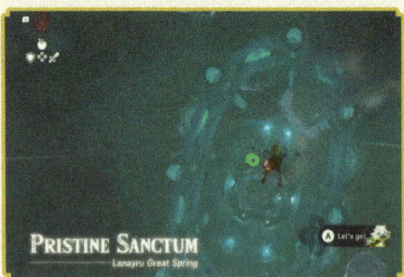

After a brief conversation, he hands over the King's Scales. If you run out, request more. Now return to the area below Mipha's Court, where Sidon awaits.

The Sky Fish & Tear Drop

Locating the Sky Fish can be challenging.

It's a fish-shaped island floating near Mipha's Court, surrounded by smaller floating rocks.

From Sidon's position, look east to spot a waterfall descending from the sky. Glide into it using your Zora Armor and ascend onto Floating Scales Island.

Cleanse the top of the island of muck to ease your movement. Facing East Reservoir Lake, moving while looking at the rocks from the right perspective aligns them into a teardrop shape.

When the teardrop is visible, affix a King's Scale to your arrow and launch it through the teardrop. A beam of light descends into East Reservoir Lake. Return to the surface and converse with Sidon.

Accompany him to the location and talk. A muck-encrusted mini-boss, a *Sludge Like*, attacks.

Employ the new ability granted by Sidon to cleanse the muck and target the beast's core. This procedure must be repeated a few more times.

After securing the Zora Armor and launching a fused arrow through the teardrop, the *Ancient Zora Waterworks* is your next stop.

Here, you've to unblock three pipes within this mini-dungeon.

Finding Your Way Through

You start by landing in a pond from which you'll move forward to dry land. You'll then encounter a blocked drain pipe which you'll need to clear using a bomb or a rock.

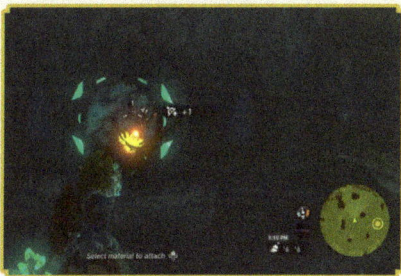

Clearing it elevates the water level, granting you access to the main room of the Ancient Zora Waterworks. The subsequent room has a low water level.

Upon looking down, you'll notice floating planks and the second blockage which you need to clear. Then, spot the third blockage which is slightly elevated.

With the help of Ultrahand, build a makeshift ladder using nearby planks, and climb in to clear the fourth pipe.

After dealing with the blockages, find the giant pipe that leads you through the system. Beware of Chuchus who attack en route.

Aim to reach the center of the pipe system where you'll see water gushing from above.

Stand in the middle, use Ascend to reach to the fourth blockage and clear it.

Move through the pipe, pull the lever using Ultrahand to open the gate.

In the center ruins, interact with the glowing stone table which opens the path to the sky islands and teleports Link back to Sidon.

Climbing Wellspring Island

To access the Water Temple, you must scale Wellspring Island, a group of islands floating over Zora's Domain accessible post the Ancient Zora Waterworks completion.

Waterfalls, bubbles, and Wings will aid Link to reach the Temple. Once you've ascended the large waterfall, you're at Wellspring Island, beneath the Water Temple.

Interact with Sidon, and then locate a machine producing bubbles on your left.

Glide through these bubbles to the next island, where you'll find a Zonai device spewing water on a pillar.

Collect it and clear the blocked waterfall further up the path using Ultrahand. This action allows water to flow. Wear the Zora Armor and jump into the waterfall to reach the next island.

You'll notice several floating pillars with waterfalls. The idea is to glide to the waterfalls and gradually swim and glide higher from one waterfall to the next, reaching the subsequent island.

Activate the Igoshon Shrine for a fast travel point. On the next island, you'll find Zonai Wings. Equip fans if available, then set the glider on the track.

If you don't have fans, a Device Dispenser down the stairs on your right will provide them. Hit the fans and glide to the next island.

Defeat the Constructs and move to the next set of waterfall pillars. Navigate past three more Constructs and a treasure chest, for a **[Soldier III Blade]**.

Create a ramp using Ultrahand where the bubble is stuck and use it to get high enough to glide to the next sky island.

On reaching another island with Gliders, you'll need to give the carts wheels. Attach at least three fans on the back and position the device near the top of the ramp.

Swiftly activate the fans before it rolls down to start flying towards the next island. When you're high enough, jump off and glide down to the next island.

Locate Sidon, have a chat, and then move forward to face a powerful Construct armed with two fuse items.

Grab them before the Construct can use them, and vanquish it. Finally, jump into the waterfall ahead to enter the Water Temple.

The path to the Temple involves unblocking pipes, navigating through the complex system of pipes, and activating the portal to Wellspring Island.

From there, it's about skillfully navigating the skyward islands. This includes gliding between bubbles, ascending waterfalls with the Zora Armor, activating Shrines, and utilizing gliders and fans.

An array of Constructs stands in your path, demanding both cunning and combat prowess.

Once you've dealt with these challenges, your final leap into the cascading waterfall will deliver you straight into the heart of the Water Temple.

It's a journey of resourcefulness, skill, and relentless determination, all culminating in an encounter with the powerful Constructs guarding the Water Temple.

So, arm yourself with the Zora Armor, join Sidon, and embark on this challenging journey, -one waterfall at a time.

THE WATER TEMPLE

KEY: Water Wheel   Weapon   Gem

1F

B1

Unleashing the Temple's Boss requires the activation of four Water Wheels. Here's how you can pull that off.

1st Water Wheel

Head to the island in the bottom left. Climbable rubble will guide your path. Constructs and a pond await your arrival. Conveniently, a swift nudge into the pond will quickly put an end to the enemies.

Next, set your sights on the nearby island. An intriguing bubble contraption smeared with muck catches your attention.

Sidon's power comes handy to clean up. Scuttle back to the pond, snag the orb, and place it in the next bubble. It'll carry you upwards.

Arriving on the new island, call upon Ultrahand. A lever materializes across the waterfall. Locate the Hover Stone, connect it to the lever and tug the lever up with Ultrahand, draining the pond.

Place the orb in its socket, and voila! The gate opens. Use Sidon's power to rotate the Water Wheel.

2nd Water Wheel

From the first island, spot the central temple. There, on its side, stairs descend to a fiery doorway. Employ Sidon's shield to sprint through the flames.

Inside, to your left, a switch waits. Execute a weapon-assisted slam dunk to douse the flames and invite Sidon inside. Another gate guards the water wheel.

Venture deeper, where Hover Stones and a spiky pit lie. Ultrahand, your bridge constructor, helps you secure the orb.

On the return journey, place the orb atop the Hover Stones and jump across. Beware, the Hover Stones can run out of energy and fall!

So, once you've ascended with the orb, use Ultrahand to cradle the orb in its holder. Let it roll for a bit, then engage Rewind.

Stand by the gate and watch the orb resume its holder. As the gate swings open, activate the second wheel.

3rd Water Wheel

On the Water Temple's right, a bubble maker carries you to the island nearest the Water Wheels. Watch out for a pesky **Flame Like** that hurls fireballs.

The next bubble machine, hanging upside down on floating rocks, creates your elevator. Hop in, engage Rewind, and ascend to the wheel's island.

A sealed gate and an outer wheel near it pose your next challenge. Manipulate Ultrahand to move one stone piece until it touches the waterfall, prompting the wheel to rotate.

Back at the sealed wheel, observe a gap in the wall. Behind it, a bubble maker awaits your command. Employ Ultrahand to position a bubble in the gap, triggering an electrical signal and the gate's opening.

The bubble's short lifespan requires a quick entry to activate the third wheel.

4th Water Wheel

Embark towards the end of the third wheel's island. Ride a bubble high enough for a glide to the last island.

Watch Constructs and Chuchus duel. When Constructs prevail, send them swimming. Use Hover Stones to get reach the sludge.

At the tower, use Sidon's power or a Water Fruit arrow If arrows are at hand jump up and use the slow down time to line up your shot.

Hit the opening twice; first with a water-filled arrow to clean, and then with a normal arrow to trigger the switch and grant access to the final water wheel.

Mission accomplished! Return to the Water Temple's core and commune with the statue. Water cleanses the gunk, unmasking the boss, Mucktorok!

As the battle begins, the boss disguises itself within a shark.

Though its gunk attacks may seem overwhelming, they aren't too hard to avoid. Dodging or leaping over the mess often does the trick.

Now, the key to damaging the boss itself is using Sidon's power. Use it on the shark to reveal the boss.

Seize this opportunity and swing your weapon like there's no tomorrow. The boss, however, isn't one to stick around. It darts away, but a swift pursuit or a well-aimed arrow can trip it up before it retreats back into the shark.

When Mucktorok's health dwindles by half, it mixes things up.

The arena becomes a muck-filled quagmire, slowing Link's pace. This makes it more challenging to close in on Mucktorok and its shark alter ego, which now spits out even more muck than before.

Your task? Clear the muck, and douse the shark with water, forcing Mucktorok out of hiding. This time, rather than running, it swims rapidly between muck pools, evading your attacks.

Only a perfectly timed arrow or a swift muck removal can make it vulnerable.

Mucktorok's resilience doesn't change - it succumbs to the same amount of damage when exposed.

Your priority is to eliminate the newly spread muck swiftly and finish off the boss.

Gerudo Highland

Gerudo Desert

Caution! *The Gerudo Valley is blisteringly hot during the day, before temperatures plummet to ice-cold at night-time. Make sure you've got your heat and cold-resistant armor to hand (or, cook up some Hydromelons for some cooling effects).*

Head for the *Gerudo Canyon Skyview Tower* and then proceed towards the *Mayatat Shrine*.

Located close to the *Kara Kara Bazaar*, this serves as your final safe haven before you brave the *Desert Rift* and reach *Gerudo Town*. You can speed your travel up using a Sled Zonai device and a Fan.

Navigating the Sandstorm

Upon reaching *Kara Kara Bazaar*, your next mission is to traverse the desert rift towards the southwest. A constant sandstorm engulfs the entire pathway between the *Bazaar* and *Gerudo Town*.

This storm not only hinders your vision but also obscures your mini-map, making the journey rather challenging.

Nonetheless, if you're savvy with your directions, finding *Gerudo Town* isn't as tough as it seems.

Venture into the storm, maintaining a southwestern course until you hit the rift. Any enemies along the path? Simply ignore them. Combat may disorient you, and the foes here aren't exactly speed demons.

At the rift, veer left, following the chasm until its end. Then navigate around it, persisting more or less southwest.

Keep a lookout for a hot air cyclone on your left. These air pockets elevate you above the storm momentarily, allowing you to orient yourself.

However, the hot air cyclone post-rift is all you need. Hop into it and deploy your Paraglide, letting the hot air carry you skyward.

Look out for Gerudo Town's shrine's green glow atop its highest building, marking the town itself.

With a bit of luck, *Gerudo Town* will be within easy reach, enabling you to glide most of the way to its walls.

If it seems too distant, you might have strayed off course. But using the hot air cyclones as vantage points should guide you towards your destination eventually.

Arrival at Gerudo Town

Once you reach the town walls, seek an entrance gate (or simply scale the walls). Inside, hunt for the largest building. Spotting it, approach and you'll find stairs leading upwards.

Ascending these won't introduce you to the townsfolk, but it leads you to the *Soryotanog Shrine* atop the building.

Activating this shrine secures a fast travel point, saving you from crossing that sandstorm again.

Descend the stairs and notice the conspicuous hole mid-staircase. It leads to the *Gerudo Sanctuary*, where Gerudo Town's residents seek refuge from the external phenomena.

Where to find Riju

To start off, make your way towards the town's end to the palace, descending the stairs. A Gerudo will stop you.

Turn around and ascend the second stairway to access the palace throne room.

Behind the throne lies a box adorned with a sand seal's head; use Ultrahand to move it, then hop inside.

Inside, you'll encounter the townsfolk, lead by captain **Buliara**. She reveals everyone has taken refuge under the palace since the sandstorm struck.

Initially wary of Link, Buliara identifies him from Riju's (the Gerudo chief) depiction and discloses Riju's location in the town's northern ruins.

Take this chance to explore the shops and restock on arrows, food, and elemental items.

Exit via heading north to the *North Gerudo Ruins* where **Riju** hones her lightning abilities.

Assist her by firing two arrows, one at the target, another close by. This showcases Riju's skills as she emits an electric wave.

Fire an arrow into this wave, and it transforms into a potent lightning strike causing extensive area damage.

After a bit of practice with Riju, a Gerudo soldier interrupts with news of an attack on *Kara Kara Bazaar*.

Protect Kara Kara Bazaar

If you activated *Mayatat Shrine* earlier, teleport back to the Bazaar directly. Upon arrival, a battle commences, with Riju as your ally.

This isn't a conventional fight but a test of your prowess in employing Riju's lightning attack. Running out of arrows isn't a concern, as Gerudo fighters will supply you with more if needed.

The aim is to repel the **Gibdos** by firing an arrow into Riju's lightning puddle.

Wait for the lightning to target a group of Gibdos, then launch an arrow near them, sending them airborne. If Riju's health bar depletes, the fight restarts.

Persist in utilizing Riju's lightning (and accepting those free arrows from the warriors) until a cutscene initiates. Riju points out the source of the Gibdos - mushroom-shaped pillars, spotted earlier in the desert.

Observe the hive center pulse and glow purple, then fire an arrow imbued with Riju's lightning to obliterate it. Head back to Gerudo Town when instructed.

Defend Gerudo Town

Back in *Gerudo Town*, chat to Riju at the stairway's summit to plan the town's defense.

Plenty of chests and weapons await, so gather what you need for the impending conflict. Rupees, weapons, and healing items are up for grabs.

Consult with **Teake** in town to block any town entrances. You can also direct the warriors to guard specific entrances.

Though not mandatory, this is useful if you find the default battle settings challenging. Speak with Riju to initiate the mini tower defense-style mini-game.

Upon battle commencement, you'll spot three Gibdo hives encircling the town - north, east, and west. Heed Riju's calls and follow her directions.

The goal is to eliminate the Hives, halting the incessant Gibdo swarm. If you've established barricades, Riju should remain safe for a while. Otherwise, monsters can reach and attack her, causing a restart if she falls.

Focus on one tower at a time, shooting an arrow electrified with Riju's power at the pulsating hive center.

Then tackle the ground Gibdos. Soldiers will also fend off Gibdos, so head towards any red markers swarming on your map.

Remember, you can use your resources to combat the Gibdos. But to destroy the Hives, Riju's lightning is a must. The battle concludes once all Gibdos have been eliminated.

Post-battle, Riju hypothesizes a link between the Gibdos and the sand.

She invites you to accompany her to a mural beneath the palace. Follow her to discover your subsequent course of action.

The Red Pillar Puzzle

Begin by heading back to the throne room. Look straight out the window, located behind the throne (and the sand seal box from before).

You'll notice a distant pillar. Make a daring jump and dash towards it.

1st Pillar

Situated straight southwest of Gerudo Town, the first pillar can be found around coordinates **-4036, -3133, 0053**. Luckily, it's buried in sand, so you can effortlessly ascend, or climb up.

Spot some breakable rocks in the center of the floor. Grab a hammer weapon (or craft one with a stone) to shatter them.

Doing so unveils a light which ascends towards a mirror, illuminating the path ahead.

2nd Pillar

Trace the trail of light (you can leverage the updrafts to keep your bearings) to the subsequent pillar. You'll trot past several large boulders en route. The light points westward.

Employ an adjacent updraft to glide over to a platform equipped with a crank.

You'll need to rotate this crank quickly, so use your Ultrahand or a fan to cause the tower to ascend from the desert until it flawlessly reflects the light in a fresh direction.

3rd Pillar

Follow this third light beam to the next tower, which already reflects the light — just not in the direction you desire.

Smash the floor to uncover Hover Stones and sticks. Use Ultrahand to affix the sticks to one of the Stones and hoist it as high as possible.

With the other Stone, suspend it mid-air, use Ascend, and then climb to the top.

Now seize the stick-covered Stone and yank it up. Detach the sticks and construct the crank using Ultrahand. Finally, give it a good push until the mirror redirects the light back to the original tower.

Finally...

With the triangle now formed, you need to navigate to the shape's center to crack the puzzle.

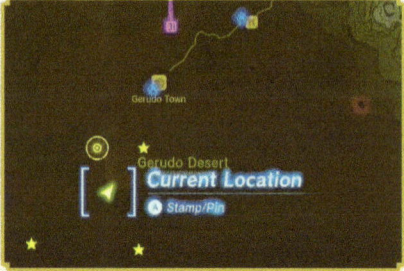

Glide northward from the third pillar until you encounter ruins with a unique stone jutting out from the center. Riju will rendezvous with you here.

Engage Riju's electric power to energize the switch — have a chat with her and loose an arrow at the tablet.

Following this, a temple will ascend from the sands - the mighty Lightning Temple.

To open up the Temple simply just fire and arrow at the ominous cocoon above the entrance.

Mini-Boss: Queen Gibdo

But, of course, you didn't think that it was going to be *that* easy to get in to it did you?

Keep this boss in mind because it's not going to be the last time you'll see it. In fact, you won't get the satisfaction of taking it down until later on.

Queen Gibdo, characterized by her speed and ability to fly, launches attacks at you via sandstorms, or by striking the ground.

However, she's not invincible - much like other Gibdos, you can peel away her outer layer by zapping her with Riju's lightning.

Keep moving, always keeping an eye on Queen Gibdo's actions.

If she rears up on her hind legs, steer clear of her, and when she fans her wings, quickly sidestep to her left or right to evade the ensuing tornadoes.

Whenever the opportunity arises, collaborate with Riju to supercharge that lightning and let fly an arrow at the Queen, consequently dissolving her outer layer. Once she's vulnerable, launch your attack using close-combat weapons.

Once you get the mini-boss' health down to 75%, it bugs off (see what we did there?).

B1

1F

2F

3F

4F

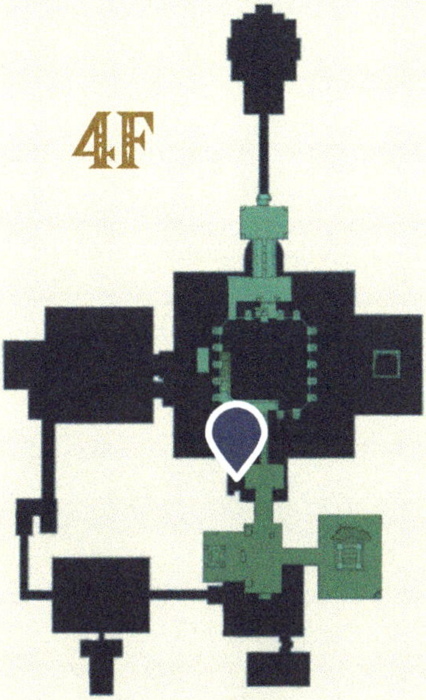

5F

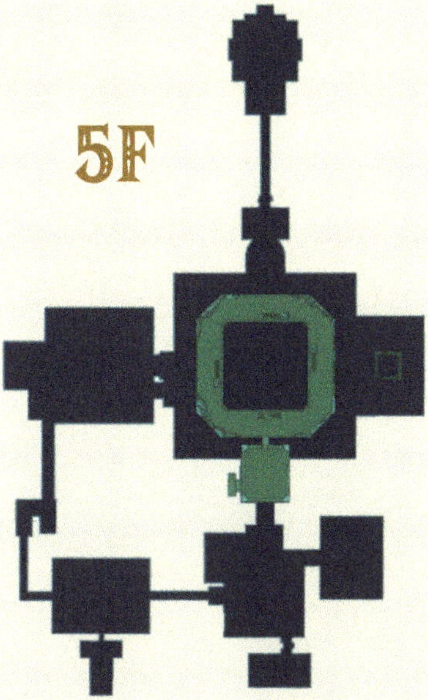

6F

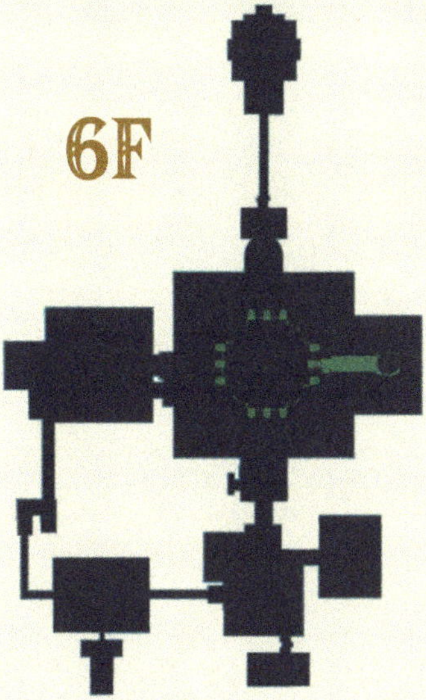

7F

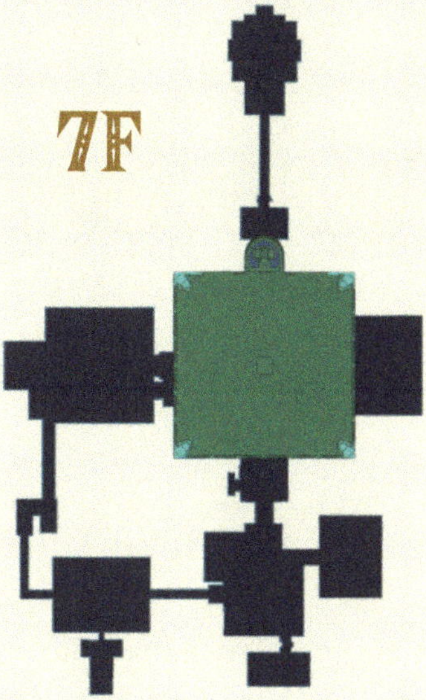

This Temple consists of eight floors and is jam-packed with puzzles to solve and battery devices to collect to open up the final room to the Temple's boss.

Power up the Batteries

There are a total of **four** batteries that require powering up. We've marked them with orange markers on the temple maps. Let's take a look at how to power up each one in turn.

1st Battery

The first battery is a cinch. Look for two sandstone blocks on the right behind the Zonai terminal on the first floor.

Use Ultrahand to shift them, step inside and zap the battery switch with Riju's lightning. Then head back to the *Room of Ascension*.

2nd Battery

Next, for battery two, the challenge starts ramping up. You'll find a breeze in the room's back corner, emanating from some sandstone bricks.

Create an updraft by lifting these bricks, then hitch a ride up to the fifth floor. A gap in the wall reveals a bright beam of light, the *Room of Natural Light*. Enter, manipulate the stone and mirror in the room using Ultrahand to reflect light into the main chamber.

Position the mirror pillar to reflect the light northeast, align the right-side pillar with the light beam to unlock a door on the third floor.

Prepare for a showdown with Gibdos and Construct enemies in the *Room of Offered Light*. Utilize Riju to annihilate the hive, take down the Gibdos with elemental attacks, and dispatch the Constructs individually.

Once the room is cleared, manipulate the light source in the room's center to open a door below, then drop down and juice up the battery with Riju's lightning.

3rd Battery

For battery three, you'll need to return to the fifth floor and adjust the pillar positions to unlock the highest room.

Carefully navigate a fiery chamber to reach a closed-off section on the second floor. Deal with two Constructs before charging up another battery.

4th Battery

Battery four demands some exploration. From the first floor, ascend to the fourth floor, find a small gap in the room's north corner, and follow a path leading to two rotating discs.

Manipulate these discs to light flood the central chamber. Glide over to the third floor and head through a trap-laden room.

Indiana Link

Deactivate the each trap to allow Riju through. Secure a sandstone block between the crushers to pass through safely, then stand on the switch beckon Riju.

The switch is on the right but isn't accessible yet. First, place another sandstone under the spiked ceiling to prevent it from crushing you.

With that in place, advance to the *Room of Light and Shade* for a showdown with a Construct.

The room's centerpiece is a light source, with a hole behind it leading to a rotating chamber. Here you'll find two stakes and a mirror that can be lifted using Ultrahand.

Position the mirror onto the light source, then grab one of the Stakes with Ultrahand. Wait until a green light appears, then secure the stake into the wall to halt the room spinning, uncovering the light source and revealing the switch door.

Leave the chamber, power up the last battery, then return to the *Room of Ascension.*

The initial phase of this boss fight is similar to your previous encounter outside the Lightning Temple.

Use Riju's lightning to weaken the enemy and rush in for an assault while evading its attacks. Hitting it twice with Riju's lightning will stun it, providing an opportunity for some free hits.

Its assault methods remain the same – sandstorms, swipes, and stomping. Once its health is halved, we move to the second phase.

This phase introduces hives that spawn Gibdos and block the light from entering the temple.

Quick action is needed here – use Riju's lightning to eradicate the hives swiftly, restoring light to the room and ceasing enemy spawn.

A bonus to note - standing in the light grants protection from smaller enemies. Queen Gibdo's assault strategy remains the same, although she will be more airborne now.

Keep moving and make the most of Riju's lightning attacks when opportunities arise. Do not hesitate to use your most powerful weapons.

Queen Gibdo will eventually fall to the storm and vanish, leaving a Heart Container and some backstory for you.

Returning to Gerudo Town, you'll find the sandstorm has dissipated (opening up the desert for further exploration), and the Gerudo have returned to their surface dwelling.

With that lengthy quest completed, fast travel back to *Lookout Landing* and *Purah's lab*.

Climb the telescope tower, chat with Purah, and voila – the *Regional Phenomena* quest concludes. This is followed by a Blood Moon rise, revealing a familiar figure by Hyrule Castle, thus enticing you to explore the castle ruins.

Preparation Phase

In case you haven't visited *Hyrule Castle* before, we'll provide some pointers to handle the castle and its residents.

The castle perimeter has a few foes including *Black Horriblins*, the trickiest ones, especially when you encounter them in groups in a cave. Luckily, they're susceptible to headshots, so stock up on arrows.

The castle is riddled with Gloom, and you'll combat a boss that deals Gloom damage. Prepare your best Gloom-healing and Gloom-

resistant meals before you go.

And remember, use your most effective weapons – you can always acquire great monster parts later.

The Path to Hyrule Castle

Hyrule Castle is floating in the air directly north of Lookout Landing.

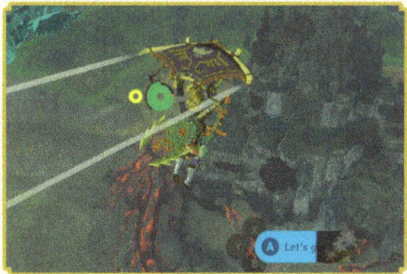

Leap off the *Skyview Tower* and glide northwards towards the castle. If your stamina is low, you can also use a Zonai Wing and a Fan to get there easily too.

Aim for the drawbridge at the castle's lower-right. Land there, and you'll receive a plea for help. Collect a **[Royal Bow]** from the chest and descend into the main chamber.

SECOND GATEHOUSE
Hyrule Field

Ⓐ Climb down

Finding Princess Zelda

In Hyrule Castle, your objective is to track *Princess Zelda* – her locations will be marked on the map, guiding you to her.

1F - Second Gatehouse

If you follow our castle approach instructions, you'll land here first. As you drop down from the roof, you're ambushed by Monster Forces, led by a *Black Boss Bokoblin*.

Defeat them, grab the **[Royal Halberd]** from the chest, and return to the roof.

Ⓐ Open

B3 - Library

Glide northeast from the roof to an open door, loot a **[Royal Shield]** from a chest, and pick up the bow and arrows.

Ascend for a **[Royal Claymore]** and a **[Korok Seed]**.

Glide north, follow the path down and around to B2, then climb rocks on your right to activate *Serutabomac Shrine*.

A staircase beneath the shrine leads to B3. Follow it to the bottom, turn left to reach the *Library*.

Inside of Hyrule Castle
MONSTER FORCES

The Library houses a *Black Hinox* and elemental *Chuchus* that can be used against the Hinox. Eliminate them, gather the loot and proceed to the next location.

B3 - Staircase

Not far from the Library, Zelda's next location is just up the east staircase.

Be prepared for a *Gibdo* swarm, which can be fought off using elemental weapons and materials.

B1 - Zelda's Room

The route to Zelda's room involves navigating through a Horriblin-infested cave and dealing with various different enemies.

Once you reach a dead end, use Ascend to reach 1F, drop into Zelda's room and battle a fresh wave of enemies.

Fire Lizalfos are easier to handle, especially when ice is used against them.

B3 - Storehouse

Collect a **[Royal Bow]** before you leave Zelda's room. Glide down to B3 where Zelda awaits along with more foes, including the dangerous *Silver Moblin*.

B3 - Corridor

Use Ascend to exit the storehouse and head for a gloom-filled area where you'll combat three *Shock Likes*. Use bombs or ice to expose their 'tongue', then attack them.

1F - Sanctum

After defeating the Shock Likes, you'll hear Zelda's voice once more. You need to make your way to the central chamber - where you previously battled Ganon in BotW.

Retrace your steps back to Zelda's room, use Ascend to appear in a room above, and then use Ascend again to reach the rooftop.

Fly towards the east, traverse some red and black gloop, and climb up to the path leading to the central hall.

There's also a **[Korok Seed]** hiding under the bridge that you can collect using Ascend. In the Sanctum, you'll spot Zelda on the room's other side.

After the cut-scene, it's boss-fighting time! Prepare for an intense boss battle.

Having all four Vows active is a wise strategy for the upcoming fight. You'll be up against not one, but *three* Phantom Ganons!

Flurry Rushes are your best tool in this fight, as each of Ganon's moves are quite predictable, making it much easier to time your dodges.

He'll either swoop down and charge at you, swipe towards you three times, or slash wildly when he's in close proximity.

To focus your attacks, lock onto one Ganon at a time and let your allies deal with the others. Keep a keen eye on their movements, time your dodges correctly to land a Flurry Rush, and be quick to sneak in some free hits.

If dodging isn't your strong suit, you can halt his charge by shooting an arrow right at his face (painful memories of the Ocarina of Time painting fight came flooding back to us during this part).

When you've successfully dwindled all of their health bars to half, you'd have overcome all three of them.

However, it's now time to face-off against **FIVE** of them at once! They all use the same moves as before, but they now come with an additional threat.

One among them will teleport to the room's end and rapidly spread gloom across the floor. This could cost you a *significant* number of hearts if left unchecked.

Fortunately, you can put a stop to this. Target the stationary Phantom Ganon's head with your bow and arrow, and if you're successful in stunning him, the gloom stops.

Keep a constant eye out for this irritating Phantom Ganon throughout the second phase.

As before, concentrate your attacks on one Ganon at a time until they're all defeated.

While speaking with Purah over the events that just occurred in Hyrule Castle, chat with her about the other village that she was investigating.

Kakariko Village

Kakariko Village lies to the southeast of *Lookout Landing* and just a tad east of the *Sahasra Slope Skyview Tower*. Chances are, you've already visited this tower or perhaps the village itself while undertaking quests like the *Gloom-Borne Illness*.

If you're unfamiliar with Kakariko, simply navigate east to the *Wetland Stable* and then head south, crossing the *Lanayru Wetlands*, until you reach the village. Once you encounter canyons, you're nearing your destination.

Upon arrival at the village, be sure to activate the *Makasura Shrine*. Make your way down to meet *Paya*, the village's new chief, and *Tauro*, the head of the Zonai Survey Team.

They will assign you a new main quest, *Secret of the Ring Ruins*.

Quest: Secret of the Ring

The quest is quite lengthy, but the initial task is straightforward: you need to enter the ruins positioned above Kakariko Village.

Once you've spoken with Paya and Tauro, the ruins overhead will be visible. Ascend the ladders until you find a section draped with a red rug. Look upward, and you'll be directly under the ring.

Use Ascend to reach inside, where you'll spot a stone tablet. Use your camera to take a snapshot of this tablet, exit the ruins, and return to Tauro. Present him the photograph and he will decode it.

The decoded message directs you to the *Zonai Ruins* situated in the Faron region, southwest of Kakariko.

Tauro and his assistant Calip request your presence at their base at the *Popla Foothills Skyview Tower,* which you can instantly teleport to if you've previously unlocked it.

Meet Calip at Popla Foothills and you'll learn that Tauro has rushed ahead. Refer to your map to locate the long dragon-shaped river known as *Dracozu Lake* (found adjacent to Damel Forest).

Utilize the Skyview Tower for a panoramic view of the region. Your desired destination is southeast of the tower, at the coordinates **0939, -2523, 0010**.

Take note to un-equip any metallic weapons and shields in this area.

Near the Zonai Ruins, you'll notice a tiny camp with a notebook.

Read the notebook to learn that Tauro has proceeded further into the ruins. Conveniently, a door stands right across from the camp.

Enter to find Tauro studying a Zonai mural. Ascend the stairs and open the mural yourself to reveal the **[Charged Shirt]**.

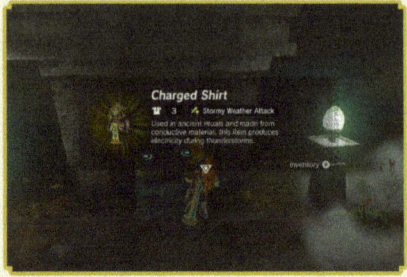

Equip the shirt and show it to Tauro. This is one piece of the "electric garb" referred to in the riddle.

Your quest isn't finished, though. You need to locate the rest of the set. If your Purah Pad is equipped with the **Sensor +** feature, it will come in handy here.

Your goal now is to find the **Charged Trousers**, the **Charged Headdress**, and the **altar**.

Journey south along the river until you reach about a third of the way down.

At coordinates **0983, -2690, 0007**, a door radiating white light should catch your eye.

Smash the rocks blocking the entrance with a hammer and open the chest within to find the **[Charged Trousers]** and equip them right away.

Keep following the river around its curve until you spot another door on your left, nestled in the river itself.

Enter the water-filled room, slice through the vines, and open the chest atop for the **[Charged Headdress]**. Don this headgear to complete the stunning armor set.

Your final task is to follow the river to its 'tail' and look straight ahead to spot a third open door. Proceed inside and approach the altar.

Ensure you're wearing the **Charged Set**. Take a **Zonai Charge** from your inventory and place it on the altar. Following the cut-scene, chart your course towards the *Thunderhead Isles*.

Thunderhead Isles

Circle back to *Popla Foothill* and utilize the *Skyview Tower* to glide southeast. *Thunderhead Isles* is fairly noticeable on your map.

Upon landing on Thunderhead Isles, ensure once more that you aren't equipped with *any* metallic weapons *or* shields!

Your next task is to navigate across a series of small islands using Zonai devices or resources provided by the islands themselves.

Starting on the initial island, position yourself on the white block, and patiently wait for a lightning strike on the adjacent rod to catapult you to the next island.

Glide to the next Island, activate Ascend, and then make your way towards some minecart tracks.

Craft a makeshift 'cart' from the nearby wood and Fans and use it to transport yourself to the next island.

Stand on the debris, employ Ascend, and find yourself in a small pond, adorned with a central pillar and a treasure chest.

Climb the pillar (use some Sticky Elixir if you need some) to obtain a **[Shock Emitter Zonai device]**.

Leap to the island on your right, demolish the Constructs, and engage another cart to traverse the tracks. Midway through, activate Ascend to reach the *Joku-usin Shrine*.

You're able to Ascend out of this chamber by ascending the stairs located at the room's rear.

You also have the option to confront the *Flux Construct* ahead.

Glide (use Tulin's wind ability if needed) to reach the structure's rooftop where you'll find a crank, a launcher, and a lightning rod.

Adjust the crank to align the two pillars with the southeastern section of the island chain. Wait for a lightning strike, which then catapults you forward.

This section doesn't require cart travel. Follow the island chain eastward until you reach the dragon's "neck."

Here, you'll need to employ a blend of gliding, climbing, and the Ascend ability.

We chose to climb to the top of the island chain, but your goal is simply to locate a stone circle shaped like an eye. Dive from here to arrive at *Dragonhead Island*.

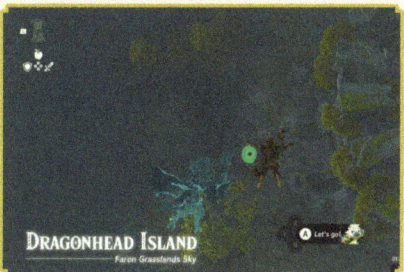

Target the eye's center to reach the *Joku-u Shrine*. Hack through the obstructing vines and approach the door.

Here's where your ten hearts become vital. Press *and hold* '**A**' to open the door, revealing an owl mask.

Interact with this mask to unveil the floor and illuminate a path below. A voice instructs you to follow this light.

The quest, *Guidance from Ages Past*, is now activated, and your objective is to transport the mask to *The Depths*.

KEY:

 Lightroot   Weapon   K. Seed

 Story Shield   Armor

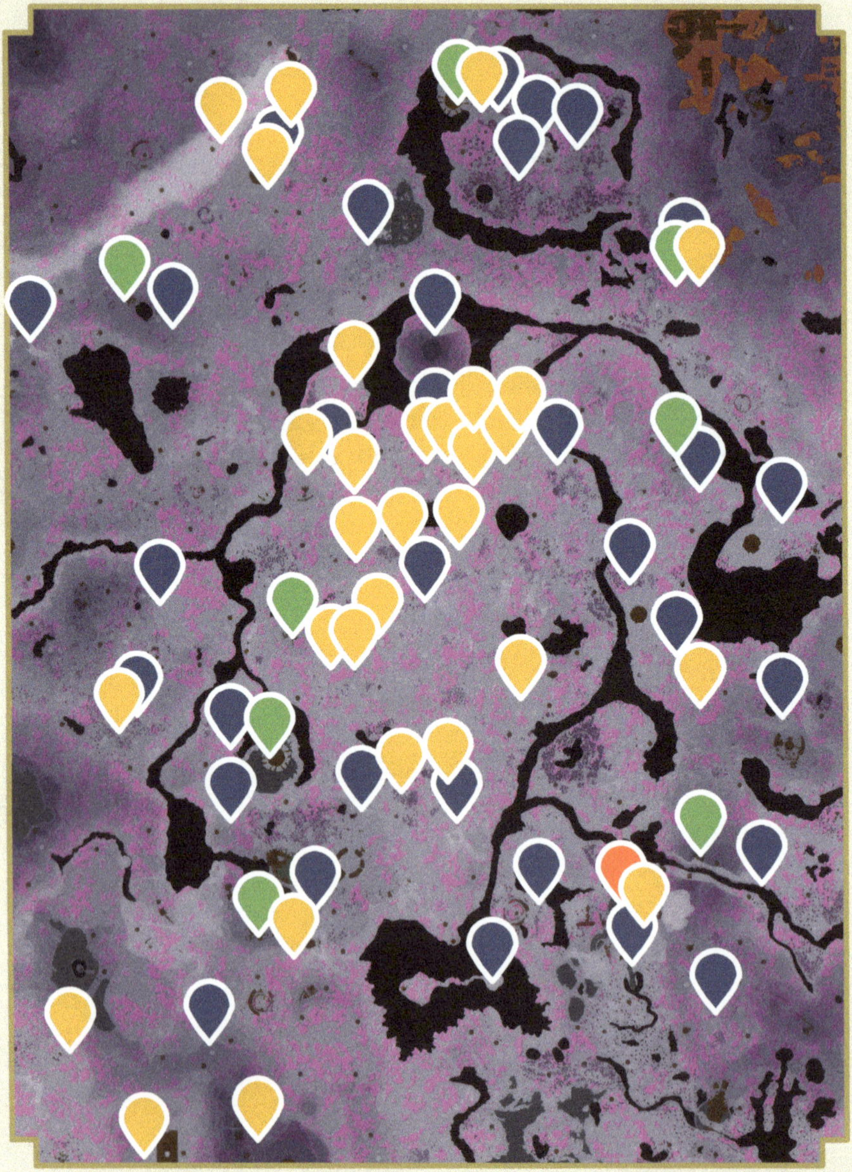

Deploy Ultrahand to seize the mask and descend the slope. Outdoors, assemble a Wing device using Fans and a Steering Stick.

Fuse the mask to the Wing's front, position your contraption on the track, and interact with the Stick to power up the device.

Follow the light northwards, descending gradually to a secluded zone with a small water body and an altar. This spot's coordinates are **1322, -2463, 0082**.

Upon landing, unhook the mask from the Wing and stand at the altar with the mask to reveal *The Depths'* entrance.

Enter *Tobio's Hollow Chasm* and descend via the elevator by positioning the mask at its center.

Once in The Depths, carry the mask towards the *Construct Factory*.

Use Ultrahand to put the mask on the altar, revealing *Mineru, the Sage of Spirit,* the fifth sage you seek.

She requests that you construct a physical form she can inhabit, which forms your next mission.

Construct Assembly

Close to the Construct Factory, you'll find four 'depots' each housing a distinct piece of the Construct — *Right Leg, Right Arm, Left Leg,* and *Left Arm*.

Each depot must be visited to collect the specific Construct piece and then returned to the Construct Factory for attaching.

Firstly, return to the elevator you arrived on and hit the *Muokuij Lightroot* to illuminate the entire area, simplifying your Construct assembly task.

Right-Leg Depot

This is located northeast of the Construct Factory. Use Ascend to reach the rooftop and glide northward towards the *Uisihcoj Lightroot*.

From the Lightroot, follow the path to the damaged ruins and glide across to the luminescent door, landing at the *Right-Leg Depot*.

Interact with the Zonai terminal, dropping a box containing the Right Leg. The doors behind you will lock. Transport the box using Ultrahand to the elevators on the left and go up.

In the subsequent room, you'll observe some rails and a "hook". Link the box to the hook using Ultrahand and attach a Fan to it.

We opted to attach the box to the elongated side to allow the hook to move along the rail. Any other method requires you to manually thread the box, which could induce unnecessary stress.

Move to the room's rear and use Ascend to reach the door. Seize the box and use the lift.

Position the box near the Wing track and head up the following lift. Open the chest to find **[3 Zonaite]**. Construct a flying vehicle, attach the box to it, and then return to the Factory.

Deliver the box to the Construct and insert the Leg.

Left-Leg Depot

Head southeast from the Construct Factory to find the *Left-Leg Depot* entrance. Enter, interact with the terminal, acquire the box, and the doors will lock.

Carry the box and ride the rocket lift. To the right, you'll find a Zonai Dispenser — use it to obtain Zonai devices if needed.

In the opposite direction, you'll see a vertical ramp and a crank. Position the box at the ramp's base and attach a Rocket Zonai device (or two) to it - which can be found in the room's corner.

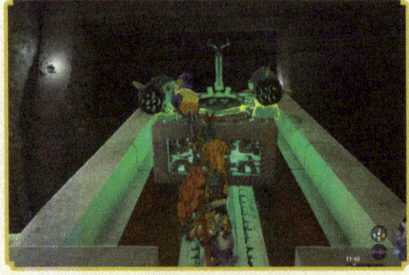

Turn the crank counter-clockwise until the ramp aligns with the upper ledge. Stand on the box, activate the rockets, and you should be propelled onto the open ledge.

Place the box in the depot's exit pathway, then turn to see a lift and some lasers. Ascend and remove the chest behind the lasers with Ultrahand for **[3 Zonaite]**.

Go back down and, if preferred, connect a Cart to the box along with a Steering Stick. Alternatively, simply carry the box from the depot to the Construct.

Left-Arm Depot

Located southwest of the Construct Factory, you'll find the *Left Arm depot*.

Go up the stairs, interact with the device, collect your box and the doors lock closed.

To the left, strike the wheel to open the door - memorize this particular setup as you'll need to replicate this later. on You'll now enter a room filled with lava.

Attach the Steering Stick and the two Big Wheels from the back of the door to the box. Activate your makeshift car and cross the lava. We're not sure how the wheels can survive the lava, but let's just run with it anyways…

In the following room, you'll encounter a narrower path unsuitable for your wheels.

The vehicle needs to be disassembled and rebuilt. Once rebuilt, you can cross.

Climb the ladder and glide over to a chest containing **[5 Steering Sticks]**. Return to your vehicle, disassemble it, and remember the wheel door from earlier? You'll need to recreate it again (we did warn you).

To accomplish this, attach both wheels to the door such that the arrows face opposite directions. Then, attach the chain to the wheel.

Strike the wheel, and the door will open. If you prefer not to do this, you can use Ultrahand and Recall to hold the door open (with the box) and slide on through.

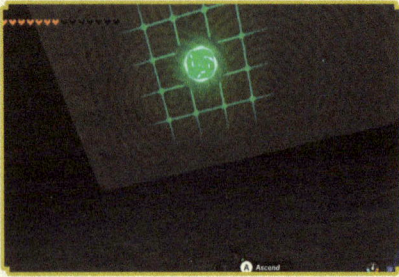

Open another chest containing **[3 Zonaite]**, then collect the Fans from beneath the propellers and the steering stick on the far right to create a small raft with your box.

Place the box in the water and ride it to the river's end to reach the Factory. Carry the box to the Construct and install the arm.

Right-Arm Depot

The final depot is situated northwest of the Factory. Walk in that direction until you reach some elevated stone platforms, then use Ascend to enter the depot.

Interact with the device to obtain your box and the doors will - predictably - lock shut.

To your right, you'll observe a conveyor belt made with **Small Wheels.** Place the box onto it and it'll automatically ascend. Follow it up.

There are more wheels and an electrically conducting pillar up here. First, go down and open the chest in the cave containing a **[Large Zonaite]**.

Then, attach two Small Wheels from the conveyor belt to the box's sides. Place the box on the pillar and ride it across to the other side.

In the following room, your box needs to be transformed into a four-wheeled car.

You can either attach two more wheels to the box (and a Steering Stick of course) or use a stone slab to build an even larger car.

Then, ride it out of the depot and towards the Factory to install the robot's final piece.

After successfully assembling the Construct, it springs to life, with Mineru expressing her gratitude. She quickly points you towards your next destination – the Spirit Temple, located southeast from your current spot.

The journey may seem daunting due to the pervading gloom, but worry not – you have a formidable new companion on your side.

By approaching the Construct and hitting 'A', you can hop on and guide it. Keep in mind that steering the Construct uses Energy Cells, but it allows you to navigate through the gloom unharmed.

Journey to the Spirit Temple

Head south towards the lift from which you originally descended, where you'll learn how to outfit your Construct with armaments.

This part of your adventure is essentially a Construct operation crash course – and it's worth your while to explore all the weapon stores scattered around.

Feel free to equip your Construct with whatever tools you fancy. Spiked balls and Flame Emitters make excellent arm attachments, although they eventually wear out with use.

Moving east, reach the next armory, experimenting with your new attacks en route. Once there, Mineru suggests focusing on speed enhancement – mounting a fan on the Construct's rear is an effective way to boost its pace.

Simply keep trekking south, aiming for the marker on your map. On your way, make sure to light up the *Sitoju Lightroot* (coordinates **1215, -2540, -0612**).

You might encounter a Blue Hinox – engage in a skirmish for some valuable monster loot if you're up for it.

Use your Construct's power to shatter any obstructing rocks — either with spiked ball arms or Cannon hands.

Ultimately, you'll arrive at an armory equipped with Rockets, positioned right before the *Spirit Temple* (coordinates **1391, -3118, -0638**).

Finally, activate the altar and descend via the lift to reveal the secret stone you've been seeking. As you venture onto the gloom-engulfed platform, brace yourself for an ambush.

Mineru lets you in on a crucial limitation — the Construct lacks climbing capabilities. Affix a Rocket to your Construct's back to bypass this issue.

Approach the fractured pathway, engage your Rocket, and soar your way up to the Spirit Temple!

SPIRIT TEMPLE
The Vessel of Spirit's Resting Place

It's showtime – a high-stakes duel in a boxing arena with electrified ropes awaits you and the boss.

The trick to inflicting substantial damage is to force the boss against these charged boundaries.

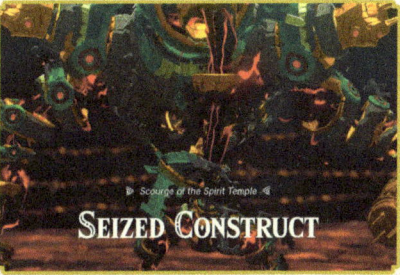

SEIZED CONSTRUCT

You have a couple of strategies at your disposal: either patiently parry its attacks, leaving it vulnerable to a series of punches pushing it into the ropes, or go all-out and pummel it relentlessly until it recoils into the ropes.

The boss, named Seized Construct, has relatively predictable moves. It shields itself by raising both hands, while the direction of incoming punches can be gauged by the movement of its corresponding arm.

Be cautious, as it can attach Zonai devices to its arms and unleash a flurry of attacks, wildly swinging its arms.

Maintain a safe distance, especially if it's equipped with Shock Emitters, as they can immobilize you.

Upon reducing its health to half, the boss grows an additional pair of arms and attaches a Rocket to its chest, granting it flight within the arena.

Keenly observe its motion, and once it halts, entice it towards the ropes. As it lunges at you, sidestep, causing it to crash-land.

Seize this opportunity to strike and propel it into the ropes once more. You can also attach the dropped items onto your Construct.

Rinse and repeat these steps until you have defeated the boss.

Next up on your adventure is your subsequent quest - *Trail of the Master Sword*.

The Master Sword is - technically - an optional extra and isn't required to beat the game.

Although, thinking about it, seeing as you can also technically go to the final boss not long after touching down on the Hyrule Surface, most of the game is technically optional!

Anyways, if you're looking to bag yourself Link's iconic sword then there's three options available to you:

Find all 12 Dragon Tears

This option is the one that we cover over the following pages as it's the one that allows you to enjoy the story-line to its fullest.

You have likely seen the large white Dragon flying around Hyrule's sky and this is where the Master Sword is located!

BotW players will be used to the mechanic of needing *loads* of stamina to pull the sword out of its resting place and it's no exception here either.

You require **two stamina wheels** to pull the sword out. This requires a minimum of **20 Lights of Blessing** to be converted to stamina.

> **Top Tip!** *If you're short on stamina, then you can convert your hearts to stamina at the Horned Statue in the Emergency Shelter at Lookout Landing for 120 rupees.*

Saving the Deku Tree

This option requires you to save the Deku Tree. However, you can't reach the Lost Woods via the Surface. You must reach it by traveling through the dreaded Depths and looking for the Lightroot of the Shrine that's closest to the Deku Tree on the Surface.

Dive into the chasm inside the Deku tree and then be ready for a fight against some Gloom Hands and when you're victorious, the Deku Tree spills the beans.

Or...

Just build a crazy flying device and go Dragon hunting in the skies! As long as you have the two stamina wheels, you can - technically - get the Master Sword anytime you like!

The Master Sword can't break (but has a cooldown period) and it *can* be fused with other items too!

KEY:

D. Tear

Elixir

Story

Zonai Gear

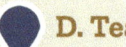

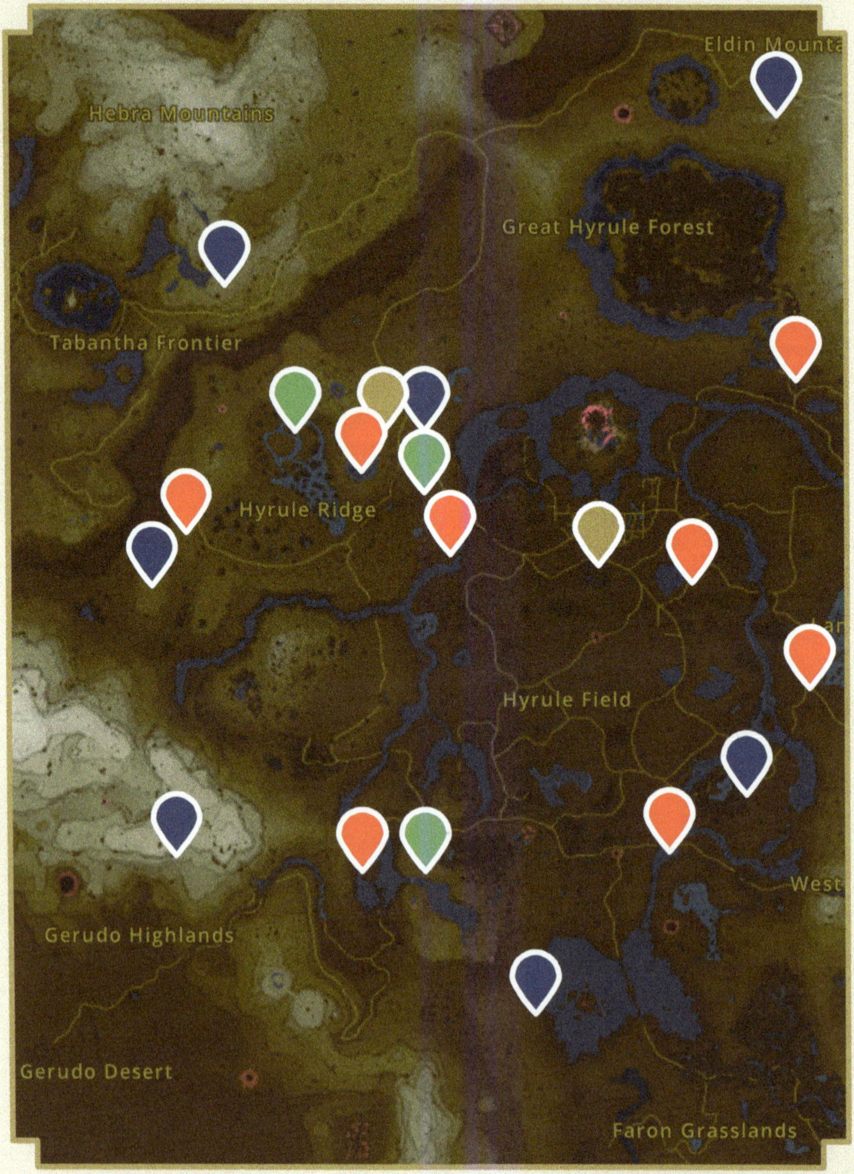

Eldin Mounta
Hebra Mountains
Great Hyrule Forest
Tabantha Frontier
Hyrule Ridge
Hyrule Field
West
Gerudo Highlands
Gerudo Desert
Faron Grasslands

The *Impa and the Geoglyphs* quest might naturally cross your path during your initial ventures across the vast expanse of *Hyrule*.

But, if your journey isn't intertwined with the other major story quests, it's fairly easy to overlook.

In case you haven't stumbled upon it yet, you'll find this quest nestled in the *New Serenne Stable* situated in the *Hyrule Field* area, a stone's throw away from the *Sinakawak Shrine*.

Seek out **Cado** standing guard opposite the stable entrance, who will advise Link to update **Impa** about Zelda's situation, thus marking the commencement of the *Impa and the Geoglyphs* quest.

After accepting the quest, approach **Impa** positioned on the nearby platform.

Impa informs Link of her desire to investigate the peculiar geoglyph that has surfaced in the vicinity of the stable, but the repair of her hot air balloon is required before she can observe the glyph from higher up.

To restore functionality to Impa's hot air balloon, you need to utilize **Ultrahand** to hoist the top balloon part from the ground beneath the platform, reorient it to a vertical position, and then secure the balloon to the lower part near Impa.

After rectifying the hot air balloon, have a chat with Impa. Following a fruitful conversation, Link is now entrusted with kindling a fire beneath the balloon to get it airborne.

If a **Fused** fire weapon is part of your inventory, it will serve the purpose. However, there's a torch, conveniently located nearby, which can be ignited at the campfire and swung at the balloon to lift off with Impa.

After chatting with Impa in the balloon, paraglide down to the surface and navigate towards the geoglyph's head, where a **Tear** awaits discovery.

Although it may resemble a mere puddle at first glance, upon closer inspection, Link will trigger the **'Where am I?'** memory, thus successfully completing the *Impa and the Geoglyphs* main quest.

Here's the locations of all 12 Dragon Tears.

Tear 1: Where Am I?

The first Tear is automatically found during the *Impa and the Geoglyphs* quest.

Tear 2: An Unfamiliar World

Your destination is *Tabantha Hills*, nestled to the east of *Rito Village*. However, be sure to arm yourself with some Cold Resistance Food or wear some Cold Resistant armor to weather the chill.

Once you're geared up, take a graceful glide from *Lindor's Brow Skyview Tower*.

Upon arrival, embark on an uphill climb until you hit the coordinates **-2549, -1888, 0319**.

Engage with the tiny pool at this location to activate the cutscene.

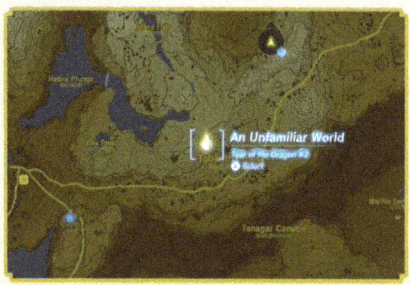

Tear 3: Mineru's Counsel

Fast travel to the Eldin Canyon Skyview Tower. Spotting the upcoming Geoglyph is as easy as looking southeast.

Soak in the view, then make your descent and beeline to the coordinates **1827, 0737, 0089**.

Interact with the water pool to set off the cutscene.

Tear 4: The Gerudo Assault

Next destination: Sahasra Slope Skyview Tower. Find it southeast of Lookout Landing, hitch a skyward ride, then crane your neck slightly west to spot the upcoming Geoglyph.

Fly over, then home in on the coordinates **0697, 1309, 0053**, perched atop the hill.

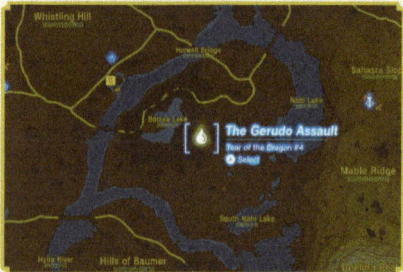

Tear 5: A Show of Fealty

Next up, the *Gerudo Canyon Skyview Tower*. Hitch a skyward ride and glance west to spot the subsequent Geoglyph.

Touchdown on the second-highest ledge, leg it up to coordinates **-3178, -1702, 0419** and begin the next cutscene by the water pool.

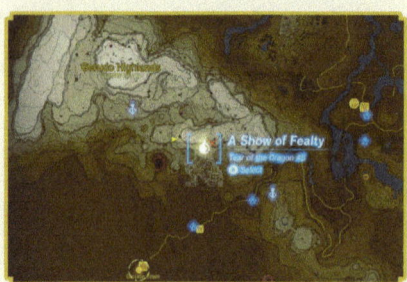

Tear 6: Zelda and Sonia

Now, venture to the *Gerudo Highland Skyview Tower*, take to the skies, then coast north to the next Geoglyph perched atop a mountain.

Upon landing, run until you hit the coordinates **-3091, -0078, 0211**.

Tear 7: Sonia is Caught By Treachery

Onwards to the *Rebella Wetland Skyview Tower*. Skyward, then southeast glide finds you a Geoglyph, snug on the island's edge.

Land, then meander left to coordinates **3324, -3566, 0004**.

Tear 8: Birth of the Demon King

Next stop, *Pikida Stonegrove Skyview Tower*. A skyward hop and northeast glide takes you to the next Geoglyph. Go to the left to coordinates **-1864, 3618, 0237**.

Tear 9: The Sages' Vow

Set course for *Mount Lanayru Skyview Tower*. A skyward leap and northeast glide lands you at the next Geoglyph. Climb the hill to coordinates **4472, -0305, 0075**.

Tear 10: A King's Duty

Next, go to the *Popla Foothills Skyview Tower*, take a skyward spin, and glide east to the next Geoglyph. Climb the hill to coordinates **-0649, -2685, 0068**.

Tear 11: A Master Sword in Time

Head to the *Thyphlo Ruins Skyview Tower*, ascend to the skies, then glide east to the next Geoglyph. Tread uphill to coordinates **0887, 2951, 0363**.

Tear 12: Tears of the Dragon

Finally, warp to the *Ulri Mountain Skyview Tower*, then go into the heart of the *Rist Peninsula*. Touch the final pool of water to bring this quest to a satisfying close.

This is it. You've traveled far and fought exceptionally hard to reach this point, so there's no turning back now.

To trigger this quest (versus just going and doing it) you'll need to speak with Purah in Lookout Landing after finishing the *Recovering the Hero's Sword* questline.

> **Top Tip!** *You're <u>definitely</u> going to want to come to this battle properly prepared. Stock up on 3 or more meals with four Ironshrooms (for Defense UP UP UP), plus around 15 meals containing Sudelion (the flower found on Sky Islands) to restore any broken hearts.*
>
> *<u>Don't</u> make any meals with any other buffs as they'll remove the far superior one you've got now.*
>
> *Also bring a ton of arrows (around 140 or so) and as many Gibdo bones as you can to attach onto said arrows (their damage boost is insane).*

Head to Hyrule Castle

It shouldn't come as a surprise to learn that the final boss can be found at Hyrule Castle. Well, not *in* the castle, but *underneath* the castle in the Gloom-ridden Depths. And getting to it *won't* be fun (or easy).

Fast travel to the *Serutabomac Shrine* and then fly down into the Depths under Hyrule Castle from there.

Hyrule Castle Chasm

Glide northwards until you see the orange hue of the *Camobatures Lightroot* below you. Set yourself down beside it and activate it, creating a new fast travel point.

Grab all the Poes while you're here, then look for the marker on your map and drop down *even deeper* into the chasm until you trigger the next area - *Gloom's Approach*.

It goes without saying that you'll want your best Gloom-resistant gear on while navigating this gloom-packed cavern system. You won't have an opportunity to reclaim any hearts broken by the Gloom!

Fly to the base and make your way to the corner in the southwest. There, you'll spot a red foe on the wall, hurling electric spheres at you.

Dodge this and and navigate through the gap underneath.

Upon touching down, climb the wall ahead where a few enemies are scaling the surface.

There's a Gloom-covered Lynel standing in the middle of a huge open area. Tackle it for some strong loot, or glide over to the exit on the left - it's up to you.

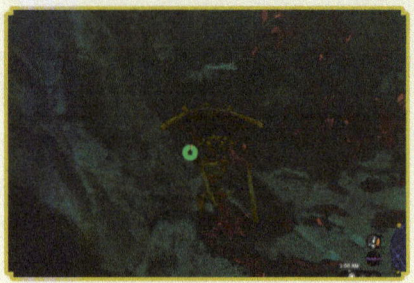

Stick to the rightward path, but at the first opportunity, take a left towards the Ice Keese and ignore the other enemies stuck to the wall.

Sprint to the corridor's end where the final stone crumbles beneath you, stick to it, and descend to the lower level.

Post-touchdown, proceed straight from the staircase and descend into the next room. You'll spot a foe stationed on the upper-level opposite you.

Clamber up the gloom-less pillar located next to it.

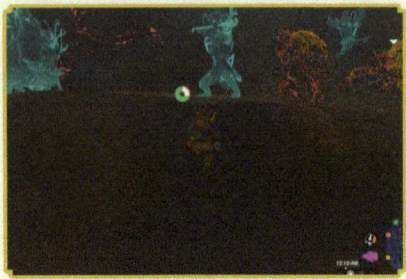

Continue deeper into the zone that's teeming with electric Keese, swiftly making a beeline for the opening on your left.

Stepping on the stones triggers their descent, so hold tight. This will usher you into a chamber where stones are falling from above.

Position yourself atop these stones and employ Recall to hoist them back up, hopping off once you reach the pinnacle.

Head down the path behind this foe, leading further downward. The corridor concludes with breakable rocks which require a melee weapon combined with a rock to shatter.

In the subsequent room, veer right, and break the rocks to make an exit. This pathway ushers you into the *Imprisoning Chamber*. Plummet down the abyss.

Upon landing at the bottom, there's only one route to follow. At its end, leap down the murky abyss, ensuring you land on the red roots to trigger the final sequence of boss battles.

The Demon King's Army

This boss battle entails tackling a horde of lesser adversaries, with your Sages lending a hand.

Seize opportunities when the foes are distracted by your Sages to strike with the Master Sword, then dash away and repeat.

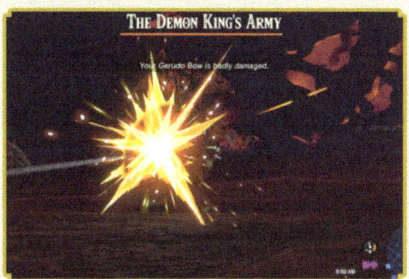

The bulk of the workload falls on your Sages, so just maintain distance from the major enemy.

First, direct your efforts towards the arches; a single blow from the Master Sword will finish them. As enemy numbers shrink, the battle eases.

Reserve the big guy for last, then your Sages can assist with him.

Wave two brings forth lizard enemies who can lob water at you, so stay alert to their ranged assaults. Focus on the weak ones, picking them off one at a time. The battle lightens as their numbers decrease.

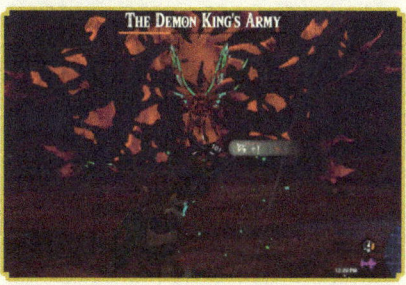

The third wave introduces flying and crawling enemies, who zero in on you, not the Sages. Rush to Riju and deploy her lightning strike ability, striking the floor with an arrow to detonate it.

These enemies shrug off regular damage but are vulnerable to lightning damage. While waiting for Riju's attack to recharge, just keep circling the enemies.

The fourth wave comes with some big foes (including potentially Phantom Ganon). Your Sages will eventually obliterate them, so just circle them to stay out of harm's way.

Once the horde is vanquished, run down the tunnel ahead of you to initiate the Demon King Ganondorf boss fight.

Demon King Ganondorf Boss Fight

This boss fight hinges on well-timed dodging. Opt for a shield and a one-handed weapon combo (two-handed weapons prohibit shield use).

The fight's difficulty level depends on your meal choice. Better to spend an hour prepping than be stuck here for two.

Phase 1

Begin the fight by consuming your DEFENSE UP UP UP meal to limit damage to 1 per hit. Snipe him with your bow, quickly dodge his attacks, and repeat.

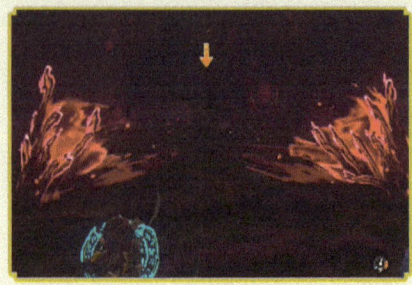

Attach items like Gibdo bones to arrows for additional damage.

The boss has three weapons at his disposal: Sword, Spear, Club. His weapon switch is random but always starts with the Sword.

Phase 2

Ganondorf summons more phantoms. Keep circling the arena, your Sages will arrive to help shortly.

With the phantoms distracted by your Sages, you can concentrate on the main boss.

Phase 3

The third phase leaves you on your own, with Ganondorf employing new ranged attacks. His orbs permanently reduce your health heart which can't be replenished with Sundelion meals.

Keep scoring headshots with your arrows, attaching strong materials like Gibdo Bones for added damage.

Maintain a safe distance when he charges for an attack.

Once you've exhausted his health bar, the Demon Dragon boss fight commences immediately.

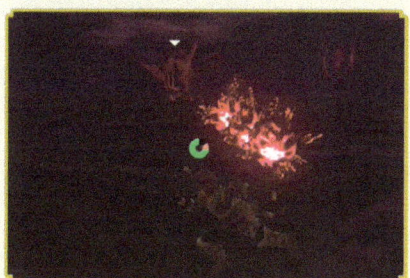

Demon Dragon Boss Fight

You'll find yourself riding the Light Dragon, tasked with defeating the Demon Dragon beneath you.

Destroy the four crystals on the red dragon's back, then attack the crystal on its head for the final blow.

Save Princess Zelda

Post-Demon Dragon defeat, you'll be in free-fall. Glide towards Princess Zelda, who is also plummeting, catch her and relish the concluding cutscene!

Congratulations!

You've defeated Ganon and freed Zelda! Once you've watched the ending, the game saves the fact that you've beaten it, but it also puts you back at your last *manual save*.

Get the True Ending?

As we mentioned before, if you stuck it out and completed all 22 **main** quests, you'll be treated to a **much** longer ending! Enjoy.

BOSSES

 ## The Bigger They Are...

There's a fair few bosses that Link can take on during his quest to save Zelda.

We already covered the main story-line bosses in our section dedicated to the main quest line, so we've reserved this section to cover all of the *other* bosses that either stroll around like they own the place, or the bosses that are tucked away and hidden out of plain sight.

What makes this section more interesting with Tears of the Kingdom is the fact that you can generally use Zonai devices against them, potentially making the fights - even against bosses such as Lynels - pretty trivial.

So, we'll cover the bosses with easy-to-repeat strategies that allow you to fight them in the spirit of the game.

However, we'll also cover a few key Zonai-based contraptions-of-ultimate-doom™ that, should you *really* find yourself struggling, you can build and use to annihilate the most irritating of enemies.

Some of these bosses make a return from Breath of the Wild (such as Lynels), but there's a few new ones added into the mix too.

Here's a list of the boss-types that we'll be covering in our guide:

- *Flux Constructs*
- *Hinox*
- *(Battle/Frost/Stone) Talus*
- *(Obsidian/Blue-White) Frox*
- *Gloom Hands*
- *Lynels*
- *Gleeoks*
- *Stalnox*

Still struggling? No worries, at the very end of this section well provide the designs for a couple of Zonai contraptions-of-ultimate-doom™ for you to have fun building and then exacting your revenge.

Enjoy…

Co-ordinates

- I: 0492, -1516, 1440
- II: 1337, −1548, 0801
- III: 3064, -2800, 1201

Flux Construct I

The key strategy here is to use Ultrahand to pull the gold and green block away from the boss, causing it to crumple to the ground in a heap.

Now's your chance to jump in there and smack that cube around without risking your health.

Each time you manage to do enough damage, it'll reform and form a different shape. Keep your distance, lock on with Ultrahand, pull it away, then hit it hard and repeat until it's finished!

Flux Construct II

Located *directly underneath Jindok Shrine*, the strategy required here is almost the same.

However, this time you need to gain height when it begins floating in the air. Use Fuse and your Zonai devices to get the height needed to attack the boss when it starts floating high in the sky.

This version has *a lot* more health than the first, so bring plenty of weapons (along with one that you can fuse your reward to...)

Flux Construct III

Pretty much the same strategy as for the previous two. However, you can use the conveniently placed springs here to launch up high into the air to get on top of the boss as it flies around the arena.

Back from causing pain in BotW, Hinox's are big, slow, but also very strong and they can hit you hard.

They can also be found fast asleep on the ground, providing you with the *perfect* opportunity to sneak up behind them and give them a surprise with the sharp end of your strongest weapon.

Once they're finally up on their feet, get some elevation and use your best bow and some bomb arrows to get a clean eye-shot in.

This should stun it for around five seconds, presenting your next opportunity to hit it hard with your strongest weapon. Repeat until it's gone.

Co-ordinates

1. -4195, -1288, 0428
2. -0799, -3026, 0119
3. 1699, -3877, 0002
4. 1643, -2908, 0260
5. 1888, -2959, 0231
6. 2032, -3064, 0095
7. 1277, -2171, 0247
8. 1561, -2412, 0192
9. 2064, -1998, 0018
10. 0692, -1078, 0009
11. 1307, 0906, 0027
12. 3405, 0274, 0247
13. 4418, 0763, 0293
14. 4646, 1774, 0029
15. 4607, 3533, -0065
16. 0838, 3358, 0199
17. -1241, 2108, 0105
18. -0749, 1263, 0081
19. -1079, 0470, 0035
20. -2224, 0760, 0102
21. -2737, 1328, 0159
22. -2826, 2440, 0403
23. -3656, 3804, 0230

New to this game, these mobile rock-fortresses have only one weak spot - the black rock on the top.

Ideally, you'll want to keep your distance and use a load of bomb-fused arrows on this rock.

However, if your arrow-count is low, you can use the Ascent ability to get up to the platform at the top and then use a close-range melee weapon on it instead.

Co-ordinates

- -1447, 1038, 0137
- -1360, -0790, 0010
- -0104, -0787, 0041
- -1360, -0790, 0010
- -0774, 0793, 0001
- 0206, 0534, 0001
- 1258, -1181, 0111

However, you'll need to keep a very close eye out for those Bokoblins who are only too eager to throw some painful rocks in your direction if they see you.

These large rocky toads are hidden deep within the Depths (so, expect a *lot* of Gloom to navigate).

One of the easiest ways to take one down to is to hold a **Hylian Tomato** and it'll suck them out of your hands, causing it to stand still. Switch to your bow, shoot it in the eye, and then quickly jump up on its back.

Use your strongest weapons to smash every crystal on its back. If it throws you into the air, glide back down onto its back and finish off the job.

Locations

- *Near Abandoned Eldin Mine*
- *Near Grove of Time*
- *Two Near Gleeok Den*
- *Near N. Lomei Depths Lab*
- *Near Sherfin's Lavafalls*
- *Near Abandoned Hebra Mine*
- *Abandoned Gerudo Mine*
- *Great Abandoned C. Mine*

GLOOM HANDS

These nightmarish creatures normally only spawn at night (unless you're at Kolomo Garisson Ruins) and they are fast, strong, and can destroy your hearts with Gloom.

Therefore, it's imperative to use a load of Bomb/Fused arrows and, *ideally*, take them out *before* they see you!

Co-ordinates

- *3321, 1436, 0425*
- *1063, 1281, -0495*
- *0437, 2094, -0588*
- *-0426, -1269, 0031*

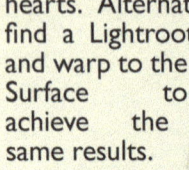

You need to work quick as any remaining hands can bring any destroyed hands back to life!

It's also worth cooking some meals with **Sundelions**, as they allow you to restore broken hearts. Alternatively, find a Lightroot and warp to the Surface to achieve the same results.

Lynels are back and they're just as aggressive as they were in BotW.

Different Lynels have different health levels. From Red-Maned (lowest at 2000HP) to Silver (5000HP). This effectively makes them very nimble tanks.

The easiest way to take these out is to take down a Red-Maned version and collect the **[Lynel Bow]** it drops.

Use a Zonai spring to get some airtime! Use this bow as it fires off three shots at once! Now fuse some bombs to it for **serious** damage *and* the ability to set the grass on fire (creating an updraft).

Now use a some Gibdo Bone-fused arrows and the updraft from the fire to life your paraglider back into the air. Three or so more rounds should do the trick.

Locations

- *West Hyrule Plains*
- *Deep Akkala*
- *Ukuku Plains*
- *Lanayru Heights*
- *Rabia Plain*
- *Kamah Plateau*
- *Wetlands*
- *Risoka Snowfield*
- *Lake Illumeni*
- *Tama Pond*
- *South of Hebra West Summit*

Gleeoks originally appeared as the very first boss in the very first Zelda game on the NES!

These three-headed dragons come in their own elemental versions: Frost, Flame, and Thunder.

Flame Gleeok

There;s a number of these dotted around the map, so it's worth starting off with these first (as their reward allows you to take down the Frost variants much more quickly).

Firstly, they do **serious** damage, so make sure you have your best armor on and the appropriate elemental resistance (*especially* for any desert battles).

Keese homing arrows are your friends here as they will home straight for each dragon head.

Hit all three heads with two shots to make it hit the ground hard.

Locations

- **Flame:** *Spectacle Rock, Bridge of Hylia, Trilby Valley, Rayne Highlands*

- **Frost:** *Gerudo Mountain, Biron Snowshelf, South Tabantha Snowfield*

- **Thunder:** *South Akkala Plains, Herin South Lake, Coliseum Ruins*

- **King:** *W/Hebra Sky Archipelago, S/E Necluda Sky Archipelago, N/ Gerudo Sky Archipelago, Gleeok Den (The Depths)*

This is your cue to rush in and hit it with your toughest weapons. Once it gets back up, run away and get some cover! It'll use lasers and/or gusts of wind to push you away.

Once it reaches 1/3 or less of its health, get ready to hide from its Meteor-of-Death™ fireball! Rinse and repeat until it's dead. Use its Gleeok Flame Horn on the Frost Gleeoks!

Frost Gleeok

Firstly, make sure you've got your best Cold Resistance meals at the ready for these battles as you'll be in *seriously* cold temps as you fight.

Secondly, stick with homing Keese Eyeball arrows on the heads to make it drop to the ground.

Once it's hit the ground, use your strongest Gleeok Flame Horn-fused weapon on its head! Ideally, you'll have killed every Flame Gleeok so you have enough horns to take out every Frost Gleeok!

Things get much more interesting at 1/3 or less health. It'll start to fire down icicles at your head!

Wait for one to land, then, climb on it and immediately use Recall to get high into the air for another round of arrows to its heads!

As with the Flame Gleeok, rinse and repeat to collect your prizes.

Thunder Gleeok

By now, you should have a fair idea of what to do. It's form of attack for 1/3 or less health are focused lightning strikes around you, so use the Rubber Armor, or be quick at dodging!

It doesn't have any elemental weakness, so just go all out with your strongest melee weapons.

King Gleeok

Alright, this hidden boss is basically all three versions combined!!!

There are also **four** of them to defeat if you want to complete the quest for obtaining all four **Sages Wills**.

Now, one option here is to try and fuse a flame and frost horn to separate items and use them on the opposite head.

Or, you can use a strong weapon, such as a **Silver Boss Boko Two-Handed Axe**, and it'll work *very* well against *all* three heads.

A **Savage Lynel Bow** will be your preferred choice of bow for the early part of these fights.

However, try and bag the **Zonaite Bow** from the *Kumamaun Shrine* as that will be *super* helpful in the frantic final third phase of these battles (as it fires *much* further than every other bow).

The King Gleeok will come at you with a battering of flame + ice + lightning homing beams from high above.

Homing arrows from your Savage Lynel Bow will bring them down quickly, then lay into them when they're down.

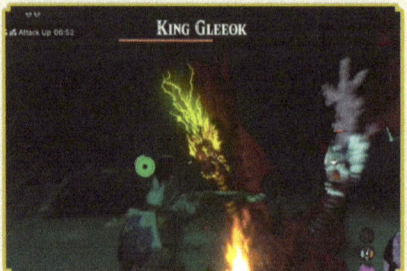

However, it's the 1/3 health left part where things start to get *really* interesting (and by interesting, we main most likely very painful).

You see, it will throw a combination of lightning strikes at your feed **and** start showering you with loads of icicles from the sky!

And while you can use the lightning to get some air up, not only will it not be high enough, but you then also have to look up and dodge the icicles aiming for your head!

If you want to make this part much easier, we recommend bringing in around 10 Zonai Springs and fusing two stacked on top of each other.

The goal is to bounce off of this and use your Zonaite Bow and Keese eyes to reach the boss as it's *way* up above you in the sky.

Keep your cool and rinse and repeat these strats and you'll be rewarded with *loads* of powerful monster parts for fusing *and* another **[Sage's Will]**! Wohoo!

Another returning foe from BotW, the Stalnox can be fought in two locations - with the second one that's found in The Depths being potentially *much* more annoying to fight (due to its attacks causing Gloom damage).

Phase 1

Start by working on stating behind the Stalnox and strike it from behind.

If you see it bending, run away and get some distance, as it's about to do a butt-slam move and you *don't* want to get hit by its bony butt!

Stay away from its feet and keep getting a few hits in and backing off until it's under 50% health.

Phase 2

This time, get your Keese Eyes ready and go to the front. Use a Homing Arrow to strike its now-vulnerable eye and if it doesn't block it, you can make the eye pop out.

Locations

- *Royal Hidden Passage*
- *Akkala House of Bones (Via Skull Lake Chasm)*

Hit the eye with a few melee attacks to make swift work of this bony boss.

The House of Bones one drops a special **[Biggoron's Sword]** too!

ADVENTURES

Extra adventures on the side

Side Adventures are new to the series and they're optional missions that often flesh out key character backstories, add more history to the main story-line, and they usually offer decent rewards for completing them.

Hestu's Concerns

Speak to: Hetsu
Reward: Inventory Upgrades

Find **Hetsu** near *Lindor's Brow* or *Lookout Landing*. Take out the trees that are bullying him, then talk to *Hetsu* again, exchange Korok Seeds for 1 extra slot, he changes location after every two upgrades:

- **Bows:** *+9 Extra slots max*
- **Shields:** *+16 Extra slots max*
- **Weapons:** *10 Extra slots max*

Bring Peace to Hyrule Field!

Speak to: Captain Hoz
Reward: 100 Rupees

Speak to **Captain Hoz** as he patrols around *Hyrule Garrison Ruins*. Join him in his battle against the Bokoblins and larger enemies.

After bagging 100 Rupees for your help, you can join him at *Fort Hateno* in *Necluda* to start the **Bring Peace to Necluda!** mission.

Bring Peace to Necluda!

Speak to: Captain Hoz
Reward: 100 Rupees

Team up with **Captain Hoz** once again to take on those pesky Monster Forces!

Lend a hand and after wiping out every enemy, you'll be rewarded with another 100 Rupees for your efforts.

Bring Peace to Faron!

Speak to: Captain Hoz
Reward: 100 Rupees

Another area and another Monster Force to take care of! Time to team up with **Captain Hoz** once again!

Lend a hand and after wiping out every enemy, you'll be rewarded with another 100 Rupees for your efforts.

Bring Peace to Hebra!

Speak to: Captain Hoz
Reward: 100 Rupees

Unlocks after completing the Faron mission. Fuse the spiked ball that's blocking your way to a sword as it'll come in very handy soon.

Start the battle, take out the **Boss Bokoblin**, and use the explosive barrels here to take out the smaller enemies quickly.

The Flute Player's Plan

Speak to: Pyper
Reward: 100 Rupees

This quest involves helping the missing flutist **Pyper** at the *Highland Stable* in *Faron*. Find *Haite*, then speak to Pyper who's up a tree.

Get him **10 Sunset Fireflys** (found in *Pagos*, *Faron*, and *Finra Woods*) to complete this mission.

An Eerie Voice

Speak to: Penn
Reward: 100 Rupees

Part of the **Potential Princess Sightings** quest. Meet with **Penn** outside *Highland Stable*, then explore the stable grounds to find the source of the voice.

The voice is coming from *Haran Lakefront Well*. Speak with **Sagessa**, then inform *Penn* for your reward.

Honey, Bee Mine

Speak to: Beetz
Reward: 100 Rupees

Go look for missing horn drummer **Beetz**, located near *Kakariko Village*. Speak with **Mastro** at *Dueling Peaks Stable*, look for Beetz hiding in his tent near an alcove en-route to *Kakariko*.

Find him three **Courser Bee Honeys**, then give them to him to finish this quest.

The Hornist's Dramatic Escape

Speak to: Eustus
Reward: Courser Bee Honey

This quest involves finding **Eustus** whose fallen in a pit on the road to *Rito Village*. *Mastro* kicks this quest off. You'll find him in a huge hole at *Tabantha Great Bridge*.

Safely fly him out with the tools at hand and he'll give you the honey.

A Call from the Depths

Speak to: Goddess Statue
Reward: Health or Stamina

Head to -0552, -1500, 0019 and smash open the rock to the entrance to *Gatepost Town Ruins*. You need to bring her four eyes back to her. You'll find them at:

- *-0469, -1991, 0072*
- *-1432, -2004, 0231*
- *-0661, -1521, 0067*
- *-0938, -2312, 0168*

Hateno Village Research

Speak to: Robbie
Reward: Shrine Sensor

Head to the *Hateno Ancient Tech Lab* at *3747, -2021, 0189*. Speak with Robbie, get your upgrade, exit, then head inside *Walnot Mountain Cave*.

Fight your way to the Mayahisik Shrine, activate it, then warp back to Robbie to finish this mission.

Who Goes There?

Speak to: Jerrin
Reward: 20 Rupees

After finishing at least one Temple, speak with **Jerrin** in *Lookout Landing's* emergency shelter. Head down the tunnel, take the right-hand path, and talk to the statue.

The statue allows you to swap hearts for stamina, and vice-versa. Speak with *Jerrin* to end this quest.

Gloom-Borne Illness

Speak to: Lasli
Reward: Energizing Veggie Porridge

Speak with **Lasli** in *Kakariko Village.* You need to make the Armor shop's sick grandma a special porridge. Cook a **Sundelion, Hylian Rice,** and **Fresh Milk** together to make *Sunny Veggie Porridge*.

Give it to Lasli to end this quest.

Codgers' Quarrel

Speak to: Trissa
Reward: Endura Carrot

Speak with **Trissa** in her shop in *Kakariko Village.* She tasks you with heading to *Ring Ruin,* found at: 1657, -1164, 0214.

Clear the ruins out of all enemies, speak with the two old men on the hill, then fast travel back to Trissa who rewards you, and puts **Swift Carrots** on sale at her shop!

Follow the Cuccos

Speak to: Trissa
Reward: 50 Rupees

Trissa tasks you with finding 10 **Bird's Eggs**. They're often found in nests up in wide trees, or they can also be found from Cuccos.

If you follow them to *Cucco Hideaway* at *1876, -1163, 0200*. Fill your pockets here, then head back.

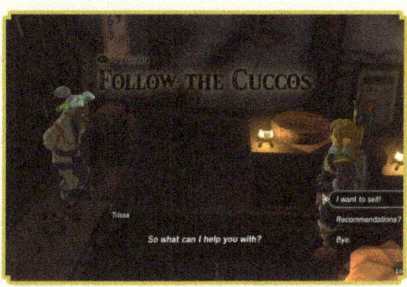

The Hunt For Bubbul Gems!

Speak to: Kilton
Reward: Mask Shop

The brother's, found at *1220, 1210, 0020* are looking for **Bubbul Gems**, which are found when you defeat a **Bubbul Frog** (found in caves). Head inside the cave, defeat the frog, and claim your **[Bokoblin Mask]** from the brothers.

Give them more Bubbul Gems for masks at *Tarry Town*.

Hero's Path Mode

Speak to: Robbie
Reward: Hero's Path Mode Upgrade

Once you've completed: *Camera Work in the Depths*, *A Mystery in the Depths*, and *Hateno Village Research*, speak with **Robbie** again for the prototype upgrade.

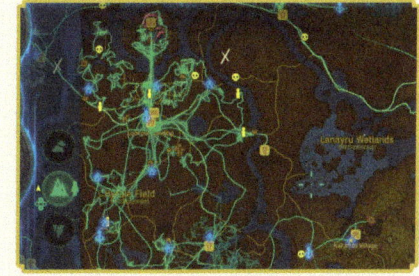

Once it's installed you have to visit 15 Shrines for the quest to be completed. You can now track where you've been on the map!

Lucky Clover Gazette

Speak to: Traysi
Reward: The Froggy Armor! :)

Starting this adventure effectively kick-starts 12 additional side-adventures that are only available once this one has been.

Speak with **Traysi** *at the Lucky Clover Gazette,* just outside *Rito Village*.

Potential Princess Sightings!

Speak to: Penn
Reward: See above

This side-adventure is basically a culmination of all linked side adventures (once they're all completed, this one is finished).

Your reward for doing so is the **Froggy Armor**, which grants you *Slip Resistance*. **Note:** All linked quests are started at their relevant stable.

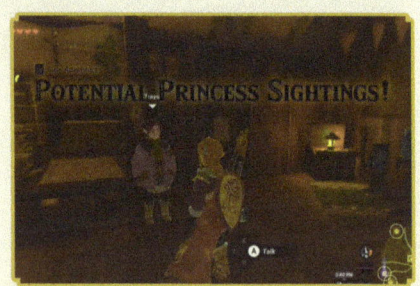

Gourmet's Gone Missing

Speak to: Penn
Reward: Rupees

Head to *Riverside Stable.* You goal here is to create a **Meat and Rice Bowl** meal to heal Agus' sick men. You need to cook some **Raw Meat**, **Salt**, and **Hylian Rice** together.

Give it to his men for some nice rewards and the quest is over.

White Goat's Gone Missing

Speak to: Penn
Reward: Rupees

Talk to **Penn** at *Tabantha Bridge Stable*. Speak with **Chork** and follow the trial of *Hylian Pine Cones*.

Eventually you'll come across the White Goats, finishing the quest.

The Beast and the Princess

Speak to: Penn
Reward: Rupees

Talk to *Penn* at *New Serenne Stable*. Once the quest has started, head to *Lakeside Stable* (near *Lake Floria*).

Chat to **Shay** then head across to **Sima**. Once finished, Penn arrives, signaling the end of this quest.

Zelda's Golden Horse

Speak to: Penn
Reward: Zelda's Golden Horse!

Talk to pen at *Snowfield Stable*. Once the quest starts, make your way to -1823, 3382, 0236 which is where the horse is located.

Now, *before* you sneak up on it, make sure you have **at least** 1.5 - 2 wheels of stamina to tame it! (Or Stamina Elixirs). Take it back and register the horse to keep it!

Keep your eyes open for purple smoke near some of the stables:

- *Woodland Stable,*
- *Dueling Peaks Stable,*
- *Outskirt Stable,*
- *Snowfield Stable.*

In a twist from Breath of the Wild, Great Fairies now want to hear delightful music before they'll emerge. You can only kick-off this questline once you're a Lucky Clover Gazette reporter (see page 160).

First Fairy

As a reporter, head towards *Woodland Stable* and chat to the musical group who want to serenade the Great Fairy Tera, but their cart needs repairs.

Use Ultrahand to fix the wheels and get a Towing Harness Key Item with 3 Pony Points from any stable.

Now, attach the Towing Harness to your horse and hitch the cart.

Finally, head up the hillside to the Great Fairy to unlock your first of four Great Fairies and start enhancing your armor in exchange for some rupees and ingredients.

However, not all armor can be upgraded, and if you're after set bonuses, you'll need to unlock more Great Fairies.

Remaining Three Fairies

The remaining Fairies appear on the map. The musical group will also show up at the next stable you need to visit, and you can unlock the Great Fairies in any order.

Each Fairy is picky about their music, so you'll need to track down the right musicians.

The relevant quests solutions can be found on pages 156 and 157:

- *The Flute Player's Plan*
- *Honey, Bee Mine*
- *The Hornist's Dramatic Escape*

Side quests are much smaller in size and scope and are usually quicker to finish (and can even be finished in parallel with side adventures, if the conditions match). Here's a list of the side quests we came across on our adventure:

Quest Name	Co-ordinates
Mired in Muck	2846, 0585, 0375
Crossing the Cold Pool	-3217, 2456, 0347
Molli the Fletcher's Quest	-3616, 1793, 0214
A Bottled Cry for Help	3945, -2508, 0000
The Incomplete Stable	-0245, 0060, 0019
Misko's Treasure: Pirate Manuscript	2603, 1319, 0150
Misko's Cave of Chests	2606, 1325, 0150
Piaffe, Packed Away	-2802, -2226, 0029
Today's Menu	-0266, 0098, 0008
An Uninvited Guest	0865, -0171, 0025
The Never-Ending Lecture	3322, 0548, 0163
The Heroines' Secret	-3884, -2970, 0033
Dantz's Prize Cows	3626, -2075, 0178
Misko's Treasure: The Fierce Deity	2582, 1426, 0134
Misko's Treasure: Heroines Manuscript	2603, 1319, 0150
The Horse Guard's Request	-1449, -1251, 0032
A Token of Friendship	3307, 0488, 0150
A New Champion's Tunic	3306, -2297, 0112
The North Lomei Prophecy	-0799, 3534, 0235
One-Hit Wonder	3085, 1672, 0201
Home on Arrange	3946, 1596, 0128
Misko's Treasure: Twins Manuscript	2603, 1319, 0150
Horse-Drawn Dreams	-1333, 0723, 0085
The Lomei Labyrinth Island Prophecy	4655, 3682, 0129

SHRINES

Puzzling Opportunities

Shrines are effectively self-contained puzzle areas and they task you with reaching the statue at the end for the reward.

What's important to remember is that while there's likely a "main" way to solve each Shrine's series of puzzles (or challenges), the developers allow *plenty* of room for you to go nuts and solve these puzzles in any way you wish (some of the puzzles can be skipped altogether, with devices taking you *straight* to the end!).

Outside of the first four Shrines (which we covered earlier as they're story-line critical), the remaining Shrines are used for collecting the **Light of Blessing** that's awarded for completing each Shrine.

You can then trade four of these in at a statue for either an extra **Heart Container** or **Stamina Vessel** upgrade. The choice is yours.

Shrine entrances also double up as fast travel points, so they're definitely worth activating.

There's a whopping total of 152 Shrines in this game. 120 of them can be located on the Surface, with the remaining 32 being located in the Sky region.

Shrine's are effectively broken up into two types:

- **Shrine Puzzles/Combat:** *Where a key theme exists for opening the door to the exit.*
- **Shrine Quests:** *The puzzle is in **how** to get the Shrine's green crystal back to the Shrine.*

The final reward for completing *every* Shrine is very cool looking, has *seriously* good defense stats and also plays a key part in the lore told throughout the game (*especially* the murals…).

However, every Shrine also has a secret area with a chest (or two) containing some goodies, so they're usually worth finding.

So, let's take a look at how to beat every Shrine in the easiest, most efficient, or down-right bonkers way possible!

Shrine: Ishodag

Caution: *You must first unlock the Paraglider at Lookout Landing Skyview Tower to complete this Shrine.*

Upon entering the shrine, you'll notice a fan situated near the left wall. Equip **Ultrahand** and transport the fan beneath the ledge.

Lift onto the Ledge

Position the fan such that its blades are directed upwards, then strike it to set it in motion. Equip your paraglider and ascend using the updraft generated by the fan.

A Fan-tastic Boat

For the boat construction, your task is straightforward: equip **Ultrahand** and employ it to secure the fan to the rear of the wooden plank.

Position the plank on the ramp to elevate its rear end. Then, you can set the fan at the center of the back edge - if it's not centered,

then your boat may exhibit make a beeline for the nearest wall!

Once your boat is ready, release it into the water and give the fan a solid whack to sail across the water to the opposite side.

Link Lift

Two fans will be required to propel the cart up the wall. Stick both under it and then use **Recall** to bring it back down. Turn it off to head up to the top.

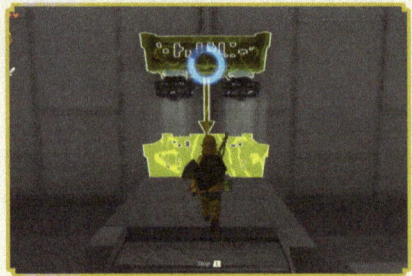

After guiding the cart to the wall's peak, you'll arrive at the end where you can collect your **[Light of Blessing]**!

Shrine: Jiosin

> **Caution:** *Be careful not to stay in the red **Gloom puddles** too long. They'll temporarily remove your hearts as you do!*

The first object to lift is located in a room to the left. This object is elongated and features three square segments arranged diagonally.

Awkward Fit 1

To maneuver it through the gap in the fence, you'll need to orient it lengthwise and align the squares with the cross (see the image below). Upon successfully passing the shape through the hole, exit the other side and position it over the floor's gap to form a bridge.

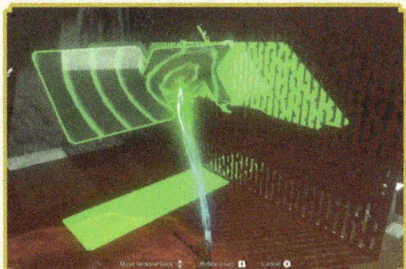

In the subsequent room, you'll need to venture over to the right and locate the dual-cube object. Adjust the object's orientation so that the cubes align horizontally, enabling them to pass the same-shaped gap.

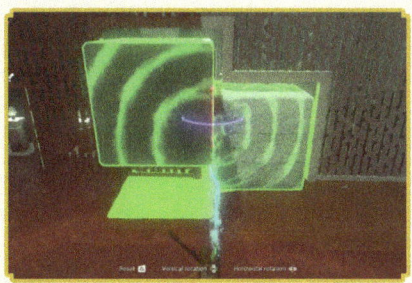

Awkward Fit 2

Now adjust the object to fit through the double diamond-shaped hole in the wall to the left. Rotate it such that the two top surfaces of the cubes face *towards* the gap.

This object can then be carried over and aligned with the blocks on the wall's side, allowing you to climb up them as if they were a set of stairs.

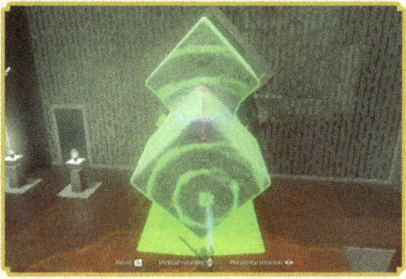

Upon reaching the top of these blocks, you'll find the shrine's end, where you can acquire another **[Light of Blessing]**!

Shrine: Kamizun

Caution: This is a combat-focused Shrine. You must defeat **ALL** enemies here to complete this Shrine.

Once you enter the Shrine, run down, and collect all of the items on the right.

A Solid as a Rock

There are four Constructs waiting for you down in the arena below. You should notice a large boulder there - *perfect* for fusing to that sword right?

Well, you *could* do that (and then risk it breaking thanks to the swords durability). Or... you can use Ultrahand to lift it up and drop it down on a Construct's head!

This method not only deals decent damage, but it also ensures that the rock never breaks (because you never fused it to anything). Sneaky! Use this method to get rid of the smaller Constructs first.

Long-Range Construction

Once they've been defeated, use your bow to get some eye-shots on the Construct up on the pillar at the back of the room. Two to three direct eye shots should see it go down.

The Final Fight

The last remaining Construct is the toughest one (indicated by the bigger horn on its head).

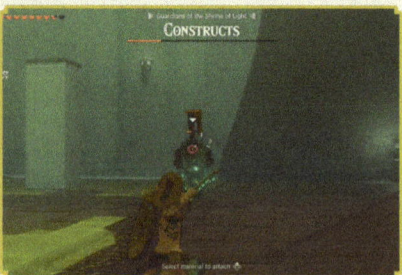

Hit it hard with some well-timed arrow shots, or fuse your sword with the boulder now to defeat it.

Collect the **[Spring Shield]** from the chest and then the **[Light of Blessing]**.

Shrine: Kyononis

To beat this shrine, you **MUST** complete each technique at least once!

The Side Hop

To side hop, first lock onto the enemy, followed by moving sideways, and then pressing **X** to jump.

Timing is everything. Ideally, side hop *just* as the Construct's weapon is about to strike you! Perfect timing presents an opportunity for a Flurry Rush, achieved by rapidly pressing **Y** during the slo-mo phase.

The Backflip

To backflip, you first need to lock onto the enemy, move backwards, and *then* jump (at the start of the enemy's attack animation).

When this maneuver is executed flawlessly and with precise timing, you'll be granted another opportunity for a flurry attack.

The Parry

To parry, you need to hold your shield up, followed by pressing **A** to block the attack *just before it connects with your shield.*

The Charged Attack

Finally, hold down the attack button for a few seconds to charge your sword. Let go to complete this final challenge.

Proceed to the end of the shrine to loot the chest for the **[Zonaite Sword]**, and claim your **[Light of Blessing]**!

Shrine: Susuyai

If you want to grab the chest containing **[5 Arrows]** from the central moving cart, fire an arrow at its wheels to stop it.

Now use **Ultrahand** to pick it up and carefully carry it across to the other side.

Rolling Road Crossing

To cross this part, turn the cart around so the green arrows are facing towards the back of the room and then place it down in front.

Get on top and hit a wheel to activate the device, surfing it until you reach the other side.

Wheely Good Time

Finally, lift the zip-line off of the metal poles with **Ultrahand** and place one of the wheels in the middle of it.

Lever Recall

Run up to the lever, turn it anti-clockwise (so the gate raises up), then use **Recall** when you let go to keep the gate open so you can pass under it in time.

Place it back on the metal railing and then strike the wheel to activate it.

You'll now be carried over the railing to the end of the Shrine where you can collect the next **[Light of Blessing]**.

Shrine: Teniten

This is a very short and simple Shrine to beat. All you need to do is throw a weapon (any weapon) at the Construct up ahead of you to defeat it (twice).

First Throw

However, throwing your weapon is a *really* good way to break it! Therefore, we recommend that you pick up one of the **[Rusty Halberds]** nearby and throw one of those instead!

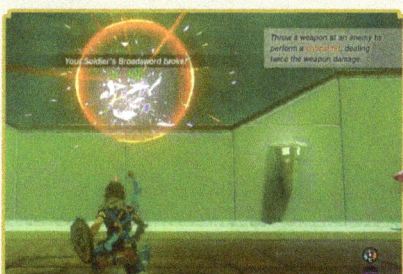

Second Throw

This time the Construct moves up and down the platform firing arrows at you. Simply wait for it to stop at either end and then throw your next lest-useful weapon at it to complete this Shrine!

Be sure to open the chest here for a rather handy **[Zonaite Spear]**! Go collect your **[Light of Blessing]**.

High-Stakes

After entering, run down the steps, pick up the wooden paddle from the ground and use **Ultrahand** to stick it to the pole that's moving up and down on the left side of the platform.

Use this platform to reach the other side, then detach it, and lift it over to the grated platform located near the fan.

Your goal is to stick the wooden stake to the moving circle so that it acts as a "scoop" at the bottom.

A way to line this up is to have the paddle horizontal and stick it to the edge of the circle pattern.

Heavy Lifting

Now wait underneath the falling metal ball and *very quickly* grab one using **Ultrahand**. You'll want to drop it in the middle of the curved metal railing (where your paddle passes around).

All being well, the wooden panel will scoop up the metal ball, pushing it high enough so it lands in the bowl at the end, opening up the pathway to the Shrine's exit.

Now all you have to do is jump back over to the nearby fan and use it to paraglide over to the Shrine's exit where your **[Light of Blessing]** awaits.

Shrine: Yamiyo

Map: 0324, 0477, 0027
Region: Central Hyrule

This is a very short and simple Shrine to beat. All you need to do is throw a Material (in this case some **Fire Fruit**) at the Construct up ahead of you to defeat it (twice).

First Throw

Take aim with your regular weapon and then press **UP** on the d-pad to select the **Fire Fruit** that you want to throw.

Be sure to open the chest here for a rather handy **[3x Bomb Flowers]**! Go collect your **[Light of Blessing]**..

Second Throw

This time the Construct moves up and down the platform firing arrows at you. Simply wait for it to stop at either end and then throw your next **Fire Fruit** at it to complete this Shrine!

Shrine: Sinakawak

Full of Hot Air

The goal here is to create a number of Hot Air Flower chase to carry Link up.

Begin by fusing together the wooden panel, a burning candle, and one of the Flower chase (called an "Envelope") in the middle of the room by the wall. Ride it up to the next level.

Once you're up here, fuse a candle and a balloon and release it so it hits the green target located directly above the door.

Bigger is Better

Slide down the really long ladder to the ground below.

The goal now depends entirely on whether or not you want the chest with the **[Opal]** in it.

If you do, you need to fuse the small ball to the top of the large ball and then use *at least* three hot air Flower chase to lift them all up to the level above (see the screenshot below).

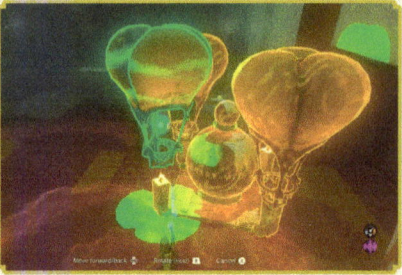

If you don't care about the Opal, then you only need to take the smaller ball up to drop into the bowl.

Just be careful to line the balloon with a solid part of the ceiling above. Drop the ball(s) into the bowl(s) to open the gates and the exit to the Shrine.

Shrine: Mayachin

Map: -0704, -0880, 0030
Region: Central Hyrule

Begin by stepping onto the rotating platform and ride it to the other side.

Go stand on the orange switch ahead of you to reveal a giant target on the left.

Pinball Puzzle

The goal now is to pick up the stake that's in the middle of the room and attach one of the poles on the ground to the side of it.

From here, you need to fuse that to the back of the device that's nearby. Doing so turns it into a giant pinball lever.

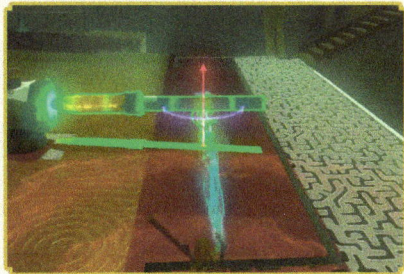

Home Run Time

Run up to the orange crystal behind you and you now want to strike it when the next ball reaches the very last white marker on the floor.

It may take a couple of goes, but the right angle causes the ball to hit the target, opening up the door to the Shrine's exit.

However, there's also a second target here that you can hit (leading to an **[Energizing Elixir]** in a chest) , but it's obscured by the panel on the right.

To make a path for the ball, pull out the peg, stick it in the nearby ceiling, and then fuse the panel to the ceiling/peg. Now time your shot to hit the target, opening up the door to the chest inside.

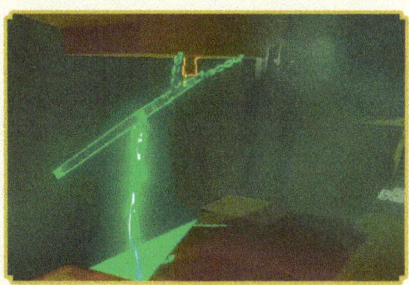

Either way, leave the Shrine now.

Begin by paragliding across to the gap to the ladders opposite.

Rock and Roll

Pick up the nearby metal ball and drop it onto the metal railings so it slides all the way down to the next platform. Paraglide down to the platform to join the ball.

Stuck in the Middle

Fuse the two poles together at their ends and then fuse the ball to the middle of this longer pole. Place it in the middle of the bars to evenly distribute the weight as it slides down to the next level.

Paraglide down to join it for the third main puzzle.

Heavy Metal

Now, the chest here only contains a regular **[Construct Bow]**, so we're going to focus on the final puzzle instead.

There's *loads* of ways to do this. One of the most reliable we found was to stick the ball to the top of the V-shaped piece on the ground.

Now fuse the metal ball to the top of the V and - very carefully - line it up so the middle of the V keeps the weight balanced in the middle.

If you're quick, you can also fuse a

flat panel to the bottom of the V to prevent it from tipping off.

Claim your **[Light of Blessing]** from the Shrine's exit statue.

Shrine: Sepapa

Map: 0220, 1083, 0028
Region: Central Hyrule

Begin by using **Recall** to change the direction of the platform so it goes upwards.

Jump off, run to the back of the room and collect the torch from the ground.

Shining Light

Carry it onto the raft on your left and use the torch here to light it. Follow the flow of the water (lighting the torch as you go) and light the leaves on the wall at the end to reveal a **[Strong Construct Bow]**.

Use your Recall ability to take the raft back across (re-lighting the torch as you do so). Use it to light the wicks at either side of the door to unlock it.

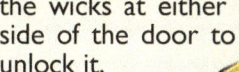

Uphill Struggle

Run to the right of the room and pick up the metal ball. The trick here is to drop it into the hole in front of you first, then lift it up and place it into the next hole behind you.

Leave it and run through the first open door on the hill. Turn around and use **Recall** on the ball to take it back up to the first hole where the next door opens up.

Now all you have to do is leave the Shrine to collect your **[Light of Blessing]**!

The goal here is to use your Ultrahand ability to fuse logs together to make it up and over several different obstacles.

Use the wooden log on the floor to create a vertical pillar that you can climb up to the slanted floor.

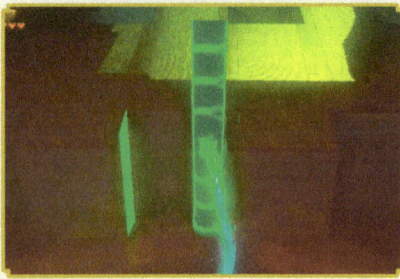

Hylian Ninja

Fuse a couple of nearby logs together and use them to create a makeshift bridge between the two pointed platforms.

You'll want to try and position the middle of the logs on the top of the upper point to keep things stable.

Lift the fused logs up and take them with you to use on the next two water crossings. You may want to make the logs three pieces long just to make sure you've got enough length for the second crossing that goes up.

Hover-crafted

Look to your right for a couple of Zonai Fans and loads of logs. It's time to create a sturdy makeshift hovercraft!

Glue 3-4 logs together and stick both fans on the back.

If you want the **[Spiky Shield]** from the chest on the left, then make sure to drop it in the water at the correct angle.

Otherwise, just sail across the water to the exit at the other side!

Shrine: Kiuyoyou

Map: -1106, 20886, 0104
Region: Hyrule Ridge

This Shrine requires you to play around with both fire and ice elements.

Ice Ice Baby

Lift the large square ice cube from the floor and then **very quickly** pass it through the corner of the flames on the right, causing it to melt *rapidly*.

If you make a mistake, don't panic! Another Ice Cube will form, allowing you to try again.

Place the smaller ice cube on top of the pressure plate on the left (by the gate).

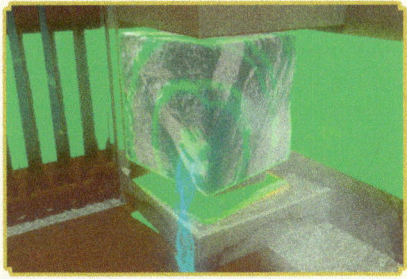

Now use your paraglider with the wind turbines to fly all the way up to the other end of the room.

Lift the large square metal plate, turn it vertically, and then place it in front of the flames.

To the Point

Lift the giant ice cube out and then fuse the metal plate to the top of the ice cube and then drop it on top of the spikes on the right so they slide down together.

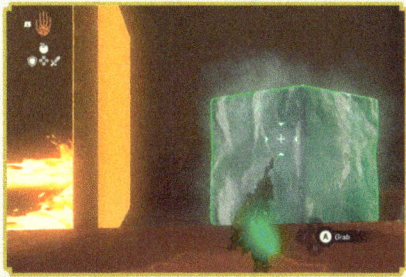

Follow the ice cube down using your paraglider to cross the gap.

Under Pressure

Finally, carry the ice cube and metal plate back into the main room and place it into the flames (**metal plate at the top!**). This allows the ice to trigger the pressure plate, opening up the exit to the Shrine.

Shrine: Taki-ihaban

The challenge of this Shrine isn't so much the Shrine itself (it's pretty much empty), it's the fact that it's *so well hidden* that it's very easy to miss.

How to Find This Shrine

First travel to *Lindor's Brow Skyview Tower* and then head to the co-ordinates at the top of this page, it'll take you to *Lindor's Brow Cave*.

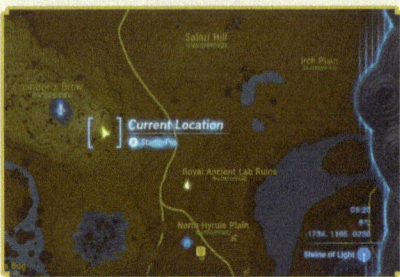

Assuming your approach is from the east, a chute will be present that drops down. Jump into it to find yourself in a body of water, then head southwest to reach dry land.

Follow the downhill path and take a turn towards the northwest upon reaching a cliff. You'll see the Taki-ihaban shrine situated on another ledge across a chamber towards the northwest.

However, an unexpected issue arises - the trench separating you from the shrine is swarming with troublesome Gloom Hands.

Their appearance isn't immediate, but if you casually wander around the chamber's floor, they'll soon make their presence known.!

These enemies can be quite a menace even under the best circumstances.

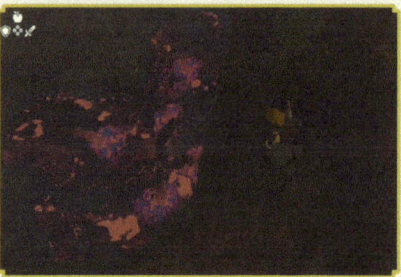

Your most effective strategy is to make a swift descent and dash across the chamber to reach the cliff where the shrine is located, climbing it as rapidly as possible. Thankfully, the Gloom Hands can't reach you once you've ascended high enough off the ground.

Navigate across the chamber filled with Gloom Hands, enter the deserted Shrine, and clear it out. Now fast travel back out.

Shrine: Ren-iz

Map: 0746, 0822, 0081
Region: Central Hyrule

This Shrine requires you to help a metal ball fly across the gaping chasm, and land in the metal basket in the distance.

First Ramp

This one is easy enough, lift up the nearby flat piece of metal and then lay it at an angle opposite the basket, so it forms a ramp.

Now strike the nearby crystal and watch as the metal ball soars majestically through the air and into the basket, opening the gate.

Second Ramp

Alright, now it's time to get a little more creative. Firstly, fuse the two nearby metal plates together at the edges to form a bridge.

Carry it across to the right and place it down here. Walk across and open the chest for a very useful **[Mighty Zonaite Shield]**.

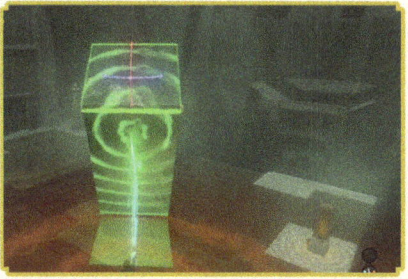

Now pick the bridge back up and carry it over to the left. Stand by the switch, drop the metal, unfuse it, and then fuse it back together at a right-angle.

Rotate the metal around so it forms a ramp and then place it down into the groove in the ground.

Hit the nearby switch and watch as the metal ball zooms down the ramp and over the chasm to the safety of the basket.

The gate to the exit opens up, allowing you to collect this Shrine's **[Light of Blessing]**.

Shrine: Anedamimik

Map: 4184, -2314, 0003
Region: East Necluda

Use Recall on the ball as it passes the gate and quickly hit the orange switch to move the platform so the ball goes into the hole.

You can also ascend up the right-hand section to open the chest that contains a **[Large Zonai Charge]**. Turn off recall and exit the Shrine.

Shrine: Apogek

Map: 3887, -0217, 0164
Region: Lanayru

Pull a Zonai Wing over to you and Fuse the ball to the middle of the Wing and fly it down to the hole below. Detach and put the ball in.

Rise up to the next platform and use both Fans on the nearby Wing and fly from the middle railing to the exit at the end.

Shrine: Bamitok

Map: 3285, -3355, 0064
Region: East Necluda

Dive into the water, swim into the cave, and you're in *Mount Dunsel Cave*. Defeat the enemies in the cave, collect the **[Royal Bow]** from the chest.

Now use a wooden panel and Ascend to reach the **[Royal Shield]**, go through the tunnel, enter the Shrine, collect the **[Big Battery]**, and leave.

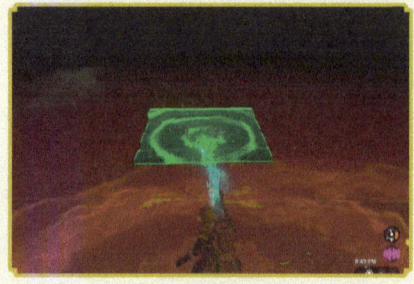

Shrine: ChiChim

Map: -3132, -3068, 0090
Region: Gerudo Desert

Fall into the sand pit and fight your way through the windy, but linear underground temple. Follow the statue's swords for directions.

Ascend by the fire-lit gate, open the chest, lift up the panels, pull the lever, drop down, claim the **[Mighty Zonaite Spear]**, and then leave the Shrine.

Shrine: Domizuin

Map: 3305, 1443, 0426
Region: Akkala Highlands

Ascend, hit the switch once, stand in the middle, turn around, shoot an arrow at the same switch, turn back around and then hit the arrow here to turn the block around you **three** times.

Run into the corner with the tall pillar, ascend up it, then jump across to the Shrine's exit ahead.

Shrine: Ekochiu

Map: 1062, 1279, 0045
Region: Central Hyrule

Hit the switch then use Recall to bring the block back. Stand on the block that falls down and use Recall to take you up the ledge.

In the next room, drop down to the right, push the block onto the large switch, climb up, stand on the switch, climb onto the block, and use Recall to launch you into the air, glide down to the exit.

Shrine: En-oma

Map: 0012, -2629, 0040
Region: Faron Grasslands

Use the *Popla Foothills Skyview Tower* and glide to the *Faron Sky Archipelago* island. Lift the green crystal and drop it into the hole.

Dive down the hold and *straight* into the middle of the whirlpool! In the cave, carry the rock to the Shrine's spot. Open the chest for a **[Mighty Zonaite Sword]**.

Shrine: Eutoum

Map: -3506, 3570, 0387
Region: Hebra Mountains

This is a combat Shrine that requires you to take out **five Constructs** of increasing difficulty.

Use your beam lightning-fused weapons to make light work of the Constructs. Collect the **[Sapphire]** from the chest before leaving.

Shrine: Eshos

Map: 1506, -1903, 0288
Region: West Necluda

Found tucked right into the mountain ridge. This is a tutorial Shrine. Perform shield parries back at the Constructs to complete the tutorial.

Collect the very handy **[Mighty Zonaite Shield]** from the chest then exit the Shrine.

Shrine: Gasas

Map: -4152, 0098, 0040
Region: Hyrule Ridge

Use your bow to cut the strings of the items suspended in the air. Make a double-length bridge, then use the large square as a counter-weight to put your panel under the chest with the key in it.

Finally, swing the ball in the last room and shoot it down when swings in, Drop it in the hole, exit.

Shrine: Gatakis

Map: -3650, 1805, 0168
Region: Hebra Mountains

Use your Paraglider to fly around this Shrine by using the gusts of wind. Stick to the left to dodge the lasers, time your dive-bomb through the rotating floor, and smash the ice with your weapon.

Dive down and glide forwards to the opening. Fly up and then touch the exit to complete this Shrine.

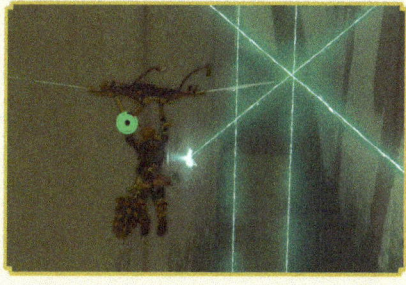

Shrine: Ga-ahisas

Map: -3598, 0970, 1701
Region: Tabantha Frontier Sky

This Shrine is hidden high up in the sky on *Lightcast Island*. Clear the rocks in the middle cave, then rotate the mirrors so they're pointing at the next mirror in the room.

Defeat the Construct, use the Mirror Shield on the green icon, run down the steps, take the **[Star Fragment]**, then leave.

Shrine: Ganos

Map: -3374, 0461, 1696
Region: Tabantha Frontier Sky

Grab the green gem from the top of the **Flux Construct III** boss, carry it to the nearby pre-built Zonai device, and follow the green line up to the flying island above.

Detach the stone, drop it in its place, grab the **[Diamond]** from the chest and exit the Shrine.

Shrine: Gatanisis

Map: 4496, 0822, 0095
Region: Akkala Highlands

Use Recall on the middle platform *after* the ball rolls off of it, so that it drops down as the next ball lands on it.

Wait until gets to near the end and finish the Recall path to send the ball into the target. Pick up the next ball, Ascent *through* the target, glide to the exit.

Shrine: Gemimik

Map: 4513, 2116, 0001
Region: Akkala Highlands

Fuse the propeller to the central column, grab the metal panel and complete the circuit on the floor. Fly up the air-stream, grab the **[Mighty Zonaite Shield]**.

Fly to the other corner, and fuse the flaming head to the propeller to quickly light all the candles and open the exit.

Shrine: Gikaku

Map: 4512, 2152, 1156
Region: Akkala Sea Sky

Grab the green stone that's located *very high up* on a small sky island that's *just* beside the giant stone floating ball. Use the Gerudo Highlands Tower and rocket devices to reach the stone.

Drop it down to the flying island located directly below you. The Shrine contains a **[Ruby]**.

Shrine: Igashuk

Map: 4645, 3530, 0098
Region: Akkala Sea

In the floating *Lomei Labyrinth* Island, opposite the entrance, place a wooden panel by the Gloom. From there, Ascend up twice, turn, run around the corner, drop down in-between the walls, glide left, climb, ascend, and turn around.

Follow the path to the Shrine with a **[Large Zonai Charge]**.

Shrine: Igoshon

Map: 3480, 0664, 1326
Region: Lanayru Great Spring Sky

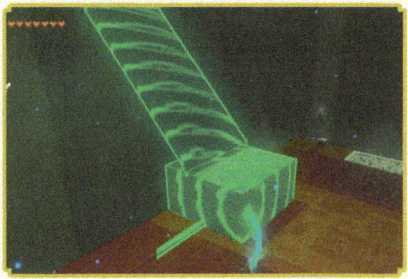

Found on *Wellspring Island*. Use the water bubble to reach the next area, then use a water bubble to catch the falling chest on the left for a **[Large Zonai Charge]**.

Use Recall on the next bubble up, then cross the gap, and build a ramp on the top level. Pull it into the middle, then get high enough to jump and glide to the exit.

Shrine: Ihen-A

Map: 3791, 0576, 0485
Region: Lanayru Great Spring

Clean the entrance, then activate the Zonai blocks as flying steps/platforms. To cross the large gaps, fuse the long metal platform to the top of an activated Zonai block.

Finally, attach the ball to the nearby block, activate it, and hit the switch with an arrow to cross the gap, use the ball, and exit.

Shrine: Ijo-o

Map: -3862, 2679, 0702
Region: Hebra Mountains Sky

Destroy the Construct, grab its **Flame Shield**, use it on the ice and the next Construct, use the **Stone-Slab Shield** to block the flames, then defeat the final Construct.

Fuse a Zonai Rocket to a Rusty Shield and use it to fly up high, then glide over to the Shrine's exit!

Shrine: Ikatak

Map: -3950, 1138, 0112
Region: Tabantha Frontier

Drop down into the nearby *Gisa Crater Cave* and fuse the two nearby Zonai Rockets to the green crystal. Place it in the middle of the room and set it off.

Ascend back up to the Surface, pick up the rock (follow the green beam), then claim the **[Big Battery]** from the Shrine's chest.

Shrine: Irasak

Map: -4126, -3922, 0023
Region: Gerudo Desert

Located at the *Arbiter's Grounds*, this Shrine simple requires you to jump across the moving sand and to the Shrine in the middle.

Use a Zonai Spring to leap up, float across, and collect the **[Large Zonai Charge]** inside the chest.

Shrine: Ishokin

Map: -0565, -3525, 0129
Region: Faron Grasslands

Baddek requires you to find him a large golden horse. Head to 0745, -3724, 0081 and make sure you have **two** health bars to tame it!

Sneak up on it, then ride it back to Baddek. Take the green crystal and drop it by the Shrine's entrance. The chest contains a **[Topaz]**.

Shrine: Isisim

Map: 1762, 2818, 0398
Region: Death Mountain

Come here **after** completing the *Yunobo of Goron City* main quest. This is a combat-focused Shrine, so use Recall to send the Zonai Time Bombs back at the Constructs who throw them.

Otherwise, fuse the Time Bombs to swords and throw them at the Constructs, and use the bombs to clear the rubble to the exit.

Shrine: Iun-orok

Map: -3295, 0789, -0103
Region: Tabantha Frontier

You must smash your way through *many* levels of rocks in *Tanagar Canyon West Cave*. Once there, roll the first ball into the target. Next, fuse both metal balls together and roll them right down the middle.

Finally, fuse all 3 balls side-by-side, walk down with them, then drop it so it touches the target as it falls.

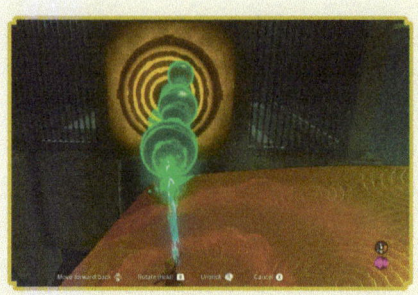

Shrine: Jikais

Map: 4266, -1674, 0182
Region: East Necluda

Slide the blocks so you can use Ascend to get up high, glide down, then use Ascend to go up to the next floor.

Pick up the plank and place it so 2/3 of it is on the ground. Ascend up and then use the final plank up here to create a ramp out of the "jail cell", leave by the nearby exit.

Shrine: Jinodok

Map: -1257, -1490, 1007
Region: Central Hyrule Sky

Use Ultrahand to turn the floating dial (that controls the floating island opposite) so the long side faces the green crystal's location.

Bring the crystal onto the floating island, then turn the dial back so that the platform faces the dial. Take the crystal back to the shrine and collect the **[Diamond]** inside the chest.

Shrine: Jiotak

Map: 1590, 3075, 0393
Region: Eldin Canyon

Equip the *Flamebreaker Armor* then enter the lava-filled cave. Build a fan minecart, ride the tracks, and then use an arrow on the sign to change tracks to go left.

After jumping between tracks, get ready to leap, glide, and finally climb to the Shrine located to your right.

Shrine: Jirutagumac

Map: -0565, -3525, 0129
Region: Lanayru Spring Sky

Use the *Upland Zorana Skyview Tower* to glide inside the floating round island. Now push the glider between each stage and glide behind.

Add the wheels underneath first, slide it down the ramp, then add the fan, and use this to reach the exit at the far end of the Shrine.

Shrine: Jiukoum

Map: 0867, -2279, 0141
Region: Faron Grasslands

Fuse two panels together to make a wide sled and slide down the first railings. Next, attach one panel **vertically** under the middle of the next railing.

Finally, create a "W" shaped platform, flip it onto the rails, then attach three fans. This keeps you on the track to the exit at the end.

Shrine: Jochi-ihiga

Map: 3809, 1216, 0090
Region: Akkala Highlands

Go to *Tarrey Town* and speak with **Hagie** who will sell you the green crystal and also let you use the rail device. Use this to take the crystal down to the edge of the lake.

Get as close to the Shrine as you can by hand, then build a hovercraft with panels and fans to take it across the water.

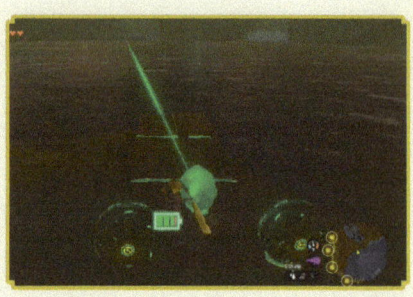

Shrine: Jochi-iu

Map: 4346, 2875, 0165
Region: Deep Akkala

Take the bottom-right and lower-middle pillars out of the Jenga tower to keep it all balanced. Create an electrical connection on the floor with both of these pillars.

Use Recall to go out far enough to collect the metal ball with Ultrahand, then drop it in the hole to open the exit.

Shrine: Jochisiu

Map: 0938, -1898, 0017
Region: West Necluda

Head to *Squabble River*, light the campfire here, and fire some ice-type materials into the water to create square ice panels.

Melt each of the ice panels *just* enough to fit them into the diamond-shaped holes in front of you. Once all three are down, Ascend up and enter the Shrine.

Shrine: Jogou

Map: 3347, -1195, 0057
Region: Mount Lanayru

Glide into the cave located under the *Lanayru Road East Gate* bridge. Make your way to the circular cave at the end.

Use some Bomb Arrows on the breakable blocks to reveal the entrance to the Shrine. Swim across and open the chest inside for a very handy **[Hearty Elixir]**!

Shrine: Jonjon

Map: -0565, -3525, 0129
Region: Lanayru Spring Sky

Bomb/break your way through the tunnel starting at 1366, 0294. 0028. Once you reach the Shrine, you must defeat each Construct on all three levels.

Use Recall on the cogs, avoid the flame jets, and pick up the **[Magic Rod]** by the exit once every Construct has been defeated.

Shrine: Joju-u-u

Map: 1516, -3576, 0142
Region: Faron Grasslands

The trick here is to fuse the ends of the bridge to the hanging bridge panel at the other end. As long as they fuse together, they're good.

When you get to the third bridge, fuse the cube to the end and hang it off over the bar to create the bridge needed to reach the exit.

Shrine: Joniu

Map: 2912, 0499, 0154
Region: Lanayru Great Spring

Head to the cave at the bottom of the mountain at 2911, 0151, 0162. Build a steerable hovercraft using a plank, fan, and control stick to carry the Shrine Crystal on.

Carefully navigate the underground river and drop the crystal off at the end. Collect the **[Large Zonai Charge]** inside.

Shrine: Josiu

Map: 1764, -1220, 0923
Region: West Necluda Sky

Fly to the North Necluda Sky Archipelago islands. On the right side is a curved bridge that you must rotate so you can put the Shrine's Crystal on it (and reach it by gliding and climbing).

Head back to the lever and use it to rotate the bridge back. Take the crystal back to the Shrine.

Shrine: Joku-u

Map: 1376, -3342, 0429
Region: Faron Grasslands Sky

Head to 1660, -3185, 0109 and wait for a rock to fall down into the middle of the rock pool. Use Recall to take the rock back up and then glide over to *Dragonhead Island*.

Go inside the building, drop down, enter the Shrine, and collect the **[Diamond]** inside.

Shrine: Joku-usin

Map: 0170, 3346, 0785
Region: Faron Grasslands Sky

Located high up on *Thunderhead Isles*. This Shrine is packed with level II and III Constructs. You start off with wooden weapons, so fuse their horns to the sticks and use electrical weapons when available.

Use Electric Arrows on any far-off Constructs and claim the powerful **[Electro Elixir]** from the chest.

Shrine: Jonsau

Map: 1744, 0017, 0025
Region: Lanayru Wetlands

The trick is to use Ultrahand to pull the same ball *under* the water far enough so, when released, it shoots up far enough to hit both of the round targets.

In the final room, use the ball to knock the platform down, then use Recall to take it back up. Jump off and drop down to the Shrine' exit.

Shrine: Kadaunar

Map: 1900, 1202, 1251
Region: Eldin Canyon Sky

Use the cart rails at *South Eldin Sky Archipelago* to make it to the top-most floating island here. Once in the Shrine, activate and use Ultrahand on the Zonai faucets to create platforms in the lava.

In the room with the exit, extend the faucet over the lava in front of you and use Recall on the platform after it floats toward you.

Shrine: Kahatanaum

Map: -3270, 3417, 1347
Region: Hebra Mountains Sky

Located just before the *Wind Temple*. Refer to page 68 on how to scale the multitude of floating platforms and bouncing ship sails to safely reach this high up.

Once you're in the Shrine, collect the **[Large Zonai Charge]** from the chest.

Shrine: Kamatukis

Map: 3431, 3355, 0071
Region: Deep Akkala

Ready for some crazy golf? Attach the cube to the pipe and pull it back with Ultrahand. Lift the cube up high and release it into the ball.

If you take it *just* off to the right, you can get the ball to roll into the target at the far side. Repeat in the left-hand room for a chest with a **[Mighty Zonaite Longsword]**.

Shrine: Kikakin

Map: -0395, 2736, 0287
Region: Great Hyrule Forest

Pick up the Zonai light and carry it around the pitch-black maze to help you see the moving spiked walls. From the start go: Forward, right, left, then right. Lift up the middle panel for the **[Small Key]**.

Now turn around and follow your steps back to the exit.

Shrine: Kimayat

Map: 2863, 3637, 0241
Region: Deep Akkala

Keep the wooden sticks safe as there are two heavy metal spiked balls you can ascend up to and fuse to those sticks to cause some *serious* damage to the Constructs.

Finally, use an **Ice Fruit-arrow** to create a platform on the water. Smash the tower to remove the archers, exit opens when all clear.

Shrine: Kisinona

Map: 2568, 1247, 0173
Region: Eldin Canyon

Firstly, use the fan on the left to blow yourself up to the nearby chest for a **[Construct Bow]**.

Next, attach the **two** fans here to the larger fan. Stick one on opposite sides so that when you activate them, the big fan spins and activates all four outer fans together, opening the exit.

Shrine: Kitawak

Map: -1529, -2928, 0321
Region: Gerudo Highlands

Grab the metal panel from the wall and you need to re-use this for each and every bridge. Connect it to the end of the first bridge and then connect two to the second (making a slant upwards).

Finally, attach it to the end of the last panel, walk down, turn around, shoot the switch, and glide to the Shrine's exit.

Shrine: Kudanisar

Map: 4168, -2144, 0050
Region: Gerudo Highlands

Quickly use the moving planks to get across the quicksand. Use two fused planks to get over the barrier. Use the nearby sand sled to reach the back of the room.

Attach the ball here to a sand sled, open the gate, and go to the exit. Fuse 3 planks to reach the final area and drop the ball in the hole.

Shrine: Kumamayn

Map: 2855, -2863, 1212
Region: Necluda Sky Archipelago

First, reach the Shrine via the *Rabella Wetlands Skyview Tower* (starting the quest). You need to grab the Shrine Crystal from the nearby **Flux Construct III** boss.

Use the nearby double springs fused to a grating device, on the launching ramp. Launch the crystal and yourself over to the Shrine.

Shrine: Kyokugon

Map: -0838, -1482, 0025
Region: Central Hyrule

You must drop the four balls into the correct four holes. The 1st goes to the hole up the steps to the right, the 2nd at the bottom of the step.

On the other side, put the 3rd in the far left hole (lower level), and finally the 4th in the upper-left hole. The exit gate will now open.

Shrine: Makasura

Map: 1770, -1051, 1066
Region: Lanayru Wetlands

Hit the stabilizing devices to launch the fencing into the air and use it as a portable climbing frame.

Once they're standing up, cross over the left fence, put the ball into the cup on the ground, hit it, use the ball in the hole, grab the next fence, then fuse it to the bigger fence and launch yourself over.

Shrine: Maoikes

Map: 2238, 0099, 0129
Region: Eldin Canyon

Enter the stone skull to *Bone Pond East Cave* which is located high up on the cliffs northeast of *Boné Pond*.

It's a very short walk into the Shrine. Open the chest for a **[Diamond]**.

Shrine: Marakuguc

Map: 1761, 2508, 0437
Region: Eldin Canyon

First, attach the end of the broken bridge to the other side. Next, attach the wheels to the end of the bridge and hit the wheels to pass the lava. Now attach *both* wheels together and cross the lava.

Ascend up, defeat the Construct, then attach the walkway to the device to push enough balls into the target to open the exit.

Shrine: Marari-in

Map: 4168, -2144, 0050
Region: Necluda Sea

Speak with **Sesami** on *Toronbo Beach* and clear out the enemy bases of their Monster Forces. Once cleared, head to the top of the rock at 4760, -3791, 0110.

Drop down, clear the pirate hideout of enemies, then create a plank to reach the Shrine at the back.

Shrine: Mayachideg

Map: 3061, 1823, 0216
Region: Akkala Highlands

Fuse the spiked panels to the devices on the ground, then use the stick to activate them. Carry them into the main room, then immediately head for the mid-level at the back.

Fuse the laser to the device and carry it around, allowing it to quickly destroy all Constructs.

Shrine: Mayahisik

Map: 3743, -2087, 0208
Region: Lanayru

You must destroy the rocks blocking a cave entering to the east of *Hateno Village*. Drop down into the *Retsam Forest Cave* and enter the Shrine.

Finally, collect the **[Magic Scepter]** inside.

Shrine: Mayak

Map: 1270, 3733, 0106
Region: Great Hyrule Forest

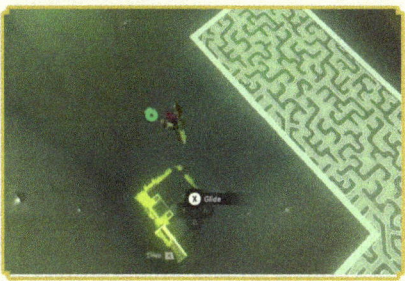

Drop the first ball onto the pipe-like platform and hit the nearby switch *just* as the ball reaches the end to hit the target.

In the next room, use the launching pillar to send you up into another launching pillar, up to the top level. Drop the ball at the start, **quickly** drop and hit the switch.

Shrine: Mayam

Map: 0340, 2814, 1821
Region: Central Hyrule Sky

Grab the crystal from the *Flux Construct I* boss on the floating Island above *Central Hyrule*. Run up the steps with the crystal, fuse it to the platform.

Lift *every* rocket and add it to your platform, use them to take you up to where you drop the crystal.

Shrine: Mayanas

Map: 4613, -0947, 1780
Region: Lanayru Sea Sky

Touch the Shrine to reveal where the crystal is. Use the nearby flying device to get up, burn the bushes down, create a mobile zonai wing device to fly the crystal back.

Use the ice devices/fruits in the water to create two ice sheets, fuse them together, slide it down the hill to hit the target. The exit is in the next room on the left.

Shrine: Mayasiar

Map: 4168, -2144, 0050
Region: Gerudo Highlands Sky

Enter the giant "Death Star"-like island up here and rotate the multiple mirrors around the room so they ultimately reach the big panel, unlocking the Shrine. Quickly move the panel right to unlock a **[Sage's Will]**.

Grab the **[Star-Fragment Staff]** from the Shrine's chest.

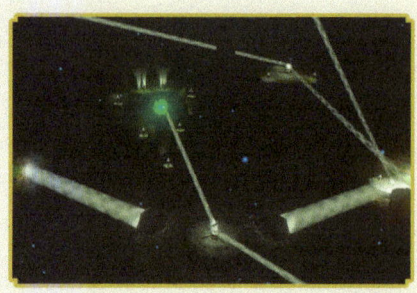

Shrine: Mayaumekis

Map: 2943, 3051, 0896
Region: Hebra Mountains Sky

Head to the *Rising Island Chain* via the *Pikida Stonegrove Skyview Tower*. First, shoot an arrow at the switch, then use the ship sails as trampolines to bounce up higher and higher.

Use your bow to initiate slow-mo and fire an arrow at the switch. Bounce over and up to the exit.

Shrine: Minetak

Map: 3743, -2087, 0208
Region: Eldin Mountains

Head to the *Deplian Badlands* and look for the cave just below 0328, 3596, 0119. Drop down into it, then fight your way past the Fire ChuChu's and other enemies.

Grab the **[Big Battery]** from the chest in the Shrine.

Shrine: Mogawak

Map: 3299, 0424, 0112
Region: Lanayru Great Spring

Take the empty electrical battery pack and drop it on the raised platform on the right. Attach the missing paddle to the wheel on the wall, use Ultrahand to put it under the flowing water to recharge the battery.

Now carry it to the platform, but the battery down, and leave.

Shrine: Momosik

Map: 2958, 2760, 0524
Region: Death Mountain

With the *Flamebreaker Armor* equipped, enter the *Death Mountain East Tunnel*, use a powered minecart to reach the **Igneo Talus** boss.

Quickly jump on top and hit the crystal to dislodge it. Take it back via the same powered minecart.

Shrine: Morok

Map: 1182, -0779, 0133
Region: Central Hyrule

Launch up to the next floor, stand on the spring, hit it to go up, then use the next spring to leap across the chasm. Use the spring to launch the ball to the other side, drop it in the hole and use the two springs to reach the **[Sneaky Elixir]** chest.

Fuse all three springs together and spring up to the exit at the top.

Shrine: Moshapin

Map: 4168, -2144, 0050
Region: Eldin Canyon

Enter the cave at 2502, 1773, 0154 wearing some *Flamebreaker Armor*. Fight your way to the lava, use the Zonai hydrant and fan here to create some rock panels to ferry the crystal across the lava.

Carry the crystal around a few more corners to the Shrine. Grab the **[Mighty Zonaite Shield]**.

Shrine: Musanokir

Map: 0408, 2133, 0144
Region: Great Hyrule Forest

Attach the ball to the side of the block, cross over, unhook the block, attach it to the bottom of the ball, and pull the block back to hit the target.

In the final room, attach the block to the ball, then then pole to the top. Pull the block back and release to hit the target, opening the exit.

Shrine: Makurukis

Map: -2847, 0629, 0233
Region: Hyrule Ridge

The goal here is to simply achieve headshots with your bow and arrow. Dispatch all four *Constructs* to open the exit.

Grab the **[Strong Construct Bow]** from the chest before leaving.

Shrine: Mayamats

Map: -4637, -1514, 0452
Region: Gerudo Highlands

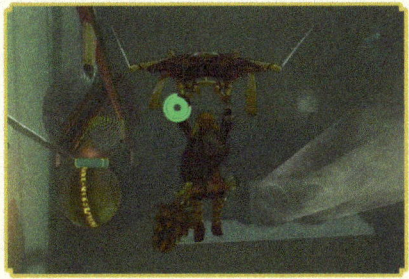

Fly up with the wind, Ascend up the left side, bring the ball down, use it to reach the **[Large Zonai Charge]** chest, then place it in the nearby slants, Ascend *through* the ball, drop it at the top of the railings so the small ball fuses to it.

Finally, slide it face down the railing and use the small ball in the hole.

Shrine: Mayaotaki

Map: -0956, 3535, 0234
Region: Hebra Mountains

Located inside the *North Lomei Labyrinth*. Follow the glittering pine cones on the floor. Be *very* careful of all the Gloom here!

You'll eventually go up a ladder, keep following and picking up the cones, and you'll eventually drop down to the Shrine in the middle.

Shrine: Mayatat

Map: -3290, -2512, 0024
Region: Gerudo Desert

Use Recall on the closest sled and ride it up to the top. Run across the sand to the steps, then add the control unit to the sled, drop it on top of the quicksand, jump across, then fuse a nearby fan to it.

Simply drive it over to the exit in the top-right corner of this room.

Shrine: Mayausiy

Map: -1165, 2602, -0083
Region: Tabantha

Found at the top of the *Tanagar Canyon*. Rotate the two sets of blocks so they form a rectangle. Defeat the **Construct**, then make steps to the **[Large Zonai Charge]** chest.

Finally, use the three pieces here to rotate and put together to build a cube, opening up the exit door.

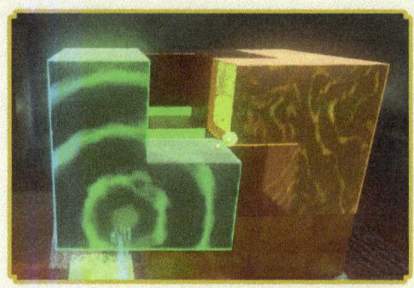

Shrine: Miryotanog

Map: -4679, -3086, 0054
Region: Gerudo Desert

Pick up all the weapons, leap the lasers, grab the **Fire Fruits** from behind the crates, run up the hill, and lure the **Constructs** down to the flamethrower trap.

Defeat the final enemy at the top and collect the hard-hitting **[Captain II Blade]** from the chest at the exit!

Shrine: Mogisari

Map: 4654, 3499, 1010
Region: Akkala Sea Sky

You'll need *loads* of stamina replenishment meals or Zonai devices to reach this Shrine. This is a cool race track where you have to drive the vehicle around the track.

When you reach the jump at the end, strap a nearby rocket to it and boost across to the exit!

Shrine: Motsusis

Map: 11785, -3310, 0138
Region: Gerudo Highlands

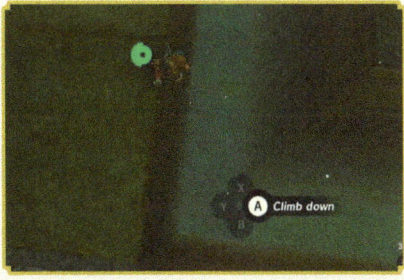

Drop down onto the **top** of the labyrinth and run along the left-central path. Drop down to the lower level at -1780, -3467, 0121.

Glide past the Gloom, keep turning left, and you'll soon reach the Shrine. Grab the **[Large Zonai Charge]** inside.

Shrine: Ninjis

Map: 0356,1894,0178
Region: Great Hyrule Forest

First, speak with **Maca** in the by the Deku Tree for the quest. Get to *Bravery Island* (*N. Hyrule Sky*) and dive down from 0243, 1993, 0753.

Dive and then glide right to the entrance of the Shrine and collect the **[Mighty Construct Bow]** from the chest.

Shrine: Nouda

Map: -2318, 2201, 0173
Region: Tabantha Frontier

Use nearby ice sheets to cross the freezing cold water to the Shrine. Collect the weapons and then head to the **Fire Fruits** on the platform. Shoot the leaves to drop the **Shock Emitter**.

Use this to quickly deal with every **Construct**, opening the exit.

Shrine: Natak

Map: 3671, 1484, 1158
Region: Akkala Highlands Sky

Use a Zonai device to fly up to the island with the Shrine on it. Turn the ejector block left once, use it to reach the giant ball, and glide inside.

Use Ultrahand to turn the device so the sunlight exits the hole. Drop the crystal on the springs and use it to send it to the Shrine.

Shrine: O-ogim

Map: 2755, -1090, 0100
Region: East Necluda

Activate the Shrine quest, follow the path leading behind the waterfall, and destroy the blue blocks for a Glider and the red for the location of the green crystal.

Build a fan-powered Glider, fuse the crystal to it, and then launch it from behind the Waterfall. Place the crystal and enter the Shrine.

Shrine: Orochium

Map: -1636, 2641, 0239
Region: Tabantha Tundra

Immediately go left, Ascend, climb the ladder, crouch walk through the gap, drop down behind the lasers, open the doors, trip the lasers, fall down, Ascend up, and collect the **[Small Key]**.

Ascend up, open the door, take the ball up the lift, attach it to the Glider, then drop it in the hole.

Shrine: Oromuwak

Map: -3079, 1618, 0243
Region: Tabantha Frontier

Use fire to get to the entrance. Place a rocket in the grove and activate it. Now attach two rockets to the minecart and activate them to go up the rails.

Finally, attach one rocket facing up. Glide over to the **[Ruby]** chest, and glide straight over to the exit.

Shrine: Oshozan-u

Map: -1405, 3677, 0288
Region: Tabantha Tundra

Fuse a rocket to a log, fuse that to the side panel, and activate it, hitting the target. Now use a log to reach the **[Zonaite Bow]** chest.

Finally, fuse that log to the end of the smaller one, and fuse a rocket *facing you* to it. Fuse it to the circle, activate the rocket, then leave.

Shrine: Otak

Map: -4428, 3767, 0225
Region: Hebra Mountains

Found deep inside an icy cave. Collect the weapons at the start and pick off each **Construct** one-by-one. There's a hanging candle right above an explosive barrel that can *really* damage a group of **Constructs**…

Once everyone's defeated, collect the **[Mighty Construct Bow]** and depart this Shrine.

Shrine: Otutsum

Map: -4468, -0670, 0509
Region: Gerudo Highlands

Put on some warm clothes (or eat a Spicy Pepper meal) and simply climb your way up to (or glide down to) the Shrine. No challenges, no quests! Sweet!

Inside you'll find a **[Topaz]** for your, err… "trouble."

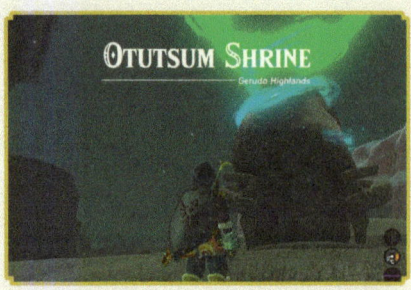

Shrine: Pupunke

Map: 0408, 2133, 0144
Region: Great Hyrule Forest

Speak to **Damia** the Korok who asks you to collect five golden apples outside *Sponapan Shrine*. Once there, cut down the trees and collect the golden apples that drop.

Give them to **Damia** and examine the crystal to activate the beam. Carry it back to the Shine.

Shrine: Rakakudaj

Map: -2036, -1852, 0064
Region: Gerudo Highlands

Touch the Shrine and follow the green light down the mini waterfalls to the crystal in the sand. Fuse two pre-made large wheeled platforms and a control panel together, fuse the crystal to this and drive it back.

Grab the **[Mighty Zonaite Longsword]** from the chest.

Shrine: Rakashog

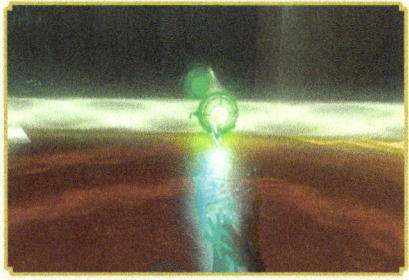

Pick up the mirror and reflect the light at the gem to open the door. Lift the mirror through the gap, reflect the light right. Reflect the next light down while by the gem.

Finally, use the two mirrors to angle the light around the barrier to hit the gem, opening up the exit.

Shrine: Riogok

Fuse the wooden pole between the cogs and hit the switch. Now fuse the log to the handle at an angle and use Ultrahand to turn it.

Lift one log up both platforms and use Ascend to get yourself up. Place the log upright by the wall and climb up the log to the exit.

Shrine: Rotsumamu

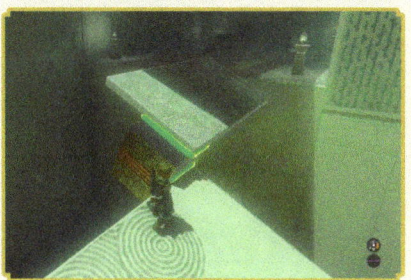

Run across the first tilting bridge, fuse a barrel to the left-edge of the 2nd bridge, and run up. Fuse the cube and panel to the edge of the next bridge for the **[Large Zonaite]** chest.

Finally, build a ramp up to the doorway and the Shrine's exit is on the left.

Shrine: Rutafu-um

Map: -2996, 3102, 0515
Region: Hebra Mountains

Enter the snowy cave at -2986, 3170, 0570 and dispatch the Bokoblins inside. Touch the Shrine, then shoot some icicles down over the water.

Fuse them together and fuse the crystal to the end of it. Lift it back and open the Shrine with it.

Shrine: Rastiakiwak

Map: 4166, 1323, 0229
Region: Akkala Highlands

To make short work of this Shrine, simply run to the near-right corner when you enter the large room.

Immediately fuse the Zonai laser and fire emitters beside each other and use Ultrahand to have an unbreakable Construct-destroying combo! Collect the **[Magic Rod]** before leaving.

Shrine: Rasiwak

Map: 4664, 3262, 0002
Region: Akkala Sea

Use an arrow on the rope to drop the bridge, then fuse the ball to it to make it float. Lift the next bridge, let it drop, then use Recall and run up it as it lifts up again.

Finally, attach a fan and a ball to the slate, then when you reach the other side, lift it out, and put it on the target to open the exit.

Shrine: Sahirow

Map: -3354, 2387, 0361
Region: Hebra Mountains

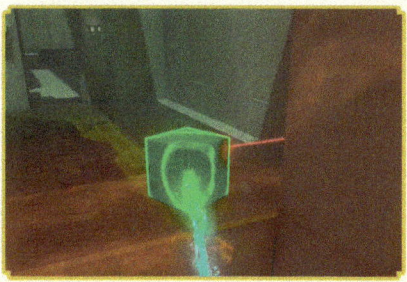

The aim of this Shrine is to jump, duck, and glide over the laser beam traps. Once you see the chest on the right, use a cube to trip the trap and collect the handy **[Spicy Elixir]**.

Now jump, duck, then Ascend up past the final three laser traps.

Shrine: Sakunbomar

Map: 0167, 2320, 0179
Region: Great Hyrule Forest

Speak to Korok *Zooki* and then fight/run through the forest behind her. Touch the Shrine, then smash the *Stone Talus* that holds the crystal on its back!

Once it's defeated, carry it back, and claim the **[Diamond]** from the chest. Sweet!

Shrine: Sisuran

Map: −2647, 3352, 0241
Region: Hebra Mountains

The crystal is on the back of a *Frost Talus*! Use a fire arrow on it to melt the ice, climb up onto its back, then smash off the crystal.

Once defeated, carry the crystal back to the Shrine and collect the **[Sapphire]** for your efforts.

Shrine: Siwakama

Map: -2445, -3345, 0042
Region: Gerudo Desert

The trick here is to use the balls as platforms between the gaps. However, after the 1st one, the 2nd ball sits on an edge. So, use Ultrahand to move the ball forwards and backwards in the gap.

Use Recall to cross and repeat this method for the last ball.

Shrine: Siyamotsus

Map: -1795, -3291, 1011
Region: Gerudo Highlands Sky

A real trek to reach, use Zonai devices, or several stamina meals. It's in front of the giant cube.

Once there, open the chest and then the floor drops away!!! Use flame arrows to light the two unlit torches, then use the launcher to glide to the Shrine's exit. Cheeky designers!

Shrine: Sonapan

Map: -1921, -0357, 0228
Region: Hyrule Ridge

A simple enough Shrine. Place the nearby cube up on the platform and Ascend through both.

In the next room, drop the cube in the middle by the wall, Ascend into the gap the cube left, glide down, then Ascend to the exit. Easy!

Shrine: Soryotanog

Map: -3881, -2961, 0123
Region: Gerudo Desert

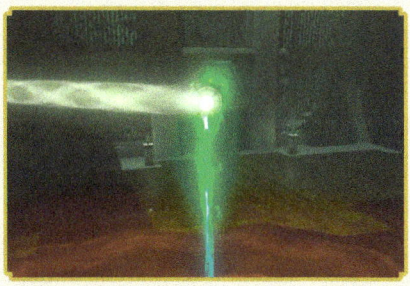

Fuse a pole to a Zonai fan and use this to blow away all of the sand piles dotted around this Shrine. Use the **[Small Key]**, look for the mirror, drop it in the room by the exit, then go left, and Ascend.

Clear the sand and reflect the light with the mirror here out. Finally, reflect that light to open the exit.

Shrine: Serutabomac

Map: -0179, 1170, 0280
Region: Central Hyrule

First, place a panel on the poles and Ascend up through the panel. In the next room, fuse both panel ends together and lay it at an angle to create a ramp up.

Finally, fuse all three panels together to make a longer ramp used to reach the exit.

Shrine: Sibajitak

Map: 2400, 3276, 0402
Region: Eldin Canyon

The goal here is to use Recall to time when the pillars pass over each other on the rotating tower. Use Recall to align the bottom two pillars, Ascend up and open the chest.

Finally use Recall to align the top pillar to the rest and Ascend up.

Shrine: Sifumim

Map: 2826, -3271, 0078
Region: East Necluda

Let's have some fun! Use Ultrahand to pull the wooden towers away that the **Constructs** are on top of. Now watch as they plummet into the water to their doom! *Laughs manically* (Sorry).

Finally, climb the ladder and sneak attack the toughest **Construct** and use the nearby **Ice Fruit**.

Shrine: Sihajog

Map: 4544, -0845, 1121
Region: Mount Lanayru Sky

Use the *Mount Lanayru Skyview Tower* to reach *Valor Island* at 4434, 0847, 1122. Speak with the **Construct**, activate the portal, and successfully skydive through *all* of the green rings into the water.

Collect the **[Diamond]** from the Shrine that appears and speak with the **Construct** for a cool prize…

Shrine: Sikukuu

Map: 0699, 2793, 0226
Region: Great Hyrule Forest

Use Recall on the first gear to get the ball that drops to drop to the right. Place it in the hole.

In the next room, grab the gear with Ultrahand and turn it **clockwise** for a few rotations. Use Recall to ride the cog up to the exit.

Shrine: Simosiwak

Map: 0163, 1972, 0759
Region: Great Hyrule Forest Sky

First, you **must** complete the skydiving challenge on *Bravery Island*. Once in the Shrine, grab the **Light Shields** and weapons and take out the left-hand **Construct** first. Fuse the **Flame Emitter** to your weapon.

Use this flame weapon on the final two enemies to unlock the exit.

Shrine: Sinatanika

Map: 3842, 2300, 0048
Region: Akkala Highlands

This is a sneak-attack training Shrine. Sneak walk past the Construct when it's not looking, hold **Block** and hit **Y** to succeed.

For phase two, it moves around, so wait for it to be facing away from you before sneaking up. Grab the **[Sneaky Elixir]** at the exit.

Shrine: Sitsum

Map: 2369, 2595, 0790
Region: Death Mountain

Drive the vehicle through the lava. Turn right at the junction, fuse the ball to the device, use Recall to reverse, drop the ball in for the **[Mighty Construct Bow]** chest.

Climb the ladder, destroy the **Construct**, put a nearby steering wheel on the Glider, then steer it left towards the exit.

Shrine: Susub

Map: 0350, -2052, -0026
Region: Necluda

Break the blocks and drop down into the *Deya Village Ruins Well* located at 0324, -1934, 0011. Watch out for the **Stone Talus** down here, and climb the nearby rock to the Shrine.

Collect the **[Magic Staff]** from the chest before leaving.

Shrine: Suariwak

Map: -2429, -1821, 0147
Region: Gerudo Highlands

Complete the Yiga Clan Exam side adventure, plus be wearing the full Yiga armor set to unlock this shrine.

To unlock this chest-only Shrine, offer a **Mighty Banana** to the following 5 frog statues: **1.** -2354, -1812, 0091 **2.** -2434, -2033, 0078 **3.** -2300, -2424, 0357 **4.** -2672, -2496, 0093 **5.** -1386, -1943, 0041

Shrine: Tadarok

Map: -1082, -2187, 0129
Region: Central Hyrule

Drop the cube in the water, cross over, pick the cube up, drop it into the lava furthest away, pull it back, then jump on it and use Recall.

Pick up the wooden crate, dip it in the water, drop it over the lava, cross back over, block the flames, fuse all three blocks together, pull the ball out of the water, Ascend.

Shrine: Tauyosipun

Map: -4539, 2881, 0262
Region: Hebra Mountains

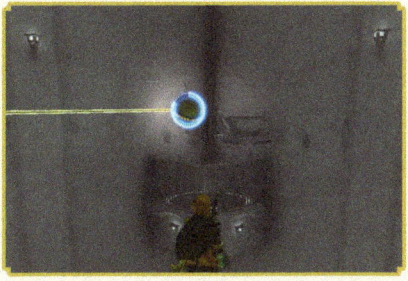

Use Recall to love the balls back up the slope. Run right, stand on the switch, drop the nearby ball in front of the one in the half-pipe, and use Recall to push it off.

Catch the ball with Ultrahand as it's falling and place it in the hole. Drop the last ball into the bowl on the left, use Recall, then exit Recall.

Shrine: Tenamaten

Map: -0073, -1115, 0021
Region: Hyrule Field

Smash open the *Elma Knolls Well*, drop down into the cave, drop down into the deeper cave, light up the pitch-black caves, stay right, and then glide and swim across the pool.

Open the chest in the Shrine for a useful **[Large Zonaite Charge]**.

Shrine: Turakamik

Map: -2658, -2236, 0067
Region: Gerudo Desert

Use Ultrahand to fuse the two charged metal balls together, completing the circuit. Climb the cog, then swing the left ball by pulling it left, and hold the right ball ready for them to fuse together.

Ascend up, grab the metal bar from the cogs, place it on the poles, fuse the ball to the bar.

Shrine: Turakawak

Map: -3496, -0197, 0066
Region: Gerudo Highlands

Use the first block as a climbing wall, the lift it up and fuse it with the second block (letting some of it hang off the side). Look up at the roof and Ascend up the grating.

Ascend once more, drop down, lift up the fused cubes, and stack with the block here. Ascend to the exit.

Shrine: Taninoud

Map: -1805, 3403, 0948
Region: Hebra Mountains Sky

Fly up/across to the Shrine and touch it to start the quest. Turn the launchpad left once, jump on, then glide to the island opposite. You can - very carefully - land on the **very** bottom rock of the island and Ascend right to the crystal!

Destroy the vines, then fuse the crystal to a flying Zonai device.

Shrine: Taunhiy

Map: -2400, 0824, 0615
Region: Central Hyrule Sky

Use *Lindor's Brow Skyview Tower* to reach *Courage Island* north of you. Speak to the **Construct**, complete the final skydive mini-game, and the Shrine now appears.

Inside, use the fans to get air, pull out your bow, fire at the enemy in slow-mo. Now repeat, but hit **all 3** enemies on the same descent.

Shrine: Tenbez

Map: -0972, 3535, 1011
Region: Hebra Mountains Sky

Drop down to the Shrine at the front of the *North Lomei Castle Top Floor* cube. Inside, hit the reverse gravity button, and place the ball on the launcher. Once it hits the target, jump into the left-hand launcher.

Run left, wait for the ball to reach the metal cage, then hit the switch.

Shrine: Timawak

Map: 1799, 1638, 0311
Region: Death Mountain

Jump across the moving platforms, destroy the **Construct**, go right, use Recall to reach the ball, pull a platform out, and fuse the ball to it.

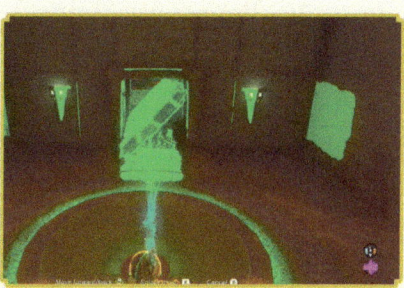

Put the ball in the hole, then pick up a platform again, carefully *squeeze* it through the hole, attach a fan, and head straight to the exit!

Shrine: Tokiy

Map: 2300, -2379, -0028
Region: West Necluda

Drop down the ledge near *Oakle's Navel*, enter the cave here, pick up the stone, and then **very carefully** carry it back *past the falling rocks!*

When you reach the small tunnel, quickly use Recall on the boulder, to move it away, enter the Shrine and claim your reward inside.

Shrine: Tukarok

Map: 0915, -0250, 0035
Region: Lanayru Wetlands

Run forwards, go down, fuse the ball to the vehicle, dive it into the lava, then stick the ball to the side of the block, drag it up as far as you can **and hold it for 10 seconds!**

Use Recall on the block, *quickly* climb up, detach the ball, use all panels to build a bridge across the water, and carry the ball over.

Shrine: Usazum

Map: -2139, -0873, 0093
Region: Hyrule Ridge

Touch the Shrine, turn around, enter the nearby cave, and take out the **Hinox** in your way, as it's carrying your Shrine crystal!

Hit its eye, then use your strongest melee weapons when it's stunned. Carry the crystal back to the Shrine and collect the **[Strong Zonaite Spear]** inside.

Shrine: Ukoojisi

Map: 1466, -2168, 0585
Region: West Necluda Sky

Glide east from the *Popla Foothills Skyview Tower*. Touch the Shrine, then turn the launcher so you're ejected towards the island to the northeast. Stick loads of batteries to the Glider here and fly over to the island ahead.

Burn the reeds, add wheels to the Glider, fuse the crystal to the Glider, add a battery, and fly back!

Shrine: Utojis

Map: 1217, -2541, 0096
Region: East Necluda

Starting at 1141, -2346, 0227, enter *Tobio's Hollow Cave* in front of you. Kill the Keese on the way down (you want their **Wings**).

Pick up the **Zonaite Spears**, fuse a Keese Wing to one, stand on the platform nearby, and throw the spear through the green ring to make the Shrine appear.

Shrine: Utsushok

Map: 0668, -3358, 0072
Region: Faron Grasslands

Use Ultrahand to pull the paddle back, release, and watch the ball go in. Next, fuse the cube to the back of the paddle, and the same again.

Finally, fuse the long panel to the back of the paddle, swing it back, re-fuse it side-ways, enter the minecart, push the panel away, then let go to reach the exit.

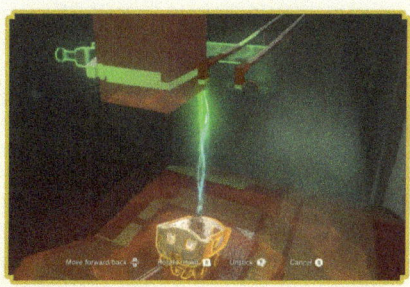

Shrine: Wao-os

Map: -3950, 2034, 0202
Region: Hebra Mountains

Fuse the bowl to the wood, place the ball in the bowl, pick up the cube, hold it up high above the panel, then let go to fling the ball at the target. Now extend the lever with the new panel, fuse the bowl to this part, and repeat as before.

Stand in the bowl, hold the cube up, let go, and glide to the exit!

Shrine: Yansamin

Map: 2350, -1782, 1475
Region: East Necluda Sky

Equip at least *one Zora armor* item, then at 2640, -1373, 0191, swim up the waterfall (*when it's raining*). Make your way to the top of *Zonaite Forge Island*. Skydive down through all the red lasers.

In the Shrine, use fused weapons and throw the explosive barrels at the **Constructs** until it's all clear.

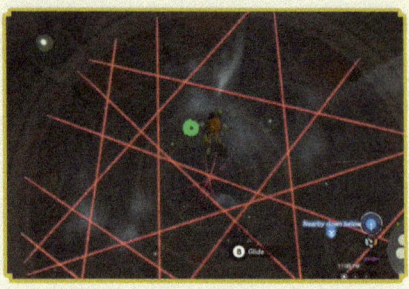

Shrine: Yomizuk

Map: 4412, -0610, 0034
Region: Lanayru Great Springs

Starting at **4480, -0836, 0053**, drop into the hole here, then swim to each rock face as they bob up and down to regenerate stamina.

Take your time (it's a decent distance), and claim your **[Diamond]** from inside the Shrine's chest.

Shrine: Zanmik

Map: 3469, -2179, 0148
Region: Mount Lanayru

Drop down to the lower floor, complete the circuit with a square panel, then start fusing a bunch of metal balls (from the left) to the cog that starts turning. Lift up the chest hidden here for a **[Strong Zonaite Longsword]**.

Climb up the nearby ladder and watch a ball roll into the hole, opening up the Shrine's exit.

Shrine: Zakusu

The final Shrine in our complete list (*finally!*) requires you to complete a lengthy side-quest to access it first. Here's how to do it.

Speak with Nazbi at *3964, -1356, 0464* to start *The High Spring & the Light Rings*.

Launch yourself into the sky from the *Mount Lanayru Skyview Tower*. Now glide to the nearest sky island South of you at *3948, -1543, 1120* and collect the **[Sled Shield]** resting by the wall.

Touch the green panel nearby to begin this fun mini-game! You have to "Shield Surf" down the course. To actually do this, hold up your shield, then jump, and press **A**.

If done correctly, Link jumps on top of shield. Nice! Now you must slide right off the sky island down to the snowy mountain peak below.

Look for the green ring which you **must** pass through (and not miss any on the way down either)!

Pass through **all six rings** to make the Shrine rise up from its hiding place! Cheeky Shrine.

You're once again stripped of all your weapons (and armor) and you're tasked with clearing out every **Construct**.

Collect your weapons, run right, then use Recall on the moving platform to go up to the higher level.

Take out the walkway Construct, fuse its **Spiked Ball** with your wooden sword, collect the **Fire Fruits**, run up to the top, take out the toughest **Construct**, glide down, and finish off the remaining enemies to open the exit!

KOROK SEEDS

A Real Turd of a Reward!

Not content with the *ludicrous* side-mission of finding **900** Korok seeds in BotW (in return for a "Golden Poo" - we kid you not), Nintendo went and upped the total to - a quite frankly **ridiculous** - *1,000* seeds.

And - spoiler alert - the "reward" for all of that *is exactly the same*. Thanks (we think?). Trying to cover all 1,000 in-depth would take an unfeasible amount of time and 441 are required to max-out all inventory slots with *Hetsu*.

We'll provide you with grid co-ordinates and the type of puzzle to expect for the **500+** seeds we've found.

As in BotW, you hand them over to *Hetsu* in return for those extra inventory slots.

There are several different types of puzzles reserved for making the Koroks appear. Once you know how to spot one, it'll be *far* easier to find others of the same type.

Area to Check	Page No
Great Sky Island	228
Faron	229
Central Hyrule	232
Hebra Mountains	235
Tabantha Frontiers	237
Tabantha Tundra	239
Gerudo Highlands	240
Gerudo Desert	244
W. Necluda + Lanayru Wetlands	246
Eldin Canyon	248
Akkala	251

It's important to note that there's quite a few different styles of puzzles that those fiendish Koroks expect you to solve if you want to unlock all those sweet, sweet inventory upgrade slots.

Some types of puzzles (such as the block puzzles) stick out like a sore thumb. Others, such as the targets or sparkles, require you to be paying *much* closer attention.

Here's the type of puzzles you can expect to come across:

Lift the rock

Lift the rock to make the it appear.

Moving Sparkle

Hard-to-spot sparkles that keep moving. Touch it to find the Korok.

Reunite friends

Take this Korok to his friend further away. Worth **2** seeds!

Tree Stump Races

Stand on the tree stump and reach the Korok fast enough to catch it.

Balloon Targets

Shoot **every** balloon that appears.

Dandelion

Inspect it then catch the seed **before** it hits the ground!

Build the roof

Fuse a roof together to the top of the structure with the statues.

Lily pad circle

Dive into the middle of the lilies.

Target

Shoot the small acorn or balloon.

Rock Circle

Put back the missing rock(s).

Ascend

Ascend up into the Korok tree stump.

Flower Chase

Catch the flower as it moves around!

GREAT SKY ISLAND

No.	Co-ordinates	Puzzle Type	Collected?
01	0464, -0382, 1418	Ascend	☐
02	0271, -0828, 1443	Moving sparkle	☐
03	0112, -1081, 1417	Lift the rock	☐
04	0022, -1271, 1416	Reunite friends (start)	☐
05	0082, -1242, 1406	Reunite friends (end)	☐
06	0020, -1557, 1452	Lift the rock (up tree)	☐
07	0346, -1756, 2280	Sparkles	☐
08	0379, -1685, 2334	Sparkles (tree trunk)	☐
09	0228, -1644, 1407	Lift rock under leaves	☐
10	0100, -3842, 0031	Target	☐
11	0310, -1456, 2060	Circle of lilies	☐
12	0494, -1313, 1416	Flower chase	☐
13	0424, -1503, 1497	Rock circle (tree)	☐
14	0464, -1531, 1358	Balloon	☐
15	0470, -1693, 1442	Reunite friends (start)	☐
16	0454, -1773, 1446	Reunite friends (end)	☐
17	0570, -1593, 1482	Block puzzle	☐
18	0764, -1344, 1604	Rock circle	☐
19	0627, -1521, 1443	Block puzzle	☐
20	0624, -1662, 1507	Dandelion	☐

No.	Co-ordinates	Puzzle Type	Collected?
01	0885, -2424, 0065	Tree Stump Races	☐
02	0791, -3341, 0081	Balloon Targets	☐
03	0951, -3477, 0021	Moving sparks	☐
04	1096, -3829, 0002	Lift the rock	☐
05	0813, -3717, 0107	Flowers	☐
06	0572, -3850, 0030	Block puzzle	☐
07	0529, -3667, 0063	Missing rock	☐
08	0594, -3726, 0061	Lily pad circle	☐
09	0259, -3891, 0002	Target	☐
10	0100, -3842, 0031	Target	☐
11	0521, -3482, 0048	Reunite friends	☐
12	0389, -3605, 0072	Missing rock	☐
13	0205, -3308, 0060	Lift the rock	☐
14	-0108, -3427, 0015	Lily pad circle	☐
15	0225, -3339, 0071	Lift the rock	☐
16	-0415, 3370, 0032	Moving sparks	☐
17	-0242, -3917, 0004	Sparkle cloud	☐
18	0222, -3529, 0068	Reunite friends	☐
19	-0799, -3259, 0089	Target	☐
20	-0464, -2900, -0014	Block puzzle	☐

No.	Co-ordinates	Puzzle Type	Collected?
21	-0152, -3068, 0037	Lift the rock	☐
22	-0038, -2962, 0111	Flowers	☐
23	0117, -2963, 0034	Lift the rock	☐
24	0699, -2953, 0014	Block puzzle	☐
25	-0711, -2625, 0099	Lift the rock	☐
26	1392, 3637, 0001	Reunite friends	☐
27	0055, -3760, 0003	Reunite friends	☐
28	0574, -3852, 0030	Block puzzle	☐
29	0782, -2763, 0006	Lift the rock	☐
30	-0124, -0937, 0041	Lily pad circle	☐
31	-1038, -2397, 0028	Missing rock	☐
32	-0307, -3290, 0024	Reunite friends	☐
33	0082, -3769, 0006	Reunite friends	☐
34	0099, -3841, 0031	Pop the cork	☐
35	0269, -3905, -0001	Target	☐
36	0397, -3862, 0000	Reunite friends	☐
37	0589, -3735, 0028	Lily pad circle	☐
38	0524, -3679, 0058	Lift the rock	☐
39	0051, -3393, 0025	Reunite friends	☐
40	0792, -3342, 0081	Target	☐

No.	Co-ordinates	Puzzle Type	Collected?
41	1449, -3530, 0117	Moving sparks	☐
42	-0038, -2962, 0111	Flowers	☐
43	0117, -2963, 0034	Lift the rock	☐
44	0699, -2953, 0014	Block puzzle	☐
45	-0711, -2625, 0099	Lift the rock	☐
46	1392, 3637, 0001	Reunite friends	☐
47	0055, -3760, 0003	Reunite friends	☐
48	0574, -3852, 0030	Block puzzle	☐
49	0782, -2763, 0006	Lift the rock	☐
50	-0124, -0937, 0041	Lily pad circle	☐
51	-1038, -2397, 0028	Missing rock	☐
52	-0307, -3290, 0024	Reunite friends	☐
53	0082, -3769, 0006	Reunite friends	☐
54	0099, -3841, 0031	Pop the cork	☐
55	0269, -3905, -0001	Target	☐
56	0397, -3862, 0002	Reunite friends	☐
57	0589, -3735, 0028	Lily pad circle	☐
58	0524, -3679, 0058	Lift the rock	☐
59	0051, -3393, 0025	Reunite friends	☐
60	0792, -3342, 0081	Target	☐

No.	Co-ordinates	Puzzle Type	Collected?
01	0624, -0752, 0021	Lift the rock	☐
02	0752, -0451, 0020	Lift the rock (tree top)	☐
03	0502, -0470, 0052	Lift the rock	☐
04	0760, 0003, 0031	Block puzzle (roof)	☐
05	0616, -0074, 0053	Dandelion	☐
06	0291, -0246, 0027	Pop the cork	☐
07	0075, -0326, 0034	Lift rock under leaves	☐
08	-0217, -0362, 0052	Lift the rock	☐
09	-0589, -0559, 0024	Lift the rock	☐
10	-0425, -0149, 0030	Balloon Targets	☐
11	-1111, -0567, 0095	Rock circle	☐
12	-1083, -0511, 055	Target	☐
13	-1109, -0419, 0062	Tree stump race	☐
14	-1093, -0197, 0041	Dandelion	☐
15	-1356, -0191, 0009	Block puzzle	☐
16	-1129, 0018, 0039	Lift the rock	☐
17	-0923, -0042, 0105	Lift the rock	☐
18	-0800, -0025, 0062	Balloon Targets	☐
19	-0753, 0198, 0028	Pop the cork	☐
20	-0944, 0347, 0023	Ascend	☐

No.	Co-ordinates	Puzzle Type	Collected?
21	-1014, 0567, 0010	Rock circle	
22	-0790, 0556, 0081	Moving sparkle	
23	-0669, 0559, 0023	Block puzzle	
24	-0530, 0693, 0034	Lift the rock	
25	-0604, 0677, 0013	Balloon (under bridge)	
26	-0679, 0856, 0014	Moving sparkle	
27	-0680, 0954, 0010	Target (water)	
28	-0770, 0940, 0017	Reunite friends (start)	
29	-0755, 1066, 0044	Reunite friends (end)	
30	-1034, 1084, 0062	Tree stump race	
31	-0948, 0580, 0055	Tree stump race	
32	-0527, 0190, 0062	Flower chase	
33	-0314, 0322, 0024	Lift rock under leaves	
34	-0253, 0258, 0046	Lift the rock	
35	-0254, 0426, 0029	Lift the rock	
36	-0086, 0400, 0027	Ascend	
37	0347, 0493, 0041	Flower chase	
38	0714, 0362, 0009	Rock circle	
39	0133, 0596, 0026	Pop a cork	
40	0248, 0692, 0023	Target (under bridge)	

No.	Co-ordinates	Puzzle Type	Collected?
41	0192, 0894, 0026	Moving sparkle	☐
42	0407, 1176, 0010	Target (under bridge)	☐
43	0536, 1105, 0016	Reunite a friend (start)	☐
44	0631, 1168, 0009	Reunite a friend (end)	☐
45	-0270, 0608, 0042	Circle of lilies	☐
46	-0237, 0631, 0079	Lift the rock (spire)	☐
47	-0273, 0752, 0130	Balloon Targets	☐
48	-0339, 0728, 0053	Block puzzle	☐
49	-0415, 0838, 0085	Moving sparkle	☐
50	-0351, 0830, 0179	Sparkles (climb tall spire)	☐
51	-0293, 0837, 0105	Lift the rock (Ultrahand)	☐
52	-0126, 0815, 0096	Lift the rock	☐
53	-0065, 0867, 0168	Rock circle (spire)	☐
54	-0467, 0848, 0100	Flower chase	☐
55	-0435, 1114, 0024	Balloon Targets	☐
56	-0126, 1189, 0033	Target (in a cave)	☐
57	-0303, 1123, 0090	Tree stump race	☐
58	-0299, 1127, 0034	Circle of lilies	☐
59	-0360, 0888, 0277	Balloon Targets	☐
60	-0889, 0938, 0314	Balloon Targets	☐
61	-0049, 0978, 0272	Block Puzzle	☐

No.	Co-ordinates	Puzzle Type	Collected?
01	-4253, 2138, 0018	Build a roof	☐
02	-0426, 2175, -0010	Reunite friends (start)	☐
03	-4117, 2411, -0013	Reunite friends (end)	☐
04	-4067, 2519, 0021	Rock circle	☐
05	-4336, 2613, 0322	Fuse 2 rocks to bell	☐
06	-4631, 2820, 0242	Balloon Targets	☐
07	-4422, 3215, 0391	Tree stump race	☐
08	-4249, 3127, 0194	Sparkles (top of tree)	☐
09	-4186, 3369, 0242	Build a roof	☐
10	-4036, 3366, 0264	Lift the rock	☐
11	-3838, 3416, 0274	Ascend	☐
12	-3835, 3350, 0316	Flower chase	☐
13	-3947, 3171, 0323	Block Puzzle	☐
14	-3797, 3023, 0246	Build a roof	☐
15	-3576, 3264, 0386	Melt ice, lift rock	☐
16	-3663, 3385, 0329	Reunite friends (start)	☐
17	-4122, 3427, 0222	Reunite friends (end)	☐
18	-4511, 3466, 0260	Block puzzle	☐
19	-4432, 3690, 0307	Lift rock (melt ice first)	☐
20	-4272, 3499, 0390	Dandelion	☐

No.	Co-ordinates	Puzzle Type	Collected?
21	-4005, 3617, 0523	Lift rock (melt ice first)	☐
22	-3992, 3836, 0220	Tree stump race	☐
23	-3772, 3840, 0268	Moving sparkle	☐
24	-3976, 3698, 0239	Balloon (while gliding)	☐
25	-3967, 3753, 0217	Balloon (while gliding)	☐
26	-3468, 3473, 0481	Balloon Targets	☐
27	-3415, 3503, 0432	Sparkles (up thin tree)	☐
28	-3428, 3799, 0245	Tree stump race	☐
29	-2890, 3495, 0246	Reunite friends (start)	☐
30	-3235, 3686, 0243	Reunite friends (end)	☐
31	-2605, 3239, 0387	Rock circle	☐
32	-2356, 3674, 0274	Balloon Targets	☐
33	-2001, 3117, 0385	Tree stump race	☐
34	-2338, 2952, 0404	Reunite friends (start)	☐
35	-2371, 3026, 0442	Reunite friends (end)	☐
36	-2470, 2760, 0513	Block Puzzle	☐
37	-2833, 2835, 0582	Reunite friends (start)	☐
38	-2798, 2879, 0600	Reunite friends (end)	☐
39	-3061, 2839, 0429	Rock circle	☐
40	-3001, 3220, 0560	Ascend	☐
41	-3352, 2992, 0515	Lift the rock	☐
42	-3157, 2691, 0594	Sparkle (top of tall tree)	☐

No.	Co-ordinates	Puzzle Type	Collected?
01	-3749, 2798, 0138	Lift the rock	☐
02	-3850, 2739, 0029	Lift the rock (melt ice)	☐
03	-3676, 2468, 0319	Destroy vines, lift rock	☐
04	-3797, 2319, 0171	Flowers sequence	☐
05	-3579, 2258, 0149	Sparkles (chimney)	☐
06	-3423, 2066, 0164	Ascend	☐
07	-3086, 2119, 0121	Lift rock (lonely pillar)	☐
08	-3635, 1809, 0167	Lift the rock (by Shrine)	☐
09	-3552, 1754, 0182	Balloon Targets	☐
10	-4036, 3366, 0264	Lift the rock	☐
11	-3769, 1866, 0260	Build a roof	☐
12	-3697, 1682, 0103	Lift the rock	☐
13	-4117, 2050, 0185	Block Puzzle	☐
14	-3955, 2038, 0206	Lift the rock	☐
15	-3944, 1969, 0209	Lift rock (up a tree)	☐
16	-4125, 1934, 0198	Flower chase	☐
17	-4479, 1943, 0162	Sparkles	☐
18	-4229, 1747, 0111	Flower chase	☐
19	-4172, 1695, 0110	Lift rock	☐
20	-4060, 1794, 0151	Ascend	☐

No.	Co-ordinates	Puzzle Type	Collected?
21	-3984, 1709, 0177	Lift rock (up a tree)	☐
22	-4005, 1651, 0173	Rock circle	☐
23	-3884, 1754, 0105	Block puzzle	☐
24	-3621, 1518, 0148	Flower chase	☐
25	-3133, 1548, 0122	Fuse rocks to pop cork	☐
26	-3105, 1327, 0219	Target (under bridge)	☐
27	-3145, 1107, 0158	Lift the rock	☐
28	-3280, 1342, 0187	Lift the rock	☐
29	-3423, 1316, 0119	Block puzzle	☐
30	-3819, 1318, 0287	Tree stump race	☐
31	-3982, 0929, 0112	Sparkle (up a tree)	☐
32	-4055, 0775, 0102	Spicy pepper statues	☐
33	-3965, 0625, 0189	Tree stump race	☐
34	−3824, 0835, 0122	Place rock on stick	☐
35	-3715, 1038, 0197	Ascend	☐
36	-3613, 0989, 0287	Reunite friends (start)	☐
37	-3559, 0773, 0187	Reunite friends (end)	☐
38	-3542, 0755, 0186	Sparkle	☐
39	-3434, 0708, 0172	Ascend	☐
40	-3443, 0663, 0250	Dandelion	☐
41	-3240, 0586, 0170	Balloon (under bridge)	☐
42	-3553, 0595, 0211	Lift the rock	☐

No.	Co-ordinates	Puzzle Type	Collected?
01	-1970, 3794, 0315	Lift the rock	☐
02	-1764, 3554, 0234	Lift the rock	☐
03	-1668, 3752, 0239	Moving sparkle	☐
04	-1385, 3633, 0256	Reunite friends (start)	☐
05	-1035, 3522, 0229	Reunite friends (end)	☐
06	-1211, 3608, 0191	Block puzzle	☐
07	-1104, 3405, 0304	Rock circle	☐
08	-1146, 3077, 0340	Put a rock on a stick	☐
09	-0997, 3084, 0200	Ascend	☐
10	-0875, 2304, 0222	In the tree trunk	☐
11	-0686, 3535, 0284	Flower chase (corner)	☐
12	-1710, 2560, 0229	Ascend	☐
13	-1648, 2443, 0237	Statues (Ice Fruit)	☐
14	-1811, 2197, 0273	Lift the rock	☐
15	-1581, 2129, -0037	Flower chase (pillar)	☐
16	-1451, 2368, 0134	Put a rock on a stick	☐
17	-1543, 2556, 0238	Reunite friends (start)	☐
18	-1358, 2783, 0205	Reunite friends (end)	☐
19	-1189, 2484, -0100	Lift rock	☐
20	-1147, 2533, -0033	Lift rock up on a tree	☐

No.	Co-ordinates	Puzzle Type	Collected?
21	-1060, 2615, 0031	Block puzzle	
22	-2085, 2591, 0301	Rock circle	
23	-2274, 2288, 0320	Put a rock on a stick	
24	-2383, 2129, 0392	Balloon Targets	
25	-2210, 2093, 0321	Build a roof	
26	-2075, 2087, 0285	Target	
27	-2291, 1913, 0296	Inside tree stump	
28	-2508, 1849, 0278	Target (up high)	
29	-2640, 2054, 0339	Block puzzle (in cave)	
30	-2801, 1948, 0272	Rock circle	
31	-2687, 1664, 0268	Sparkles (on chimney)	
32	-2826, 1595, -0019	Block puzzle	

 # GERUDO HIGHLANDS

No.	Co-ordinates	Puzzle Type	Collected?
01	-4904, -1242, 0452	Block puzzle	
02	-4691, -1285, 0522	Stand on tree top	
03	-4538, -1340, 0528	Reunite friends (start)	
04	-4510, -0698, 0510	Reunite friends (end)	
05	-4412, -0350, 0511	Put a rock on a stick	
06	-4375, -0525, 0451	Lift the rock (ledge)	

No.	Co-ordinates	Puzzle Type	Collected?
07	-4351, -0686, 0526	Balloon (up high)	☐
08	-4322, -1082, 0522	Rock circle	☐
09	-3877, -1186, 0492	Rock puzzle	☐
10	-3572, -1083, 0523	Flower chase	☐
11	-4003, -0970, 0714	Rock lift (Frost Gleeok)!	☐
12	-3970, -0607, 0656	Sparkle moving	☐
13	-3973, -0337, 0446	Build a roof	☐
14	-3621, -0403, 0239	Moving sparkles	☐
15	-03816, 0787, 0547	Melt ice, lift rock	☐
16	-3719, -0799, 0640	Moving sparkle	☐
17	-3560, -0735, 0556	Rock circle	☐
18	-3597, -0916, 0506	Lift rock	☐
19	-3489, -0977, 0598	Climb to top of tree	☐
20	-3250, -1028, 0570	Balloon Targets	☐
21	-3168, -1034, 0428	Ascend	☐
22	-3093, -1034, 0595	Build a roof	☐
23	-3065, -1291, 0498	Pop the cork	☐
24	-3191, -1176, 0478	Reunite friends (start)	☐
25	-3145, -0616, 0199	Reunite friends (end)	☐
26	-2669, -1125, 0409	Sparkles (tree top)	☐
27	-2672, -1356, 0501	Ascend	☐

No.	Co-ordinates	Puzzle Type	Collected?
28	-2497, -1587, 0535	Build a roof	☐
29	-2639, -1541, 0582	Rock circle	☐
30	-2809, -1650, 0472	Pop the cork	☐
31	-2397, -1448, 0542	Tree stump race	☐
32	-3000, -1502, 0577	Melt ice, lift rock	☐
33	-3245, -1452, 0401	Melt ice, lift rock	☐
34	-3215, -1728, 0378	Target (cliff edge)	☐
35	–3212, -1858, 0074	Block puzzle	☐
36	-3543, -1559, 0452	Rock circle	☐
37	-3674, -1563, 0464	Put a rock on a stick	☐
38	-3647, -1466, 0365	Tree stump race	☐
39	-3918, -1591, 0249	Statues: *Mighty Bananas*	☐
40	-3895, -1633, 0289	Block puzzle	☐
41	-3846, -1891, 0304	Dandelion	☐
42	-3597, -1983, 0201	Target (mid-air shot)	☐
43	-3580, -1981, 0244	Pop the cork	☐
44	-3572, -1852, 0358	Balloon Targets	☐
45	-2936, -2214, 0208	Flower chase	☐
46	-2736, -2329, 0131	Target (mid-air shot)	☐
47	-2618, -2197, 0067	Sparkles (sign posts)	☐
48	-2442, 2111, 0231	Reunite friends (start)	☐

No.	Co-ordinates	Puzzle Type	Collected?
49	-2433, -2145, 0265	Reunite friends (end)	☐
50	-2477, -2054, 0121	Lift the rock	☐
51	-2321, -1838, 0147	Target (under bridge)	☐
52	-2243, -1744, 0110	Lift the rock (tiny ledge)	☐
53	-2197, -1683, 0065	Lift the rock	☐
54	-2141, -1486, 0279	Lift the rock	☐
55	-1817, -1531, 0100	Balloon Targets	☐
56	-2276, -2167, 0250	Rock under leaves	☐
57	-2252, -2209, 0250	Put a rock on a stick	☐
58	-2250, -2359, 0275	Tree stump race	☐
59	-2015, -2468, 0222	Target (under rock)	☐
60	-1928, -2824, 0151	Block puzzle	☐
61	-1428, -2976, 0271	Ascend	☐
62	-1603, -3086, 0201	Pop the cork	☐
63	-1954, -3191, 0125	Lift the rock	☐
64	–0977, -3232, 0250	Flower chase	☐
65	-1150, -3296, 0268	Block puzzle	☐
66	-1179, -3509, 0217	Sparkles (sign posts)	☐
67	-1361, -3717, 0395	Stone circle	☐
68	-1445, -3650, 0427	Block puzzle	☐
69	-1378, -3505, 0434	Lift the rock	☐

GERUDO DESERT

No.	Co-ordinates	Puzzle Type	Collected?
01	-4685, -1965, 0059	Flower chase	☐
02	-4711, -2164, 0100	Dandelion	☐
03	-4593, -2345, 0038	Ascend (quicksand)	☐
04	-4442, -2273, 0080	Flower chase	☐
05	-4483, -2133, 0068	Tree stump race	☐
06	-4383, -2021, 0095	Block puzzle	☐
07	-4137, -2581, 0053	Moving sparkle	☐
08	-4131, -2256, 0044	Reunite friends (start)	☐
09	-4319, -1867, 0064	Reunite friends (end)	☐
10	-4356, -1849, 0073	Target (up high)	☐
11	-4149, -1934, 0102	Lift the rock	☐
12	-3751, -2286, 0077	Lift the rock	☐
13	-3756, -2442, 0043	Ascend	☐
14	-3315, -2285, 0075	Rock circle	☐
15	-3317, -2172, 0039	Moving sparkle	☐
16	-2958, -2318, 0025	Reunite friends (start)	☐
17	-3312, -2460, 0029	Reunite friends (end)	☐
18	-3266, -2610, 0120	Sparkles	☐
19	-3827, -2859, 0026	Ascend (small tunnel)	☐
20	-3854, -2861, 0058	Sparkles (chimney)	☐

No.	Co-ordinates	Puzzle Type	Collected?
21	-3860, -3017, 0085	Tree stump race	
22	-3818, -3121, 0051	Reunite friends (start)	
23	-3743, -3475, 0016	Reunite friends (end)	
24	-3610, -2843, 0070	Dandelion	
25	-3595, -3003, 0035	Flower chase	
26	-3422, -3118, 0084	Tree stump race	
27	-3346, -3056, 0041	Reunite friends (start)	
28	-3075, -3050, 0014	Reunite friends (end)	
29	-2732, -2820, 0035	Tree stump race	
30	-2247, -3272, 0041	Moving sparkle	
31	-2488, -3349, 0026	Reunite friends (start)	
32	-2543, -3927, 0014	Reunite friends (end)	
33	-2547, -3951, 0035	Dandelion	
34	-4621, -3197, 0037	Reunite friends (start)	
35	-4871, -3559, 0039	Reunite friends (end)	
36	-4906, -3771, -0034	Lift rock under leaves	

No.	Co-ordinates	Puzzle Type	Collected?
01	1071, 0848, 0017	Balloon	☐
02	0968, 1025, 0010	Lift the rock	☐
03	0616, 0754, 0077	Moving sparkles	☐
04	0689, 0626, 0059	Dandelion	☐
05	0841, 0692, 0128	Flower chase	☐
06	0974, 0674, 0084	Flower chase	☐
07	0553, 0514, 0013	Circle of lilies	☐
08	0919, 0410, 0095	Ascend	☐
09	1181, 0379, 0157	Lift rock under leaves	☐
10	1118, 0229, 0074	Dandelion	☐
11	1396, 0128, 0026	Lift rock under leaves	☐
12	1514, 0296, 0035	Balloon Targets	☐
13	0821, -0329, 0030	Sparkle	☐
14	0958, -0203, 0031	Reunite friends (start)	☐
15	1195, -0649, 0020	Reunite friends (end)	☐
16	0929, -0365, 0039	Rock circle	☐
17	0957, -0943, 0009	Pop the cork	☐
18	1486, 0441, 0008	Target (underwater)	☐
19	1304, -0179, 0008	Circle of lilies	☐
20	1441, -0537, 0012	Dandelion	☐

No.	Co-ordinates	Puzzle Type	Collected?
21	1327, -0781, 0039	Lift rock (up a tree)	
22	1825, -0459, 0012	Lift the rock	
23	1980, -0451, 0068	Balloon	
24	1505, -0332, 0014	Reunite friends (start)	
25	1700, 0009, 0010	Reunite friends (end)	
26	1891, -0150, 0009	Rock (under bridge)	
27	1115, -0732, 0062	Target	
28	1283, -0833, 0078	Lift the rock	
29	1574, -1045, 0151	Dandelion	
30	1778, -0985, 0119	Moving sparkles	
31	1759, -0984, 0140	Sparkle (on a roof)	
32	1996, -0958, 0178	Target (under bridge)	

ELDIN CANYON

No.	Co-ordinates	Puzzle Type	Collected?
01	1425, 1534, 0363	Sparkle (signpost)	☐
02	3029, 2289, 0337	Build roof	☐
03	1531, 1613, 0306	Reunite friends	☐
04	1448, 1750, 0308	Put a rock on a stick	☐
05	1543, 1808, 0283	Reunite friends	☐
06	1670, 1979, 0342	Lift the rock	☐
07	1767, 1539, 0309	Sparkle	☐
08	1699, 1753, 0343	Put a rock on a stick	☐
09	1941, 1205, 0140	Lift the rock	☐
10	2371, 1401, 0129	Reunite friends	☐
11	2639, 1109, 0158	Reunite friends	☐
12	2436, 1243, 0119	Dandelion	☐
13	2719, 1157, 0178	Block puzzle	☐
14	2677, 1073, 0156	Moving sparkle	☐
15	2431, 1708, 0149	Pop the cork	☐
16	2673, 1351, 0128	Tree stump race	☐
17	2703, 1742, 0119	Rock circle	☐
18	2264, 1835, 0332	Flower chase	☐
19	1964, 2040, 0423	Put stick on a rock	☐
20	1984, 2040, 0423	Reunite friends	☐

No.	Co-ordinates	Puzzle Type	Collected?
21	2063, 2326, 0498	Block puzzle	☐
22	1799, 2209, 0497	Tree stump race	☐
23	1574, 2465, 0408	Balloon	☐
24	1680, 2385, 0463	Balloon (under bridge)	☐
25	1722, 2419, 0390	Circle of lilies	☐
26	1251, 3007, 0422	Reunite friends	☐
27	1603, 2824, 0466	Sparkle	☐
28	1573, 2951, 0398	Target (under bridge)	☐
29	1854, 0785, 0091	Lift the rock	☐
30	3227, 2114, 0118	Reunite friends	☐
31	1380, 2835, 0361	Rock circle	☐
32	2776, 2520, 0653	Balloon (under arch)	☐
33	2638, 3468, 0362	Sparkle	☐
34	1768, 2237, 0413	Block puzzle	☐
35	2223, 3055, 0445	Target (under bridge)	☐
36	1812, 2527, 0401	Statues (offer vase)	☐
37	2224, 2356, 0515	Flower chase	☐
38	2711, 2389, 0623	Lift the rock	☐
39	2313, 1132, 0209	Ascend	☐
40	2290, 0943, 0111	Rock circle	☐

No.	Co-ordinates	Puzzle Type	Collected?
41	2232, 3680, 0232	Block puzzle	☐
42	3092, 3693, 0203	Balloons	☐
43	2405, 3327, 0435	Ascend	☐
44	2063, 2761, 0474	Block puzzle	☐
45	1724, 2556, 0499	Lift the rock	☐
46	2189, 2773, 0523	Reunite friends	☐
47	1729, 2604, 0431	Reunite friends	☐
48	1814, 2640, 0400	Reunite friends	☐
49	2196, 3006, 0507	Tree stump race	☐
50	1477, 2231, 0325	Circle of lilies	☐
51	2171, 3037, 0452	Dandelion	☐
52	1433, 1952, 0355	Ascend	☐
53	1249, 2290, 0322	Rock circle	☐
54	1577, 0724, 0077	Statues (give apples)	☐
55	1333, 1315, 0167	Inside tree stump	☐
56	0769, 1416, 0087	Lift the rock	☐
57	0939, 1553, 0150	Target (in rafters)	☐
58	0776, 1527, 0148	Tree stump race	☐
59	0987, 1803, 0210	Balloons	☐

No.	Co-ordinates	Puzzle Type	Collected?
01	3273, 1398, 0285	Lift the rock	
02	3357, 1306, 0289	Block puzzle	
03	3669, 1468, 0096	Flower chase	
04	4021, 1623, 0137	Lift the rock	
05	3972, 1612, 0127	Shoot town bell	
06	4137, 1491, 0166	Build a roof	
07	4109, 1384, 0166	Moving sparkle	
08	4048, 1284, 0216	Sparkle (tree top)	
09	4742, 1983, 0000	Reunite friends	
10	4599, 1858, 0009	Lift rock under leaves	
11	3232, 1787, 0226	Lift the rock (up a tree)	
12	3222, 2167, 0128	Reunite friends	
13	3327, 2168, 0135	Sparkle (signpost)	
14	4527, 2047, 0000	Lift the rock	
15	4278, 2337, 0020	Reunite friends	
16	4074, 2451, 0073	Lift rock under leaves	
17	4312, 2519, 0080	Sparkle (signposts)	
18	4626, 2859, 0002	Reunite friends	
19	4277, 2942, 0143	Circle of lilies	
20	4271, 2828, 0148	Lift rock under leaves	

No.	Co-ordinates	Puzzle Type	Collected?
21	3855, 2685, 0049	Reunite friends	☐
22	3767, 2696, 0018	Moving sparkle	☐
23	3542, 2636, 0077	Block puzzle	☐
24	3546, 3025, 0080	Tree stump race	☐
25	3344, 3074, 0058	Statues (give apples)	☐
26	3146, 3093, 0141.	Block puzzles	☐
27	3268, 3397, 0034	Lift the rocks	☐
28	4435, 3185, 0249	Flower chase	☐
29	4540, 3162, 0270	Sparkle	☐
30	4493, 3151, 0245	Statues: *Mighty Bananas*	☐
31	4155, 3167, 0250	Lift the rock	☐
32	4120, 3285, 0198	Target	☐
33	3448, 3175, 0054	Reunite friends	☐
34	3768, 3376, 0171	Put a rock on a tree	☐
35	3455, 3581, 0208	Balloons	☐
36	2969, 3648, 0224	Reunite friends	☐
37	3075, 3682, 0214	Balloons (climb tree)	☐
38	3183, 3456, 0088	Tree stump race	☐
39	4794, 3755, 0140	Balloons (corner)	☐
40	3647, 1796, 0111	Lift the rock	☐

ITEM TABLES

For All You Data Fans...

Over the following pages you'll find our reference tables for the armor, weapons, shields, bows, and - mahoosive - amount of materials in the game.

Note: Zonai devices were added near the start of the guide to get you more familiar with this new feature sooner.

Item Type	Page No
Armor Sets	230
Weapons	235
Shields	238
Bows	239
Materials	240

Set	Items	Set Bonus	Location(s)
Archaic	Archaic Tunic	N/A	*Great Sky Island*
	Archaic Legwear	N/A	*Great Sky Island*
Armor of the Depths	Hood of the Depths	Additional gloom resistance	5th Bargainer statue (300 poes)
	Tunic of the Depths		1st Bargainer statue (150 poes)
	Gaiters of the Depths		3rd Bargainer statue (200 poes)
Awakening	Mask of Awakening	Raises attack	*Thundra Plateau* at noon
	Tunic of Awakening		Secret passage at *Ancient Columns*
	Trousers of Awakening		Bottom floor of the *Coliseum Ruins*
Armor of the Wild	Cap of the Wild	Raises attack	Hebra Dark Skeleton
	Tunic of the Wild		Gerudo Dark Skeleton
	Trousers of the Wild		Eldin Dark Skeleton

Set	Items	Set Bonus	Location(s)
Barbarian	Barbarian Helm	Reduces Stamina required for charged attacks	Marked on map during Misko's Treasure quest
	Barbarian Armor		
	Barbarian Leg-wraps		
Charged	Charged Headdress	Faster charged attacks during thunder storms	Behind a cave at *Dracozu River*
	Charged Shirt		Top of the river at *Dracozu Lake*
	Charged Trousers		Behind cracked rocks in *Damel Forest*
Climbing	Climber's Bandana	Less stamina used when climbing	Inside *Ploymus Mountain Cave*
	Climbing Gear		Inside *North Hyrule Plain Cave*
	Climbing Boots		Inside *Upland Zorana Byroad*
Dark	Dark Hood	Increases movement speed at night	4th Bargainer statue (300 poes)
	Dark Tunic		1st Bargainer statue (150 poes)
	Dark Trousers		2nd Bargainer statue (200 poes)
Desert Voe	Desert Voe Headband	Raises heat resistance + reduces damage from electrical attacks	Sold at *Kara Kara Bazaar* in the *Gerudo Desert*
	Desert Voe Spaulder		Sold at the secret fashion club in *Gerudo Town*
	Desert Voe Trousers		

Set	Items	Set Bonus	Location(s)
Ember	Ember Headdress	Raises attack and charge attacks in hot weather	Inside *YunoboCo HQ South Cave*
	Ember Shirt		Inside *Goronbi River Cave*
	Ember Trousers		Inside *Cephla Lake Cave*
Evil Spirit	Evil Spirit Mask	Increases stealth + increased bone weapon damage + Stal-type enemies ignore Link	Complete *The South Lomei Prophecy* quest
	Evil Spirit Armor		Complete *The Lomei Labyrinth Island* quest
	Evil Spirit Greaves		Complete *The North Lomei Prophecy* quest
Fierce Deity	Fierce Deity Mask	Raises attack + charge attacks use less stamina	*Tempest Gulch* near the *Kamatukis Shrine*
	Fierce Deity Armor		Inside *Akkala Citadel Ruins*
	Fierce Deity Boots		On *Mount Daphnes*
Flamebreaker	Flamebreaker Helm	Increases flame resistance + protection from fire attacks	Goron City armor store (1,400R)
	Flamebreaker Armor		Goron City armor store (700R)
	Flamebreaker Boots		Goron City armor store (1,200R)
Froggy	Froggy Hood	Increases slip resistance + no slipping when climbing in the rain	*Lucky Clover Gazette* (Quest reward)
	Froggy Sleeve		
	Froggy Leggings		

Set	Items	Set Bonus	Location(s)
Frostbite	Frostbite Headdress	Increases attacks + charge speed during cold weather	Inside *Lake Kilsie Cave*
	Frostbite Shirt		Inside *Brightcap Cave*
	Frostbite Trousers		Inside *Hebra Headspring Cave*
Glide	Glide Mask	Easier to glide when falling + Zero fall damage	*Valor Island* skydive challenge
	Glide Shirt *sold*		*Courage Island* skydive challenge
	Glide Tights *Sold*		*Bravery Island* skydive challenge
Hero	Cap of the Hero	Raises attack	Inside the *Abandoned Lurelin Mine*
	Tunic of the Hero		Inside the *Abandoned Kakariko Mine*
	Trousers of the Hero		Inside the *Corvash Canyon Mine*
Hylian	Hylian Hood *sold*	Nothing :(	Lookout Landing (70 Rupees)
	Hylian Tunic *sold*		Lookout Landing (130 Rupees)
	Hylian Trousers		Lookout Landing (120 Rupees)
Miner	Miner's Mask	Glow effect + extra glow radius around Link	In the *Abandoned Kara Kara Mine*
	Miner's Top		In the *Daphnes Canyon Mine*
	Miner's Trousers ✓		In the *Hylia Canyon Mine*

sold (handwritten over Glide Mask)

Set	Items	Set Bonus	Location(s)
Mystic	Mystic Headpiece	Lose Rupees, not hearts, when hit	*Koltin's Shop* (5 Bubbul Gems)
	Mystic Robe		*Koltin's Shop* (3 Bubbul Gems)
	Mystic Trousers		*Koltin's Shop* (4 Bubbul Gems)
Phantom	Phantom Helmet	Raises attack	Inside *Puffer Beach Overhead Cave*
	Phantom Armor		Inside *Tamio River Downstream Cave*
	Phantom Greaves		Inside the *Ancient Altar Ruins*
Radiant	Radiant Mask	Increased bone weapon damage + Stal-type enemies ignore Link	*Kakariko Village* (800 Rupees)
	Radiant Shirt		*Kakariko Village* (800 Rupees)
	Radiant Tights		*Kakariko Village* (800 Rupees)
Royal Guard	Royal Guard Cap	Nothing :(	Inside *Zelda's room*
	Royal Guard Uniform		Inside the *Guards' Chamber*
	Royal Guard Boots		Inside the *King's Study*
Rubber	Rubber Helm	Increases shock resistance + immune to lightening strikes :)	Inside *Sarjon Woods Cave*
	Rubber Armor		Inside *Whistling Hill Cave*
	Rubber Tights		Inside *Horon Lagoon Cave*

Set	Items	Set Bonus	Location(s)
Sky	Cap of the Sky	~~Alex + Stop~~ Raises attack *IRVING70 GPL*	In *Retsom Grove* ✓
	Tunic of the Sky		In *Minshi Grove* ✓
	Trousers of the Sky		In the *Crenel Canyon Mine*
Snowquill	Snowquill Headdress	Increases cold resistance + immune to ice attacks :)	*Rito Village* (650 Rupees)
	Snowquill Tunic		*Rito Village* (500 Rupees)
	Snowquill Trousers		*Rito Village* (1,000 Rupees)
Soldier's	Soldier's Helm	Nothing :(*SOLD*	Inside the *Royal Hidden Passage* ✓
	Soldier's Armor		
	Soldier's Greaves		✓
Stealth	Stealth Mast	Increases stealth + faster movement at night-time (**Note:** *Must finish Gloom-Borne illness*)	Kakariko Village (500 Rupees)
	Stealth Chest Guard		Kakariko Village (700 Rupees)
	Stealth Tights		Kakariko Village (600 Rupees)
Time	Cap of Time	Raises attack	In *Sturnida Lavafalls*
	Tunic of Time		In *Lindor Canyon Mine* ✓
	Trousers of Time	*Next stop Apr...*	In *Gerudo Canyon Mine*

Set	Items	Set Bonus	Location(s)
Tingle	Tingle's Hood	Faster movement at night-time	In the *Statue of the Eighth Heroine cave*
	Tingle's Shirt		In the *Dueling Peaks South Cave*
	Tingle's Tights		In the *Cape Cales Cliffbase Cave*
Twilight	Cap of Twilight	Raises attack	In the *Gleeok Den* (*The Depths*)
	Tunic of Twilight		In the *Rist Mines*
	Trousers of Twilight		In the *Ancient Underground Fortress*
Wind	Cap of the Wind	Raises attack	In the *Abandoned Lanayru Mine*
	Tunic of the Wind		In the *Cuho Canyon Mine*
	Trousers of the Wind		In the *Cresia Pit Mine*
Yiga	Yiga Mask	Increases stealth + faster movement at night-time	*Great Plateau* (small shack)
	Yiga Armor		The *Akkala Ancient Tech Lab*
	Yiga Tights		The *Yiga Clan Maritta Branch*

Set	Items	Set Bonus	Location(s)
Zonaite	Zonaite Helm	Zonai devices use less power + batteries recharge twice as fast	On *Lightcast Island*
	Zonaite Waistguard		Behind the *Yansamin Shrine*
	Zonaite Shin Guards		Near the Sky Mine
Zora	Zora Helm	Faster swimming speed + use less stamina when dashing in water + swim up waterfalls :)	In a cave on *Floating Scales Island*
	Zora Armor		During *Sidon of Zora* (Main quest)
	Zora Greaves		*A Token of Friendship* (Side quest)

Name	Icon	Type	Base Dmg	Bonus?
Biggoron's Sword		Two Handed	36	-
Board Guster		One Handed	5	-
Boko Reaper		One Handed	9	-
Bokoblin Arm		One Handed	20	-
Boomerang		One Handed	6	-
Boulder Hammer		One Handed	6	-
Captain III Spear		Spear/Polearm	36	-
Cobble Crusher		Two Handed	9	-
Decayed Master Sword		One Handed	1	-
Eightfold Blade		Two Handed	6	*Improved Sneakstrike*

Name	Icon	Type	Base Dmg	Bonus?
Eightfold Longblade (*Pristine*)		Two Handed	23	*Improved Sneakstrike*
Farming Hoe		Two Handed	6	-
Feathered Edge		One Handed	6	-
Feathered Spear		Spear/Polearm	4	-
Fierce Deity Sword		Two Handed	28	-
Fishing Harpoon		Spear/Polearm	3	-
Flame-Emitter Club		One Handed	6	-
Forest Dweller's Spear		Spear/Polearm	6	-
Gerudo Claymore		Two Handed	10	*Strong Fusion*
Gerudo Scimitar		One Handed	8	*Strong Fusion*
Gerudo Spear		Spear/Polearm	6	*Strong Fusion*

Name	Icon	Type	Base Dmg	Bonus?
Gloom Sword		One Handed	41	-
Knight's Broadsword		One Handed	7	*Desperate Strength*
Knight's Broadsword (*Pristine*)		One Handed	18	*Desperate Strength*
Knight's Claymore		Two Handed	11	*Desperate Strength*
Knight's Claymore (*Pristine*)		Two Handed	24	*Desperate Strength*
Knight's Halberd		Spear/Polearm	6	*Desperate Strength*
Korok-Frond Guster		One Handed	5	-
Lizal Boomerang		One Handed	8	-
Lizal Reaper		One Handed	13	-
Lizalfos Arm		One Handed	22	-
Long Stick		Spear/Polearm	2	-

Name	Icon	Type	Base Dmg	Bonus?
Magic Rod		One Handed	6	-
Master Sword		One Handed	-	-
Mighty Zonaite Longsword		Two Handed	15	-
Mighty Zonaite Spear		Spear/Polearm	8	-
Mighty Zonaite Sword		One Handed	10	-
Moblin Arm		Two Handed	28	-
Rock Boomerang		One Handed	7	-
Rock Hammer		One Handed	6	-
Rock Sledge		Spear/Polearm	3	-
Royal Broadsword		One Handed	10	-
Royal Claymore		Two Handed	14	-

Name	Icon	Type	Base Dmg	Bonus?
Royal Guard's Claymore		Two Handed	32	-
Royal Guard's Spear		Spear/Polearm	15	-
Royal Halberd		Spear/Polearm	7	*Improved Flurry Rush*
Rusty Broadsword		One Handed	5	-
Rusty Claymore		Two Handed	6	-
Rusty Halberd		Spear/Polearm	3	-
Soldier II Reaper		One Handed	8	-
Soldier II Spear		Spear/Polearm	15	-
Soldier Reaper		One Handed	7	-
Soldier's Broadsword		One Handed	6	-
Soldier's Broadsword (*Pristine*)		One Handed	12	-

Name	Icon	Type	Base Dmg	Bonus?
Soldier's Claymore		Two Handed	8	*Charge Atk Stamina Up*
Soldier's Spear		Spear/Polearm	4	-
Soup Ladle		One Handed	4	-
Spiked-Iron-Ball Hammer		One Handed	20	-
Stone Axe		One Handed	5	-
Stone Two-Handed Axe		Two Handed	6	-
Strong Zonaite Longsword		Two Handed	10	-
Strong Zonaite Spear		Spear/Polearm	6	-
Strong Zonaite Sword		One Handed	7	-
Sturdy Long Stick		Spear/Polearm	6	Extra durability
Sturdy Thick Stick		One Handed	7	Extra durability

Name	Icon	Type	Base Dmg	Bonus?
Sturdy Wooden Stick		One Handed	7	-
Sword of the Hero		One Handed	17	-
Thick Stick		One Handed	5	-
Thick Stick		Two Handed	5	-
Throwing Spear		Spear/Polearm	3	-
Torch		One Handed	2	-
Traveler's Claymore		Two Handed	6	-
Traveler's Claymore (Pristine)		Two Handed	9	-
Traveler's Spear		Spear/Polearm	3	-
Traveler's Spear (Pristine)		Spear/Polearm	4	-
Traveler's Sword		One Handed	7	-

Name	Icon	Type	Base Dmg	Bonus?
Traveler's Sword (*Pristine*)		One Handed	9	-
Tree Branch		One Handed	2	-
Wooden Stick		Spear/Polearm	3	-
Zonaite Spear		Spear/Polearm	4	*Zonaite-Powered*
Zonaite Sword		One Handed	6	*Zonaite-Powered*
Zora Longsword		Two Handed	8	-
Zora Spear		Spear/Polearm	6	-
Zora Sword		One Handed	6	-

Name	Icon	Base Defense
Boko Shield		36
Boulder Shield		3
Dragonbone Boko Shield		25
Fisherman's Shield		3
Flame-Emitter Shield		2
Forest Dweller's Shield		30
Kite Shield		14
Knight's Shield		40
Mighty Zonaite Shield		50
Old Wooden Shield		2

Name	Icon	Base Defense
Radiant Shield		35
Royal Guard's Shield		70
Royal Shield		55
Rusty Shield		3
Shield of the Mind's Eye		16
Soldier's Shield		16
Spiked Boko Shield		10
Steel Lizal Shield		35
Strong Zonaite Shield		26
Zonaite Shield		10
Zora Shield		24

Name	Icon	Base Damage	Location(s)
Boko Bow		4	*Bokoblin Mobs*
Construct Bow		5	*South Lanayru Sky Archipelago*
Demon King's Bow		60	*Phantom Ganon*
Dragonbone Boko Bow		24	*Gerudo Highlands/ Depths*
Duplex Bow		14	*Yiga Archer drop*
Falcon Bow		14	*Hebra Mountains & Tabantha Frontier*
Gerudo Bow		25	*Gerudo Desert/ Highlands*
Knight's Bow		24	*Gerudo Desert & Akkala Wilds*
Mighty Lynel Bow		20	*Cape Cales Cliffbase Cave*
Old Wooden Bow		4	*Many locations*

Name	Icon	Base Damage	Location(s)
Phrenic Bow		10	East & West Necluda
Royal Bow		38	Hyrule Field & Central Hyrule Depths
Royal Guard's Bow		50	Hyrule Castle
Savage Lynel Bow		32	Lynel drop
Soldier's Bow		14	Hyrule Field & Hebra Mountains
Steel Lizal Bow		36	Lizalfos drop
Strengthened Lizal Bow		25	Gerudo Desert & Akkala Highlands Depth
Strong Construct Bow		11	Death Mountain Depths & Rising Island Chain
Swallow Bow		9	Hebra Mountains
Traveler's Bow		5	Hyrule Field
Zonaite Bow		30	Labyrinth chests

Materials

Materials are often used to restore health, provide elemental buffs, improve armor, create Elixirs, or fuse to weapons!

Key:

- 🧪 Elixir
- ⚔️⬆️ Attack Up
- ❤️⬆️ Health
- ⬆️ Stamina Up
- 👕⬆️ Armor Up
- ❄️⬆️ Cold Res Up
- 🔥⬆️ Heat Res Up
- Fuse

Name	Icon	Fuse/Cook Effects	Location/Enemy
Acorn		💎 👕 👕⬆️	*Great Sky Island Evermean*
Aerocuda Eyeball		🧪 + ⚔️⬆️	*Greater Hyrule*
Aerocuda Wing		🧪 + ⚔️⬆️	*Greater Hyrule*
Amber		💎 👕⬆️ ⚔️⬆️	*(Battle/Stone) Talus Chests*
Ancient Arowana		❤️⬆️	*Great Sky Island*
Apple		❤️⬆️	*Great Sky Island Hyrule Field*
Armoranth		🛡️⬆️	*Akkala Wilds Hyrule Field South Crenel Peak*
Armored Carp		🛡️⬆️ ❤️⬆️	*Lanayru Great Spring*
Armored Porgy		🛡️⬆️ ❤️⬆️	*Necluda Sea, Lanayru Sea*

Name	Icon	Fuse/Cook Effects	Location/Enemy
Big Hearty Radish		❤️⬆️ x4 💛⬆️	*Thunderhead Isles, North Necluda Sky Archipelago*
Big Hearty Truffle		❤️⬆️ x3 💛⬆️	*east of Faron Grasslands, s/w of the Utsushok Shrine*
Bird Egg		❤️⬆️	*Great Sky Island (In tree nests)*
Black Bokoblin Horn		🧪 👕⬆️ ⚔️⬆️	*Gerudo Desert Hyrule Ridge Depths*
Black Boss Bokoblin Horn		🧪 👕⬆️ ⚔️⬆️	*Gerudo Desert Hyrule Ridge Depths*
Black Hinox Horn		🧪 👕⬆️ ⚔️⬆️	*Hyrule Ridge Depths*
Black Horriblin Horn		🧪 👕⬆️ ⚔️⬆️	*Hyrule Caves Gerudo Desert Depths*
Black Lizalfos Horn		🧪 👕⬆️ ⚔️⬆️	*Black Lizalfos*
Black Lizalfos Tail		🧪 + ⚔️⬆️	*Black Lizalfos*
Black Moblin Horn		🧪 👕⬆️ ⚔️⬆️	*Black Moblin*
Bladed Rhino Beetle		🧪 + ⚔️⬆️	*Evermean*
Blue Bokoblin Horn		🧪 👕⬆️ ⚔️⬆️	*Hyrule Field Eldin Canyon*

Name	Icon	Fuse/Cook Effects	Location/Enemy
Blue Boss Bokoblin Horn		🧪 👕⬆️ ⚔️ ⚔️⬆️	*Hyrule Field Lanayru Great Spring*
Blue Hinox Horn		🧪 👕⬆️ ⚔️ ⚔️⬆️	*East Necluda Depths, West Necluda*
Blue Horriblin Horn		🧪 👕⬆️ ⚔️ ⚔️⬆️	*Death Mountain Death Mountain Depths*
Blue Lizalfos Horn		🧪 👕⬆️ ⚔️⬆️	*Mount Lanayru, Akkala Highlands Depths*
Blue Lizalfos Tail		🧪 + ⚔️ ⚔️⬆️	*Mount Lanayru, Akkala Highlands Depths*
Blue Moblin Horn		🧪 👕⬆️ ⚔️⬆️	*Hyrule Field Eldin Canyon*
Blue Nightshade		🥷⬆️ 👕⬆️	*Great Hyrule Forest West Necluda*
Blue-Maned Lynel Mace Horn		🧪 👕⬆️ ⚔️ ⚔️⬆️	*Lanayru*
Blue-Maned Lynel Saber Horn		🧪 👕⬆️ ⚔️ ⚔️⬆️	*Lanayru*
Blue-White Frox Fang		🧪 👕⬆️ ⚔️ ⚔️⬆️	*Hebra Mountains Depths Tabantha Frontier Depths*
Bokoblin Fang		🧪 👕⬆️ ⚔️⬆️	*(Black/Blue/Silver) Bokoblin Stalkoblin*

Name	Icon	Fuse/Cook Effects	Location/Enemy
Bokoblin Guts		🧪 👕⬆️	*(Black/Blue/Silver) Bokoblin*
Bokoblin Horn		🧪 💎 👕⬆️ ⚔️⬆️	*Hyrule Field Central Hyrule Depths*
Bomb Flower		⚔️💨 ⚔️⬆️	*Great Sky Island Hyrule Caves*
Boss Bokoblin Fang		🧪 👕⬆️ ⚔️💨 ⚔️⬆️	*(Blue/Black) Boss Bokoblin*
Boss Bokoblin Guts		🧪 👕⬆️	*(Blue/Black) Boss Bokoblin Hyrule Field*
Boss Bokoblin Horn		🧪 ⚔️💨 ⚔️⬆️	*Hyrule Field, Lanayru Great Spring*
Brightbloom Seed		🧪 💎 👕⬆️ ⚔️💨	*Great Sky Island Hyrule Field (Little Frox)*
Brightcap		❤️⬆️ + Glow	*Royal Ancient Lab Ruins Hyrule Caves*
Bright-Eyed Crab		❤️⬆️ ⭕⬆️	*Lanayru Great Spring Lanayru Wetlands*
Cane Sugar		Required in making cakes and other dishes.	*Nothing on its own.*
Captain Construct I - II Horn		🧪 👕⬆️ ⚔️💨 ⚔️⬆️	*Great Sky Island Rising Island Chain*

Name	Icon	Fuse/Cook Effects	Location/Enemy
Captain Construct III - IV			Lanayru Sky Archipelago Thyphlo Ruins
Chickaloo Tree Nut			Evermean
Chillfin Trout			Hebra Mountains Lanayru Great Spring
Chillshroom			Gerudo Highlands Hebra Mountains
Chuchu Jelly			East Necluda Hyrule Field
Cold Darner			Gerudo Highlands, Mount Lanayru
Cool Safflina			Hebra Mountains Tabantha Frontier Depths
Courser Bee Honey		x2	Irch Plain North Hyrule Plain Royal Ancient Lab Ruins
Dark Clump			Crenel Hills
Dazzle Fruit		Throw to blind nearby enemies.	Gerudo Highlands Hyrule Field
Deep Firefly		(Causes Glow)	Abandoned Kara Kara Mine Giant's Grove

Name	Icon	Fuse/Cook Effects	Location/Enemy
Diamond		🟩 👕⬆️ ⚔️ ⚔️⬆️	*Igneo Talus (Boss)* *Stone Talus (Boss)*
Electric Keese Eyeball		🧴 + ⚔️ ⚔️⬆️	*Gerudo Desert*
Electric Keese Wing		🧴 + ⚔️ ⚔️⬆️	*Gerudo Desert*
Electric Lizalfos Tail		🧴 + ⚔️ ⚔️⬆️	*Gerudo Desert, Faron*
Electric Safflina		Increases shock resistance	*Gerudo Desert*
Endura Carrot		🟠⬆️	*-2295, -0349, 0348*
Endura Shroom		🟠⬆️	*North Necluda Sky Archipelago* *North Tabantha Sky Archipelago*
Energetic Rhino Beetle		⚔️⬆️	*Evermean*
Fairy		Automatically heals Link after losing his last heart	*Sihajog Shrine Sokkala Sky Archipelago W Coliseum Ruins*
Fire Fruit		❄️⬆️ ⚔️⬆️	*Great Sky Island Eldin Canyon Hyrule Field*

Name	Icon	Fuse/Cook Effects	Location/Enemy
Fire Keese Eyeball		🧪 + ⚔️ ⚔️⬆️	Fire Keese, Death Mountain
Fire Keese Wing		🧪 + ⚔️ ⚔️⬆️	Fire Keese, Death Mountain
Fireproof Lizard		🧪 + 🔥⬆️	Eldin Canyon/Caves
Fire-Breath Lizalfos Horn		🧪 + ⚔️ ⚔️⬆️	Eldin Canyon Gerudo Highlands
Fire-Breath Lizalfos Tail		🧪 + ⚔️ ⚔️⬆️	Eldin Canyon Gerudo Highlands
Fleet-Lotus Seeds		❤️⬆️ x1/2 ≫⬆️	Lanayru Great Spring Lanayru Wetlands
Flint		Strike it with a sharp object by wood to start fire.	Great Sky Island Talus (Boss)
Fortified Pumpkin		👕⬆️	Carok Bridge
Fresh Milk		❤️⬆️	Parga, Lookout Landing
Frox Fang		🧪 + ⚔️ ⚔️⬆️	Central Hyrule Depths Gerudo Highland Depths
Frox Fingernail		🧪 + ⚔️ ⚔️⬆️	Central Hyrule Depths Gerudo Highland Depths

Name	Icon	Fuse/Cook Effects	Location/Enemy
Frox Guts		🧪 + 👕⬆️	*Central Hyrule Depths Gerudo Highland Depths*
Giant Brightbloom Seed		🧪 💎 👕⬆️ 🗡️	*Great Sky Island Hyrule Caves*
Gibdo Bone		🧪 + 🗡️ 🗡️⬆️	*Gerudo Desert Gerudo Desert Depths*
Gibdo Guts		🧪 + 👕⬆️	*Gerudo Desert Gerudo Desert Depths*
Gibdo Wing		🧪 + 🗡️ 🗡️⬆️	*Gerudo Desert Gerudo Desert Depths*
Gleeok Flame Horn		🧪 + 🗡️ 🗡️⬆️	*Flame Gleeok and King Gleeok (Bosses)*
Gleeok Frost Horn		🧪 + 🗡️ 🗡️⬆️	*Flame Gleeok and King Gleeok (Bosses)*
Gleeok Guts		🧪 + 👕⬆️	*Gleeok Den (Gleeok Bosses)*
Gleeok Thunder Horn		🧪 + 🗡️ 🗡️⬆️	*Gleeok Den King Gleeok (Boss)*
Gleeok Wing		🧪 + 🗡️ 🗡️⬆️	*Gleeok Den Gleeok (Bosses)*
Glowing Cave Fish		Causes Link to Glow when eaten	*Hyrule Caverns Mount Dunsel Cave*

Name	Icon	Fuse/Cook Effects	Location/Enemy
Goat Butter		N/A	*Parga, Lookout Landing*
Golden Apple		❤️⬆️ x 1 1/2	*Castle Town Island Forest Mido Swamp*
Hateno Cheese		N/A	*Complete: A Letter to Koyin side quest*
Hearty Truffle		❤️⬆️ x ALL 🟡⬆️	*Mount Flora Cave Mount Dunsel Cave*
Hightail Lizard		🧪 + ⏩⬆️	*Evermean (Tree Mimic enemy)*
Hinox Guts		🧪 + 👕⬆️	*(Black/Blue) Hinox (Boss)*
Hinox Horn		🧪 + ⚔️⬆️	*Hinox (Boss)*
Hinox Toenail		🧪 + ⚔️⬆️	*(Black/Blue) Hinox (Boss)*
Hinox Tooth		🧪 + 👕⬆️	*(Black/Blue) Hinox (Boss)*
Horriblin Claw		🧪 + ⚔️⬆️	*Eldin Canyon Depths Hyrule Caves Horriblin (Boss)*
Horriblin Guts		🧪 + 👕⬆️	*Eldin Canyon Depths Hyrule Caves Horriblin (Boss)*

Name	Icon	Fuse/Cook Effects	Location/Enemy
Horriblin Horn		🧪 + ⚔️💨 ⚔️⬆️	*Eldin Canyon Depths* *Hyrule Caves* *Horriblin (Boss)*
Hot-Footed Frog		🧪 + 》》⬆️	*Great Sky Island* *Irch Plains* *Rabella Wetlands*
Hylian Pinecones		N/A	*Bone Pond* *Garrison Ruins* *Crenel Peak*
Hylian Rice		❤️⬆️ x 1	*S/E Koto Pond*
Hylian Shroom		❤️⬆️ x 1/2	*N/E Mabe Prairie* *S/E Carok Bridge*
Hylian Tomato		❤️⬆️ x 1	*W of Horwell Bridge* *N/W Hopper Pond*
Hyrule Herb		❤️⬆️ x 1	*Castle Town Island* *Carok Bridge* *N?E Ranch Ruins*
Ice Fruit		⚔️⬆️ + ❄️⬆️	*N/E Rospro Pass* *S/W Talonto Peak* *S/W Hebra Peak*
Ice Keese Eyeball		🧪 + ⚔️💨 ⚔️⬆️ + ❄️⬆️	*Hebra Mountains* *Mount Lanayru*
Ice Keese Wing		🧪 + ⚔️💨 ⚔️⬆️ + ❄️⬆️	*Hebra Mountains* *Mount Lanayru*
Ice Like Stone		🧪	*Hebra Mountains* *Mount Lanayru*

Name	Icon	Fuse/Cook Effects	Location/Enemy
Ice-Breath Lizalfos Horn		🧪 + ⚔️ ⚔️⬆️ + ❄️⬆️	Hebra Mountains Gerudo Highlands
Ice-Breath Lizalfos Tail		🧪 + ⚔️ ⚔️⬆️	Hebra Mountains Gerudo Highlands
Ironshroom		🛡️⬆️	Koto Pond Mount Rozudo
Keese Eyeball		🧪 + ⚔️ ⚔️⬆️	Hyrule Field Multiple Caves West Necluda
Keese Wing		🧪 + ⚔️ ⚔️⬆️	Hyrule Field Multiple Caves West Necluda
King's Scale		🧪 + ⚔️ ⚔️⬆️	King Dorephan (Clues to the Sky)
Korok Frond		Attach to a stick to use as a fan	Lake Kilsie Great Sky Island Palmorae Beach
Large Zonai Charge		Apply to Energy Cells to recharge them	S/W Millennia Sandbar E Exchange Ruins
Large Zonaite		N/A	Zonaite Ore Rocks (Blue-White/ Obsidian) Frox (Boss)
Like Like Stone		🧪	Great Sky Island
Lizalfos Horn		🧪 + ⚔️ ⚔️⬆️	Electric Lizalfos Lizalfos Stalizalfos

Name	Icon	Fuse/Cook Effects	Location/Enemy
Lizalfos Tail		🧪 + ⚔️ ⚔️⬆️	*All Lizalfos Types Stalizalfos*
Lizalfos Talon		🧪 + ⚔️ ⚔️⬆️	*Lanayru Great Sprint Lanayru Wetlands*
Luminous Stone		🧪 + 👕⬆️	*Pico Pond Cave Mount Flora Cave*
Lynel Guts		🧪 + 👕⬆️	*Blue-Maned Lynel White-Maned Lynel*
Lynel Hoof		🧪 + 👕⬆️	*Blue-Maned Lynel White-Maned Lynel Lynel*
Lynel Mace Horn		🧪 + ⚔️ ⚔️⬆️	*West Hyrule Plains SW Plains Bargainer Statue Floating Coliseum*
Lynel Saber Horn		🧪 + ⚔️ ⚔️⬆️	*West Hyrule Plains SW Plains Bargainer Statue Floating Coliseum*
Mighty Bananas		⚔️⬆️	*Lake Floria Eventide Island*
Mighty Thistle		⚔️⬆️	*Koto Pond Hanu Pond W of Breman Peak*
Moblin Fang		🧪 + ⚔️ ⚔️⬆️	*All Moblin types*
Moblin Guts		🧪 + 👕⬆️	*(Black/Blue/Silver) Moblin*

Name	Icon	Fuse/Cook Effects	Location/Enemy
Moblin Horn		🧪 + ⚔️🗡️⬆️	*Hyrule Field Central Hyrule Depths*
Monster Extract		🧪 (Boosts effects)	*West of Irch Plain Moblins*
Muddle Bud		🧪 (Confusion)	*S of Canyon Mine Hyrule Field Chasm Gustaf Canyon Mine*
Obsidian Frox Fang		🧪 + ⚔️🗡️⬆️	*Gerudo Desert Depths Hyrule Ridge Depths*
Octo Balloon		Attach to items to make them float up, can attach to arrows	*Forest Octorok Water Octorok*
Octorok Eyeball		🧪 + ⚔️🗡️⬆️	*Forest Octorok Water Octorok*
Octorok Tentacle		🧪	*Forest Octorok Water Octorok*
Opal		💎 + ⚔️🗡️⬆️	*Great Sky Island North Hyrule Plain*
Palm Fruit		❤️⬆️ x 1	*East Necluda Gerudo Desert*
Puffshroom		🧪	*Hyrule Field Chasm Abandoned Lanayru Mine*
Raw Bird Drumstick		❤️⬆️ x 1	*Blue-Winged Heron Bright-Chested Duck*

Name	Icon	Fuse/Cook Effects	Location/Enemy
Raw Gourmet Meat		❤️⬆️ x 3	Wasteland Coyote
Raw Meat		❤️⬆️ x 1	Grassland Fox Woodland Boar
Raw Prime Meat		❤️⬆️ x 2	Mountain Buck Mountain Doe Wasteland Coyote Water Buffalo
Razorshroom		🗡️⬆️	Rauru Settlement Ruins
Red Chuchu Jelly		🗡️ + 🔥	Eldin Canyon Eldin Mountains
Restless Cricket		🧪 + ⭕⬆️	Helmhead Bridge
Rock Salt		N/A	N of Rospro Pass SW of Talonto Peak Selmie's Spot
Ruby		💎 + 🗡️ 🗡️⬆️	Talus Boss Battles Hyrule Cathedral Water Reservoir
Rugged Rhino Beetle		🧪	Evermean
Rushroom		🧪 + »⬆️	Great Sky Island Gerudo Heights Tabantha Frontier Depths
Sapphire		💎 + 🗡️ 🗡️⬆️	Frost Pebblit Stone Talus (Boss) SW of Elma Knolls

Name	Icon	Fuse/Cook Effects	Location/Enemy
Shard of Dinraal's Spike		⚔️ ⚔️⬆️ + 🔥	Dinraal (Boss)
Shock Fruit		⚔️⬆️ (In thunderstorms)	E Rabella Wetlands Meda Mountain Firly Plateau
Silent Princess		🥷⬆️	Akkala Wilds Rauru Settlement Ruins Floret Sandbar
Silent Shroom		🥷⬆️	Akkala Wilds West Necluda W Breman Peak
Silver Bokoblin Horn		🧪 + ⚔️ ⚔️⬆️	Silver Bokoblin
Silver Lynel Mace Horn		🧪 + ⚔️ ⚔️⬆️	Silver Lynel
Silver Lynel Saber Horn		🧪 + ⚔️ ⚔️⬆️	Silver Lynel
Silver Moblin Horn		🧪 + ⚔️ ⚔️⬆️	Silver Moblin
Skyshroom		❤️⬆️ x 1/4	Great Sky Island (very common)
Sneaky River Snail		🥷⬆️	Zora's Domain
Soldier Construct Horn		🧪 + ⚔️ ⚔️⬆️	Great Sky Island

Name	Icon	Fuse/Cook Effects	Location/Enemy
Soldier Construct II Horn		🧪 + ⚔️ ⚔️⬆️	*Hebra Mountains Rising Island Chain*
Soldier Construct III Horn		🧪 + ⚔️ ⚔️⬆️	*Lanayru Sky Archipelago*
Spicy Pepper		❄️⬆️	*Great Sky Island Hyrule Desert Gerudo Desert*
Splash Fruit		🏊⬆️	*Lanayru Great Spring West Necluda*
Stalnox Horn		🧪 + ⚔️ ⚔️⬆️	*Stalnox*
Stambulb		⭕⬆️	*Great Sky Island*
Stamella Shroom		⭕⬆️	*Great Sky Island Lanayru Great Spring West Necluda*
Staminoka Bass		⭕⬆️	*Hyrule Field West Necluda Regencia River*
Star Fragment		Sell or use to light up dark areas	*Catch as you fall through the sky (very rare)*
Sticky Frog		🧪 + ▷⬆️	*Lanayru Great Spring West Necluda*
Sticky Lizard		🧪 + ▷⬆️	*Hyrule Cathedral North Hyrule Plain S Sahasra Slope*

Name	Icon	Fuse/Cook Effects	Location/Enemy
Sundelion		❤️⬆️ + 💔✨	Water Reservoir Hyrule Field Eldin Canyon
Sunset Firefly		🥷⬆️	Buy from Beedle (New Serenne Stable)
Sunshroom		❄️⬆️	Eldin Canyon Gerudo Highlands
Swift Carrot		»⬆️	Buy from Parga (Lookout Landing)
Swift Violet		»⬆️	Hebra Mountains Tabantha Frontier Depths
Tireless Frog		⭕⬆️	E of North Hyrule Plain N Mount Dunset
Topaz		💎 + 🗡️🗡️⬆️	Selmie's Spot
Voltfruit		🗡️🗡️⬆️ + ⚡	Hinox (Boss)
Warm Darner		❄️⬆️	Hyrule Field, Akkala Highlands
Warm Safflina		❄️⬆️	Floret Sandbar
White Chuchu Jelly		🗡️🗡️⬆️ + ❄️	Great Sky Island Hebra Mountains Gerudo Highlands

Name	Icon	Fuse/Cook Effects	Location/Enemy
White-Maned Lynel Mace Horn		🍶 + ⚔️ ⚔️⬆️	*White-Maned Lynel (Boss)*
White-Maned Lynel Saber Horn		🍶 + ⚔️ ⚔️⬆️	*White-Maned Lynel (Boss)*
Wildberry		N/A	*Gerudo Highlands Hebra Mountains*
Wood		Use to make a campfire	*Great Sky Island Rospro Pass*
Yellow Chuchu Jelly		⚔️ ⚔️⬆️ + ⚡	*Electric Chuchu*
Zonai Charge		Power Zonai devices	*Great Sky Island (Constructs)*
Zonaite		N/A	*Great Sky Island (Cave Ores) Frox (Boss)*

ALSO AVAILABLE

Here's some of our other guides

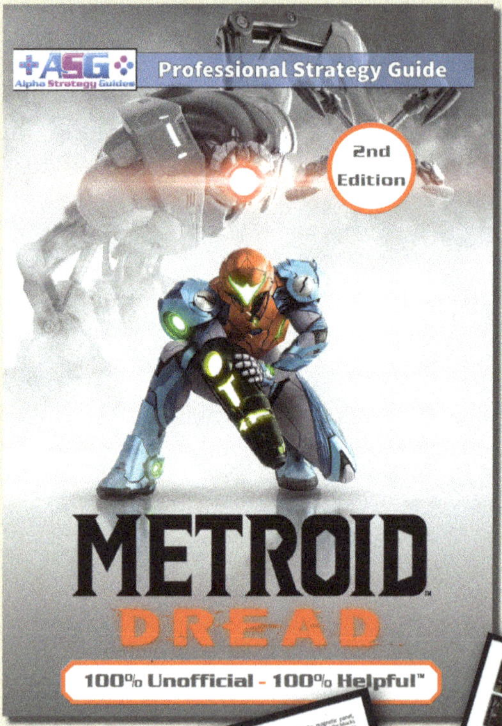

Our redesigned Metroid Dread strategy guide provides you with expert strategies from a veteran Metroid player.

Defeat every boss, master every move, locate every Missile pack, E-Tank, Power Bomb, and suit upgrade.

Break the game wide open with intentional and unintentional sequence breaks, speedruns, and a whole lot more!

Available now!

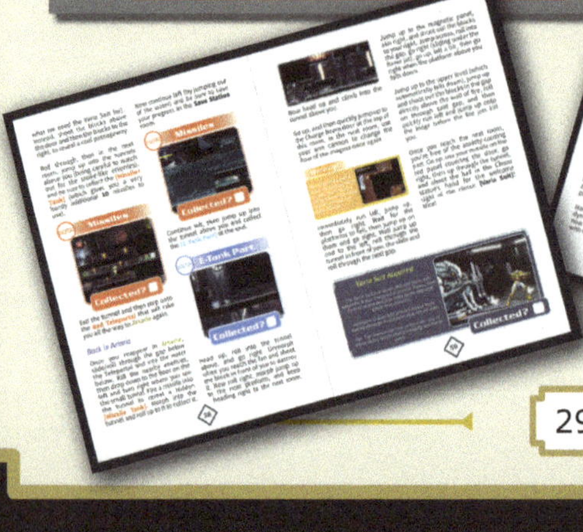

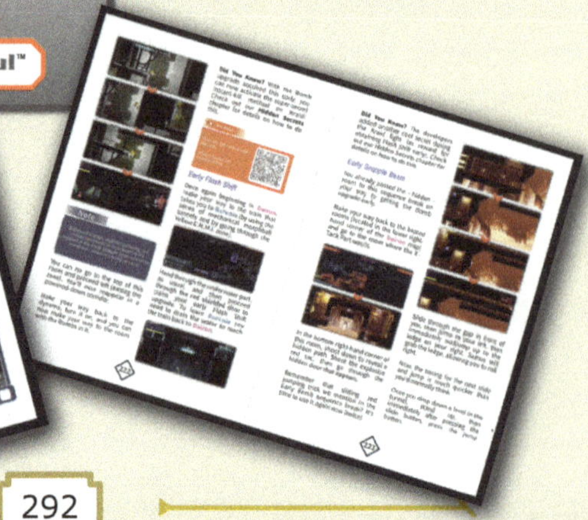

Alpha Strategy Guides presents the 3rd Edition of the No. 1 selling and highest-reviewed unofficial strategy guide to Link's Awakening, also on the Switch.

Our comprehensive guide helps you to overcome every challenge, defeat every enemy and boss, locate every secret (including every Heart Piece and Secret Seashell), uncover every hidden Easter Egg, and so much more!

Available now!

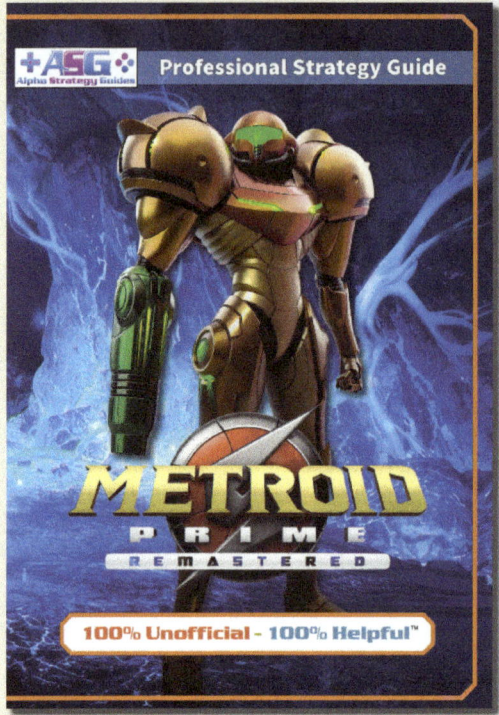

The classic Metroid Prime got an unexpected remaster in February 2023.

Our comprehensive guide, authored by a veteran Metroid Prime player, not only shows you how to beat every boss (on Hard difficulty), collect every item, and obtain every scan, but it also shows you how to sequence break the game and play it in a way you've never experienced before.

You definitely won't want to miss this guide...

Available now!

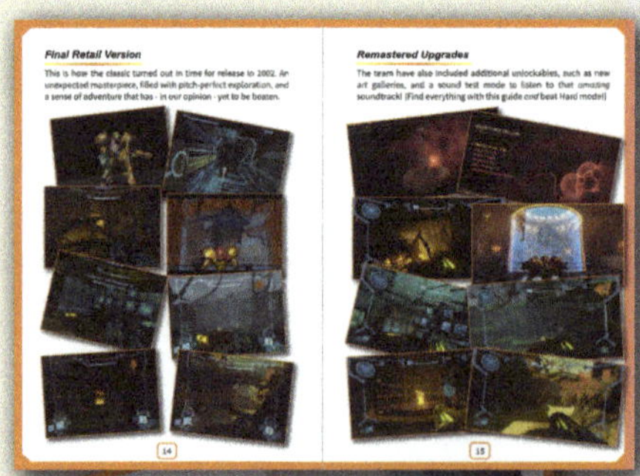

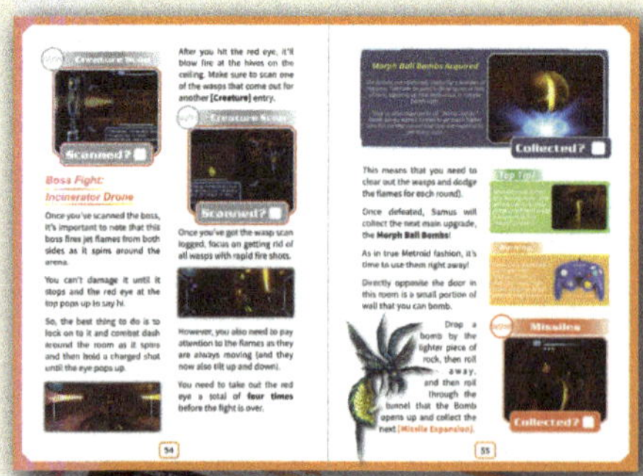

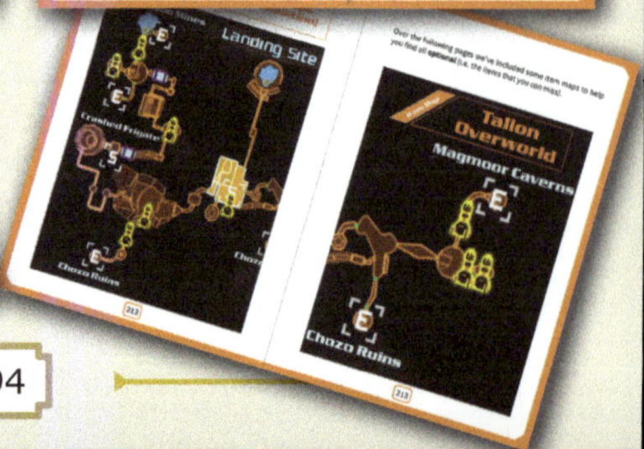

ASG
Alpha Strategy Guides
Professional Strategy Guide
Pokémon
Scarlet
Pokémon
Violet
100% Unofficial - 100% Helpful™

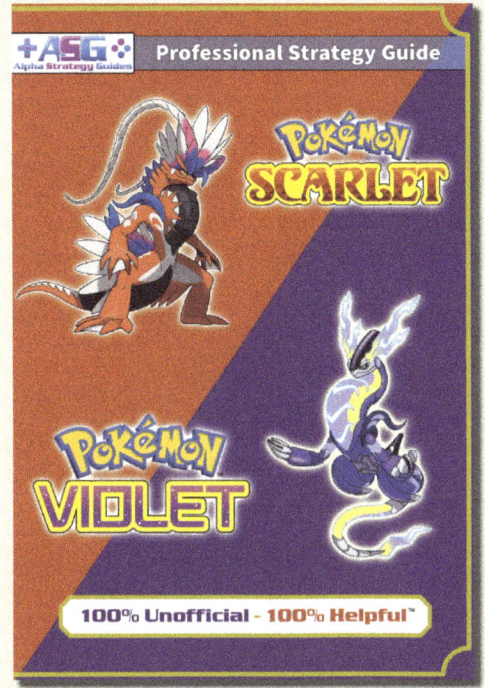

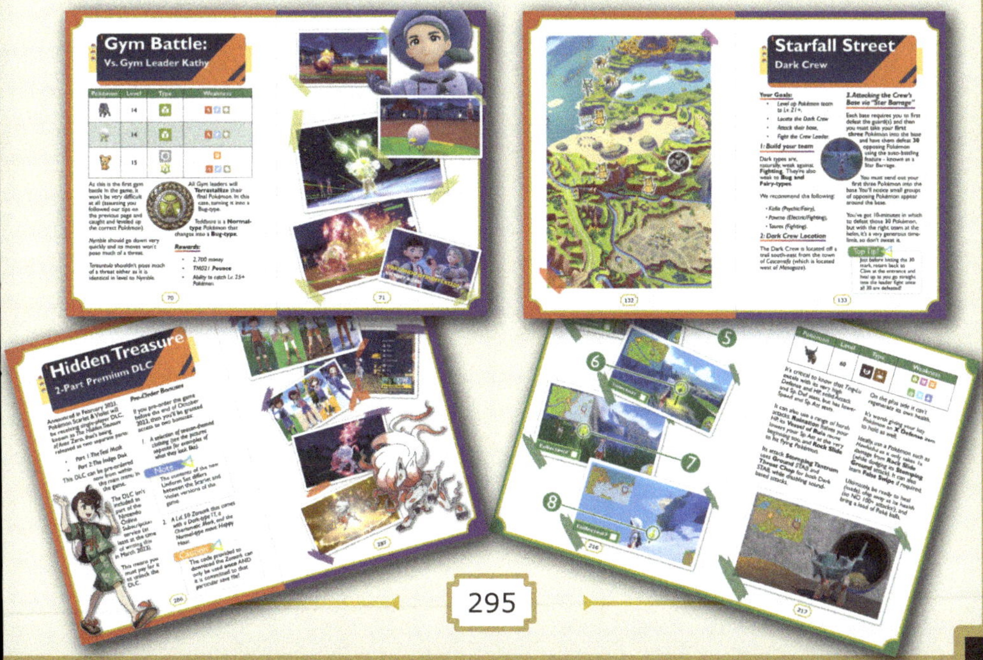
Gym Battle:
Vs. Gym Leader Katy
Starfall Street
Dark Crew
Hidden Treasure
2-Part Premium DLC

Thank you for reading!

Please don't forget to leave a review.

We genuinely read them all and take all suggestions into consideration.

Best wishes,

The Alpha Strategy Guides team.

Ingram Content Group UK Ltd.
Milton Keynes UK
UKHW050457210623
423760UK00002B/10